Markets in Profile

Founded in 1807, John Wiley & Sons is the oldest independent publishing company in the United States. With offices in North America, Europe, Australia, and Asia, Wiley is globally committed to developing and marketing print and electronic products and services for our customers' professional and personal knowledge and understanding.

The Wiley Trading series features books by traders who have survived the market's ever changing temperament and have prospered—some by reinventing systems, others by getting back to basics. Whether a novice trader, professional or somewhere in-between, these books will provide the advice and strategies needed to prosper today and well into the future.

For a list of available titles, visit our Web site at www.WileyFinance.com.

Markets in Profile

Profiting from the Auction Process

JAMES DALTON
ROBERT BEVAN DALTON
ERIC T. JONES

John Wiley & Sons, Inc.

Published by John Wiley & Sons, Inc., Hoboken, New Jersey.

Published simultaneously in Canada.

Library of Congress Cataloging-in-Publication Data:

Dalton, James F.
Markets in profile : profiting from the auction process / James Dalton,
Robert B. Dalton, Eric T. Jones.
p. cm.—(Wiley Trading Series)
Includes bibliographical references and index.
ISBN-13: 978-0-470-03909-0 (cloth)
1. Investments. 2. Auctions. 3. Risk management. I. Dalton, Robert B.
II. Jones, Eric T., 1961– III. Title.
HG4521.D1197 2007
332.64—dc22

2006030339

10 9 8 7 6 5 4 3 2 1

To all those intrepid traders who – from this day forward – will accept both the financial and emotional risks inherent in making that final decision to buy or sell.

Contents

CHAPTER 7 Short-Term Trading 99

CHAPTER 8 Day Trading Is for Everyone 141

Preface

You can manage risk but not return.
—Peter Bernstein

This book is about gaining an advantage over your competitors.

To achieve this advantage, you must first discard the belief that there is a linear relationship between risk and reward. The primary objective of investing (and trading) is to identify asymmetric opportunities. To capitalize on these opportunities, you must learn to identify imbalances that reveal themselves in evolving market structure. But that is only the beginning—you must also understand the way you process and respond to information, so your ability to act is not blocked or distorted by peripheral influences.

Markets in Profile: Profiting from the Auction Process introduces a unified theory that explains the market's auction process in relation to the human decision-making process, and the way market behavior affects human behavior. The bottom line? You are equipped to manage risk, which puts you miles ahead of the pack.

MARKETS ARE RATIONAL, PEOPLE ARE NOT

The "efficient markets" theory is half right. The market's mechanism for allocating prices is extremely fair. It's a simple two-way auction process by which price moves over time to facilitate trade either up or down—an extremely rational, efficient process.

The other half of the efficient market equation, however, is often wrong; people are seldom rational when they make financial decisions. The first step toward more profitable investing is to accept that market irrationality is due to the fact that people make decisions based on (unavoidably) incomplete information, which often results in the worst decisions being made when it is most important to be right.

Human nature is such that we tend to overweight information that supports our presupposed inclinations. We seek out a few pieces of the bigger picture that make us feel confident in our decisions. This recurring *overconfidence* is behind the idea that markets are "irrational in a predictable manner," a landmark theory put forth by Nobel Prize–winning psychologists Daniel Kahneman and Amos Tversky.

But Kahneman and Tversky didn't take this information to the next level. They didn't explore how to take *advantage* of that fact. In this book, we show you how the auction process both records and reveals market structure—and how, within that structure, predictability manifests itself in recognizable forms such as the "excess" that occurs at the end of an auction. We show you how excess is formed, too, and how to view it objectively in order to better manage risk.

All markets alternate between periods of stability and crisis. By monitoring market structure in real-time context, it is possible to recognize paradigm shifts in equilibrium. Market indicators such as excess make it possible to identify when the status quo is changing, which results in opportunities to distinguish favorable (and unfavorable) investment opportunities. In other words, it is possible to ameliorate risk by recognizing imbalances caused by irrational human behavior such as the herd instinct, which pushes price away from value.

Everyone talks about the problems of investing and market behavior. We are proposing a solution, a means of interpreting market behavior through the lens of human consciousness, and then quantifying that information in a way that enables investing on a more probabilistic basis.

IS THIS BOOK FOR YOU?

Authors' Note

While this is a collaborative work, the rest of the preface and many of the experiences shared throughout the book are written from the perspective of lead author Jim Dalton, who has spent his career furthering his understanding and mastery of the markets.

As the lead author, I'm often asked if I'm writing for investors or traders. I believe such distinctions are in many ways arbitrary for there is no line where one stops and the other ends. It's a spectrum, and every individual and every institution falls on a different point. That point changes constantly depending on the phase of activity. Even the longest-term investor should change his decision-making process in order to exit or enter a position. Trim, add, raise cash, change asset allocation—these are all timing decisions.

In *The Tipping Point*, Malcolm Gladwell could have been writing about markets when he described crime as not "a single discrete thing, but a word used to describe an almost impossibly varied and complicated set of behaviors."

Perhaps you're a growth investor. Or a value investor. Large cap, small cap—most institutional investors tend to pick a style and stick with it. The theories in this book are not dependant on the condition of the market, nor on what style is currently in favor. In fact, much of the power and appeal of these theories is that they are *totally agnostic* in terms of style, cap size, and asset class. The concepts you encounter are equally applicable to any style of investing, any timeframe, even any market, because the auction process works equally well for futures, real estate, art, even eBay.

The core idea is simple: all financial markets are measurable by time, price, and volume. This multidimensional approach to interpreting market-generated information enables you to differentiate between prices, because all prices are not equal. By extension, all opportunities are not equal, which is key in managing the probabilities of risk.

THERE IS NO CERTAINTY—THERE ARE ONLY PROBABILITIES

Markets react to countless influences other than fundamental company news. There are natural disasters, terrorist attacks, wars, and political imbroglios that cause markets to become too long or too short in different timeframes. It is often the shorter-term uncertainties that can make or break a money manager, putting sizable divots in the results investors use to choose fund allocation. One bad quarter can sink a portfolio and mar a stellar five-year track record.

Modern portfolio theory depends heavily upon diversification by asset class, sectors, individual securities, and so on. One of the core tenets of this book is that such diversification is not enough—*you must also diversify by timeframe*. Timeframe diversification is a staple for fixed income managers, who frequently diversify by owning short-, intermediate-, and long-term instruments. This approach should be natural for equity investors and investment advisors as well.

Successful timeframe diversification can help hedge against the major liquidating breaks, short-covering rallies, and other short-term market movements caused by news events that can push markets to the breaking point. What I'm getting at is that managers often throw in the towel at *exactly the wrong time*. This is undoubtedly why there's a saying that markets will trade to levels that cause the most pain for the greatest number of investors.

Change is the great common denominator. When change occurs, we are most vulnerable, and the natural human tendency is to grasp for what is familiar, what has "worked" before. That's why it is so important to learn to identify the basic structure of change through conscious attention to evolving market conditions. Recognizing the patterns that precipitate change can make the difference of a couple hundred basis points. And that, in a highly competitive world, can be the difference between feast and famine.

An investor or investment advisor who understands that markets do not change in a linear fashion, and that risk and return must be managed by interpreting change as it occurs in the present tense, is better able to recognize and capitalize on risk asymmetries. Ultimately, that is what distinguishes the successful investor from both the long-only and absolute schools of thought.

KNOW THE MARKET, KNOW YOURSELF, MANAGE RISK

The world wants absolute answers. This is why we are being careful to note that what we are suggesting is not an academic model to replace the efficient market hypothesis. The conundrum is that mathematics and factor-model approaches are more consistent than human intuition, but they don't allow for enough flexibility to respond to rapidly changing market situations. They don't allow you to distance yourself from competitors who apply similar models. It's like watching the world championship of poker—all the good players know the odds. That's why winning takes another level of understanding.

This book separates the market mechanism from the investor. While it is possible to describe the workings of any market within a single coherent framework, that knowledge represents only half of the equation. It is not enough to grasp how markets work; you must also understand how you take in and process information, and then execute based on that information. This concept has gained currency since "Prospect Theory" established that we are not rational decision makers. Our emotions can weaken or completely eliminate our self-control . . . but we'll save a thorough discussion of human behavior and neuroeconomics for a later chapter.

We're simply suggesting that traditional fundamental analysis can be enhanced with *real-time context*—time, price, and volume. By interpreting analysis in relation to market-generated information, the investor can better understand the nature of change, which can positively influence trade location. Trade location is the key to controlling risk and taking advantage of asymmetric opportunities that occur within developing market structure.

In recent years, the bifurcation of the brain has been explored thoroughly in popular media. We are not the first to suggest that successful investing (or successful *anything*) incorporates both sides of the brain. The goal is to balance the analytical hemisphere, made manifest in vital fundamental research, with the pattern recognition of the intuitive hemisphere in a present-tense process.

We're talking about *whole-brained investing*—a holistic, context-based understanding of market activity. As in all things, balance is the key to success, a concept that will appear throughout this book.

SO WHY LISTEN TO ME?

I've spent my entire career in and around the markets. That experience has resulted in two fundamental beliefs: First, that intelligence and understanding do not necessarily go hand-in-hand, and second, that patience and self control can be illusory.

I entered the industry nearly 40 years ago as a broker for a major Wall Street firm armed with a strong sales record and the belief that my success depended only on selling the stocks that my research recommended. I was a good salesman, but I was naïve and inexperienced. I didn't know it at the time, but it would take many years of learning and hard work before I could confidently say that I was consistently making money for myself, my firm, *and* my clients. I have tried to forget the financial pain I inflicted during those early years (as well as the psychological pain I endured from failing to meet my own expectations). Some of that cognitive dissonance resulted from poor stock selection, but some was from a lack of experience that kept me from cautioning customers against their own ideas.

When I first became a broker, the importance of raising capital was impressed upon me. The job was vital, I was told, because capital "nourishes our country." I quickly learned that no one really cares about the capital-raising function unless they own the company. Clients? They just wanted to purchase winners and get rich. This realization shaped the central motivation of my professional career: to independently seek profitable situations for my clients.

It was made very clear to me at the time, however, that I was expected to follow the firm's research. After all, the research department was comprised of the brightest minds on Wall Street. During my initial broker-training program, an economist who is still widely recognized told us that he wasn't interested in buying any stocks that were then available. When I returned to California after training, that economist was no longer employed by the firm. Soon after, a widely respected analyst suggested that there were very few buy candidates among the stocks that she followed. She was allowed to keep her position, but was reportedly placed on probation. Around the same time, which was just prior to the Bear Market of the early 1970s, I bought some energy and gold stocks, which were profitable for clients, only to have my commissions rescinded because the stocks I bought were not on the firm's "recommended list."

I began to observe surprising behavior in some of the stocks that were purchased from the recommended list. They declined *significantly* following higher than expected earnings. I became enamored with the slogan "buy the rumor, sell the news." The problem was that it didn't always work. Over time I observed that although the analysis of a company was often correct, the market's ensuing movement wasn't always consistent with that analysis. This is where I learned that fundamental analysis enables only a partial understanding of the bigger picture.

I changed firms with a big check in hand, as well as the assurance that the next firm's research was superior to that of the prior firm, and that my world would turn around. This was during the Bear Market of the 1970s and the market was on its way down to 500 from 1,000. Nothing worked. Right near the bottom, I learned how to short stocks and was successful with my first two shorts. The next short was Fannie Mae, which only required 25 percent margin. Do I need to continue?

One of the pivotal experiences in my life began there, at the bottom of the market: I became interested in buying and writing options. In those days, the options business was conducted through a series of independent put and call dealers who matched buyers and sellers in nonfungible transactions. During this same period, I had another introduction to the early derivatives markets when Edward O. Thorp, the legendary card counter, trader, and coauthor of *Beat the Dealer* and *Beat the Market: A Scientific Stock Market System*, opened an account with me. What his firm would do was buy stocks and sell warrants against those stocks, knowing that they would converge at expiration. My recollection is that their returns were in the 20 percent range.

In the early 1970s, my experience with options and warrants brought me a job offer from Joe Sullivan, who was the first president of the fledgling Chicago Board Options Exchange (CBOE). I gave up my memberships on both the Chicago Board of Trade (CBOT) and the CBOE to join Joe. As an executive vice president of the CBOE during its formative years, I was exposed to the various segments of the securities industry as well as the hordes of academics who were then conducting research and engaging in financial engineering involving options and other derivatives. During this period, I observed that a lot of firms and individual traders that employed single strategies—strategies that were highly successful for a while—saw those same strategies implode during economic crises caused by system abuse and overextension. I began to understand that no single strategy can work (for long) for all markets; those with superior results over the longer term were flexible, adaptive to changing conditions.

I observed how often, at major tops and bottoms, the experts and institutional investors seemed to share similar beliefs—beliefs that were simply wrong. I realized that long-term forecasting is unreliable because unforeseen events are bound to occur. I came to the conclusion, during these periods, that being skeptical, value oriented, and independent were far more important than being with the majority, especially at the extremes.

Even though I began to better understand what it takes to be successful, I was still never comfortable moving against the crowd. We are social animals after all, longing to belong. We all want to be part of a larger family, and every decision we make is in some way influenced by that desire.

In the late 1980s, I was introduced to a new theory, a method of arranging data that allowed me to see how markets are organized. I met Peter Steidlmayer, who is credited with developing *Market Profile®* for the Chicago Board of Trade (CBOT®), a graphical organization of price and time information that displays price on the vertical axis and time on the horizontal axis—the decision support tool for traders used in this book. Peter asked me if I wanted to sponsor the book that he and Kevin Koy were writing. I immediately recognized the value of this new concept and delivered a check for $10,000 to sponsor *Markets and Market Logic* (Philadelphia: Porcupine Press, 1986). My son Rob Dalton, Eric Jones, and I then expanded and elaborated on Pete's work in *Mind Over Markets* (New York: McGraw-Hill, 1990), which provides a wealth of tactical trading information. I'm happy to report that in 2005 *Mind Over Markets* has been published in a Chinese edition.

After spending several years trading on my own and mentoring other traders, UBS (Union Bank of Switzerland) Financial Services asked me if would return for a fourth time and reorganize their nonproprietary hedge fund business. This resulted in another significant pivot point in my career—as manager of Hedge Fund Research, I was in direct contact with many premier hedge funds and successful traders.

Having established an efficient process for reviewing hedge funds, my firm then offered me the position of director of research for managed accounts, a position that I was responsible for until I retired in August 2005. In this role, I was exposed not only to hedge funds but also to more traditional firms, some of which had upward of a trillion dollars under management.

I was surprised to discover how poor the actual results were for many of these relative-return firms, especially on a long-term basis. While some may have had decent relative returns (within their peer group), the absolute returns were often disappointing. I feel safe in suggesting that most hedge fund and relative-return managers could significantly benefit from the concepts in this book.

A long time ago, at the beginning of my career, I became the number-one salesman at IBM by meeting with clients, upsetting their homeostasis and then giving them a solution to resolve their state of unease. That model is still working for me today. *Markets in Profile* offers a new, holistic theory for market understanding.

For the inquisitive spirit, I believe this book provides the basis for profound insight into a more coherent form of risk management. (And it's a fun read.)

Acknowledgments

We have singled out a few individuals and organizations for having provided definitive insight or support; Markets in Profile was born out of years of teaching, research, and trading.

J. Peter Steidlmayer pioneered the original theories that served as our continual point of embarkation for both *Markets in Profile* and our earlier book, *Mind Over Markets*.

Brett N. Steenbarger was introduced to us after he read *Mind Over Markets* from the world of "protected academic medicine," as he put it (Brett was assistant professor of psychiatry and assistant dean of the College of Medicine, SUNY Health Science Center at Syracuse). Brett wrote us a two-part response to the book, spanning more than 60 pages, that was heavily focused on the, you have a healthy understanding of both markets and your *self*. Brett connected the structure of the market profile with the ways in which our brains efficiently collect and visualize information. He also introduced us to formative theories on how change occurs in both individuals and organizations. This well-reasoned response triggered several years of reading and research that led to a deeper understanding of cognition, behavioral finance, and neuroeconomics (you will notice that there are far more references to books relating to these subjects than there are to books that explicate market mechanics in *Markets in Profile*). One of the fundamental keys to successful trading, we believe, is understanding how markets change people, and how people change markets.

CQG, for their quality ongoing technical support over the years. CQG is responsible for many of the charts and data presented in this book.

WINdoTRADEr, a software utility that allows for the flexible implementation of Market Profile graphics and provides features for performing volume analysis. We have worked closely with WINdoTRADEr, consistently offering suggestions for improving this helpful, fully customizable utility.

Each of the three authors has contributed to *Markets in Profile* in a unique way. Stylistically, the book was written from the perspective of James Dalton, who has dedicated decades to an active, intense involvement with the day-to-day markets. Rob Dalton is a professional writer (and occasional poet) with an exceptional ability to translate complex ideas into a clear, compelling dialogue. Eric Jones, Jim's original trading partner, has researched, studied, and written about the markets and foreign exchange for many years. Having spent the past several years as a senior officer with one of the world's largest financial services firms, Eric contributed a wealth of experience with the Market Profile, and provided guidance in developing concepts that would resonate with other senior officers of financial services firms.

CHAPTER 1

The Only Constant

It is not necessary to change. Survival is not mandatory.

—W. Edwards Deming

My first car was a used '49 Chevy. We could pull it into the garage and change the plugs, set the timing, clean the carburetor and be on our way. Back then, it was relatively easy to understand engines and how to keep them running smoothly. Today, if someone asked me to explain the first thing about what's happening under the hood of my car, I wouldn't have a clue.

There's a parallel between that Chevy and my first excursion into the world of investing. When I became a stockbroker in the late sixties, my choices were pretty simple: common stocks, preferreds, a few warrants, limited over-the-counter options, U.S. government treasuries, municipals and corporate bonds, and cash. While there were mutual funds, they were extremely limited and many brokerage firms discouraged brokers from selling them to customers.

The financial markets have moved from simple to complex at a rate of change that is impossible to fully grasp. This accelerating complexity has been multiplied by the Internet explosion, global expansion, and myriad other factors, leaving individual traders and investors bewildered and grasping at narrow fragments of the larger picture, or subscribing to the beliefs of supposed experts who promise clarity and shelter from the information maelstrom. It's no wonder that the current financial atmosphere is one of continual change and uncertainty.

In his landmark book, *The Structure of Scientific Revolutions* (Chicago: University of Chicago Press, 1962), Thomas S. Kuhn examines the way change realigns the "received beliefs" of any given community; because a community's participants define themselves according to the ideas they share, they often take great pains to defend those ideas. In fact, it's not uncommon for this defensive posture to result in the active suppression of new theories that undermine reigning assumptions. Therefore research, Kuhn writes, is not about discovering new truths, but rather "a strenuous and devoted attempt" to force new data into accepted conceptual boxes.

In short, change threatens the very terms with which we identify who we are (and how we invest our money).

But history has proved that in all things stasis never lasts—eventually an anomaly arises that is so compelling it cannot be ignored or dismissed as a "radical theory." Inevitably, the anomaly unseats the norm, resulting in a paradigm shift in shared assumptions. These shifts, as Kuhn describes them, are nothing short of revolutionary.

Paradigm shifts force a community to reconstruct its foundation of belief. Facts are reevaluated. Data are examined through new lenses and, despite vehement resistance by those who refuse to let go of outdated ideas, the old paradigm is overthrown. A new community is established, and the "radical theories" are accepted as the new normative establishment.

The cycle of change begins again.

How important is change? Think about the many powerful institutions and intrepid individuals that once lead the fray and who are now long gone; those who recognize change early can take advantage of change, those who can't overturn their past beliefs get left behind. That pattern repeats itself endlessly in all human endeavors.

In *The Tipping Point: How Little Things Can Make a Big Difference* (Boston: Little, Brown, 2000), Malcolm Gladwell defined the way people react to change by classifying them on a spectrum:

innovators : early adopters : early majority : late majority : laggards

We are going to show you how to use market-generated information to identify and adapt to change before your competitors—once the majority recognizes that change is occurring, all assymetric opportunity is lost. This book challenges you to be an innovator, to overturn (change) many of the assumptions that now guide your perception of economic and market conditions. You may be faced with information that runs counter to the prevailing beliefs of those whom you have trusted for guidance. Daniel Kahneman said it best: "Resistance is the initial fate of all new paradigms. Often this resistance is strongest among the institutions responsible for teaching and upholding the status quo."

To begin, we address change in the financial markets from the broadest perspective, which is from the point of view of investors who operate in the longest timeframe. But it is important to note that this same process occurs for traders/investors of all timeframes—those who capitalize on five-minute price swings, day traders who make several daily decisions, short-term traders who hold positions for several days, intermediate-term traders who track bracket extremes, as well traders who hold their positions for several months or even years.

What we are addressing, across all timeframes, is how change occurs.

We believe that the financial markets—and therefore all participants, businesses, and industries dependent on the markets—are at the vortex of a truly significant change. Over the coming years, investors, traders, portfolio managers, financial advisors, pension consultants, and even academics will all have to pick their spot on the spectrum of change ... and win or lose because of it.

There is no single key driver behind the change we're experiencing. Rather, a series of developments—some connected and some not—over the past 30 years have created the evolution that is now underway. The balance of this chapter introduces these events and their implications on the financial markets and those who operate within them (traders, portfolio managers, advisors, etc.). To help you visualize the following discussion,

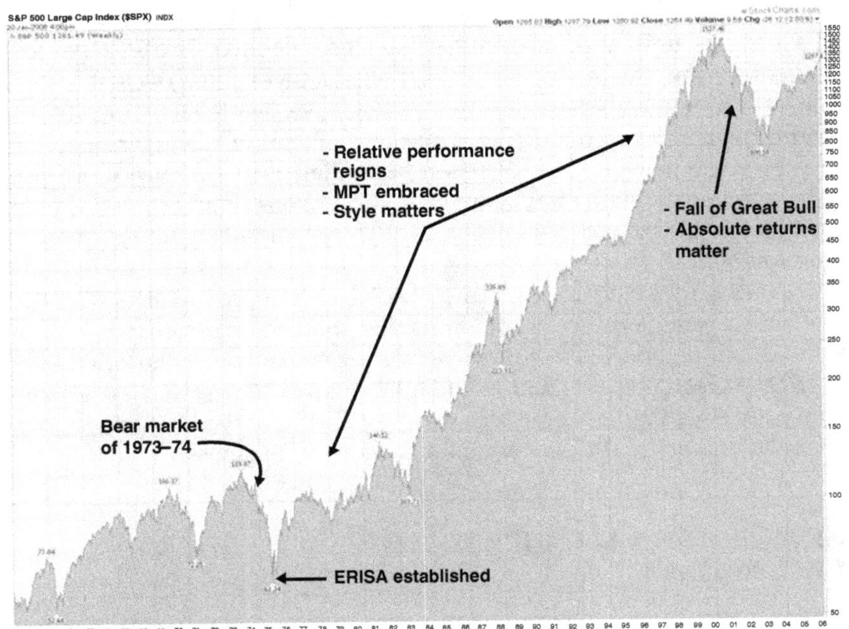

FIGURE 1.1 Events shaping market and investor behavior: S&P 500, 1965 to 2004.
Source: Chart courtesy of StockCharts.com.

Figure 1.1 illustrates several key developments of recent market history in the context of the U.S. equity market.

THE CREATION OF ERISA

The first serious change in the modern financial services business took place in the early seventies, partly as a result of the U.S. bear market that culminated in October 1974. Leading to the trend's nadir, equity valuation had decreased by approximately 40 percent (see Figure 1.1), the bond market had dropped an equivalent amount, and there was an estimated 35 percent decline in purchasing power. It should come as no surprise that innovation flourished under these extreme conditions; change demands the surrender of security, and in 1974 the very notion of security was cast in doubt.

Not surprisingly, new government regulations designed to protect employees' hard-earned retirement funds followed closely on the heels of this cataclysmic plunge. Enter ERISA (Employee Retirement Income Security Act), enacted in 1974 and designed to protect employee pensions. While performance measurement had got under way in the 1960s, ERISA increased focus on return relative to risk, which jumpstarted a new era of corporate accountability.

While this new accountability was clearly needed, ERISA was concerned more with the *process* by which pension-investment decisions were made, rather than with the investments themselves, which had the effect of ushering in an industry that focused on asset allocation, manager selection, and performance evaluation. Pension funds began to exercise more prudence when selecting money managers, hiring consultants to assist them in meeting their fiduciary responsibilities. The pension-consulting industry-began to boom.

On the surface, ERISA had many positives—it improved diversification and disclosure and promoted standards that enabled investors to better understand and compare investment performance. However, lurking below the surface was a negative that would take years to fully reveal itself: many of the processes implemented as a result of ERISA served to stifle innovation and creativity in the investment management business.

THE RISE AND FALL OF RELATIVE PERFORMANCE

The push toward improved diversification and process transparency resulted in managers developing extremely specific approaches to investing (see Figure 1.2). In turn, consultants needed improved ways to judge how

Large Cap Growth	Large Cap Core	Large Cap Value
Mid Cap Growth	Mid Cap Core	Mid Cap Value
Small Cap Growth	Small Cap Core	Small Cap Value

FIGURE 1.2 Typical U.S. equity styles.

individual managers were performing relative to the market, and relative to each other. Consultants initially used broad markets indices to gauge performance. However, as more and more specialty managers began to appear, benchmarks began to evolve and, as with all change, these evolutions became increasingly complex. Specialized market indexes were employed to gauge performance. Categories were formed so that managers could be compared against their peers. Consultants pigeonholed asset managers into distinct styles so they could more easily monitor their activity and fire them (or not hire them) if they didn't fit neatly into preconceived categories. Over time, this forced many money managers to become highly specialized, focusing on individual styles like growth or value, which in turn were further broken down into large-cap, mid-cap, and small-cap strategies, as well as a host of other variations.

Throughout the Great Bull market that began in 1982 and ran for almost 20 years, managers that attempted to be creative and innovative sometimes found that their ability to raise assets diminished—even if they had stellar track records—because they no longer fit within a convenient category.

The perceived institutional need to compare performance to peers and market benchmarks resulted in most of the focus being on *relative performance*, rather than *absolute performance*. (In short, "relative return" has to do with how an asset class performs *relative* to a benchmark, such as the S&P 500. "Absolute return" speaks to the *absolute* gain or loss an asset or portfolio posts over a certain period.) The relativistic approach to evaluating performance proved to be a boon for asset managers, in that they could now focus on constructing portfolios that had only to equal or perform marginally better than market benchmarks—*regardless of whether performance was positive or negative.*

Relativism provided a windfall for asset managers, in that it often masked poor absolute performance; an asset manager with a negative return could still win the Boeing pension fund simply by outperforming peers and benchmarks! As long as performance was measured on a relative basis, the money management industry continued to raise significant assets (upon which fees could be charged). While this wasn't so detrimental during the rising markets of the time, the relative-performance crutch did little to prepare managers to compete in the less certain markets that followed the end of the great bull market in 2000.

The tide would soon turn: Once it was clear that the market was no longer going up, clients would begin to demand that their managers do more than simply match the market.

THE FALL OF THE GREAT BULL

Coupled with an extended bull market, the enactment of ERISA had the effect of codifying *modern portfolio theory* (MPT) in the eyes of the majority of investors and investment managers. (In a nutshell, MPT emphasizes that risk is an inherent part of higher reward, and that investors can construct portfolios in order to optimize risk for expected returns.) For fiduciaries, the concept of controlled risk through diverse asset allocation is certainly appealing. When markets are "behaving" (as they were for nearly two bullish decades) the return, risk, and correlation assumptions used to generate asset allocation analyses tend to sync relatively well with market activity; a trend is predictable as long as it continues. In this environment, modern portfolio theory became the comfortable thread that held the financial markets' complex patchwork quilt together. Within this model, asset managers that performed well on a relative basis within a single, easily identifiable style could consistently raise assets. Once they stepped away from their advertised style, however, their opportunities became limited. An unfortunate result of this phenomenon was that this narrow, restrictive environment tended to limit the growth of asset managers' skill base. It's difficult to understand how talented, competitive individuals allowed themselves to remain locked into one specific management style for so long, especially when that style had clearly fallen out of favor. I saw managers literally go out of business rather than change their investment approach.

As the great bull began to show signs of strain and the equity markets began to behave with far less certainty (no longer trending up). It became apparent that the relativistic, MPT-driven business model embraced by traditional asset managers—one in which money was managed on a relative basis, track records were marketed based on relative performance, and performance was measured in relative terms—was plagued by significant weaknesses.

Alexander M. Ineichen of Union Bank of Switzerland (UBS) estimated that total global equity peaked at a little over $31 trillion at the top of the bull market, falling to approximately $18 trillion at the 2002 low—a decline of approximately 42 percent. As during the 1974 period, the investment community reluctantly began to embrace change in order to cope with the divide that opened between the objectives of traditional money managers and the needs of their clients.

One of the prime causes for this divide was that MPT depends on "reasonable" assumptions for each asset class. Implicitly, this requires a very long-term view; investors must plan on holding their investments for a long time in order to reap the desired rewards. Unfortunately, when markets failed to cooperate toward the end of the bull market, it became evident that most individuals and institutions have a vastly different perspective of what "long-term" means, especially when short-term performance is on the line. During times of market stress, the correlations between asset classes often fall apart, which often results in unexpectedly poor performance.

THE RISE OF ABSOLUTE RETURN

There appears to be a dearth of insight into how investors respond when the shorter timeframe delivers significantly different results than was advertised and expected for the longer term. But there is no lack of evidence that long-term-minded investors, when confronted with unexpectedly poor short-term results, tend to liquidate their holdings at precisely the wrong time.

As the markets became more volatile and uncertain, traders and investors who had broken free of the relativistic herd, embracing an absolute-return philosophy, continued to produce positive returns at a time when the majority of traditional asset managers were posting consistently negative returns (along with the market). Because absolute-return investors measure themselves against the risk-free rate, rather than relative to a market index, they must be more flexible and nimble. They must have the ability to employ a much broader arsenal of investment strategies in order to achieve their goal of delivering consistently positive performance. This group can employ all styles across all capitalizations. They can also short securities, which creates even more opportunities and enables portfolio managers to exploit both overpriced as well as underpriced securities.

The end of the great bull served as the catalyst for a much more adventurous and entrepreneurial environment. In today's atmosphere, it's harder for the traditional money management firms to hold on to talented traders and portfolio managers, as the financial rewards for stepping out solo can be extremely large for truly capable individuals. The firms that want to survive and prosper in the absolute-return milieu must adapt and find new incentives for attracting and retaining such innovators. An article in a leading U.K. newspaper, the *Observer*, reported that Dillon Read Capital Management, the new hedge fund unit established by UBS in 2005, earmarked $1 billion in bonuses for its first three years in business to ensure that it continued to attract and retain successful traders. When the article appeared, there were only about 120 employees in that unit, which would work out, on average, to about $3 million per employee. It's no wonder that we continue to see a steady exodus of portfolio managers from the traditional asset management firms toward those organizations that offer more challenging opportunities in the new world of *absolute return*.

SUCCEEDING IN AN ABSOLUTE RETURN MARKET ENVIRONMENT

Following a strong rise or bubble, markets historically remain within bracketing ranges for many years. As most equity markets peaked in early 2000, we are in the fifth year of a bear market at the time of this writing. Although the term "bear," in this context, is misleading, it is more useful to think of current conditions as indicative of a "consolidating," "trading," or "bracketing" market. The high-to-low range of a consolidating market offers excellent opportunities for traders who are adaptable enough to trade them. John Mauldin, in *Bull's Eye Investing: Targeting Real Returns in a Smoke and Mirrors Market* (Hoboken, NJ: John Wiley & Sons, 2005), states that the shortest bear on record is eight years, with the average being 16 years. During these periods, it seems as if the market's actions are guided by some shrewd NFL offensive coordinator—just when it looks like the market is going long it pulls up short, jukes left and rolls right, leaving a pile of stunned investors in its wake.

Consolidating markets are tricky. Just when you think you've got them figured out, you end up the wrong way on a big move and you feel like you've been betrayed by everything you know. Many traders begin to think of the market as a cunning adversary who tries to foil their best-laid plans, or perhaps a tempting siren, bent on luring them to the bottom of their bank accounts.

In a long-term bull market, or a "relative-return market," you can succeed by simply staying fully invested and matching the market's steady rise. In a bear, or consolidating market, such as the one we're in now, savvy traders seek to identify and profit from mispriced securities, both on the long as well as short side of the market. Achieving "absolute returns"

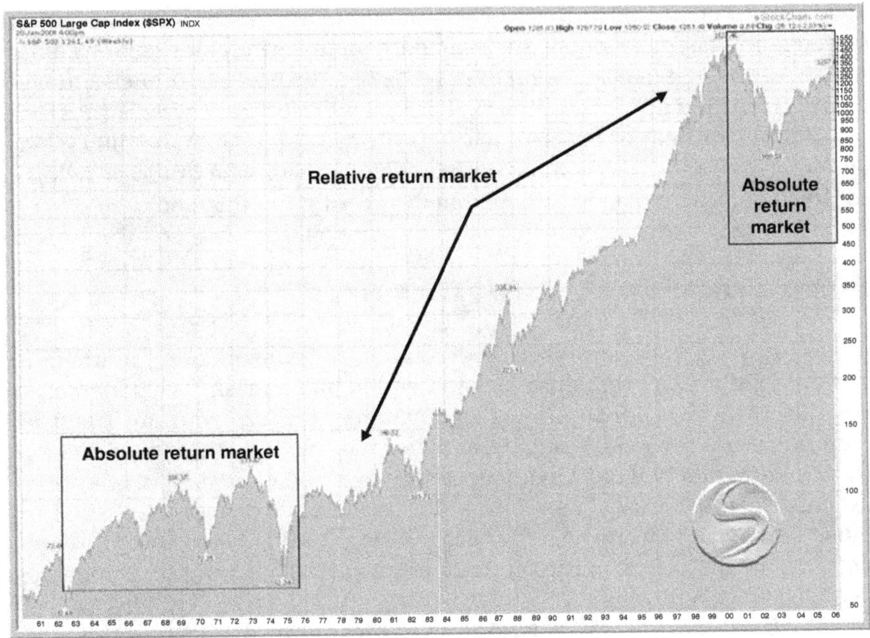

FIGURE 1.3 Absolute vs. relative return market conditions: S&P 500, 1965 to 2004.
Source: Chart courtesy of StockCharts.com.

(returns that consistently exceed the risk-free rate, regardless of market direction) requires skill, self-knowledge, an understanding of market and investor behavior, and trading maturity. The point here is that the relative and absolute approaches exist at opposite ends of the spectrum, and bracketing market conditions reward absolute-return investors—those individuals who are concerned with the value of their portfolios *at every point in time*, not just at some predetermined maturation (see Figure 1.3).

If history continues to repeat itself, as it has for the past five years, then the 20-year bull run will fade farther into the past, and a substantially different approach to market understanding will be required to consistently succeed.

It is worth noting here that *Mind over Markets*, the first collaboration between these authors, was written in the middle of the great bull market, when most investors had already climbed aboard the relative-return train. The theories and practices prescribed in that book are as applicable today as they were then—there is still unexpected volatility in bull markets, and *Mind over Markets* provided a detailed treatise on taking advantage of such volatility. Since the great bull, market mechanics and human behavior have not changed, although much around them has. With the proliferation of hedge funds, for example, there is more short-term momentum trading, which means that markets tend to move faster and go further once a movement has started.

But bull or bear or bracket, markets always conform to the fundamental dictates of time, price, and volume. We'll revisit some of the principles set forth in *Mind over Markets* within new context in this book.

PURE, UNBIASED INFORMATION

As you have already surmised, the volatility of consolidating markets is generally far greater than that experienced in bull markets. This increased volatility provides both risk and opportunity. Traders who are ruled by their emotions (or led by nearsighted analysts) will continue to chase upward swings and bail out on downward swings, which results in temporarily mispriced securities, as well as the financial destruction suffered by those who get whipsawed. This progression between bracket extremes provides prime opportunities to take advantage of fleeting discrepancies between price and value.

Markets in Profile is in large part dedicated to explicating this phenomenon in the clear light of *market-generated information*—not the deluge of hype and conflicting information that serves only to fuel the emotional panic behind most market movement. Those individuals who have the trifecta of market experience, self understanding, and skill can avoid the classic "panic in/panic out" whipsaw and take advantage of those who don't. Absolute-return investing is a zero-sum game, with a few highly skilled professionals taking from those who run, generally terrified, with the pack.

Who are those few? They are investment professionals with the experience to take a long-term view while capitalizing on short-term inequities in market structure; those who understand their own foibles, so they don't fall prey to the slings and arrows of doubt, anger, and fear; those who have the discipline to focus solely on relevant, market-generated information while the data explosion rages on around them.

Market-generated information is the pure, unbiased information that comes directly from the market itself. Structuring and interpreting this information is an excellent way to get a truly objective opinion about what's driving market movement, as it's based solely upon real order flow. Market-generated information represents a composite of all available information at any given moment—from macro and micro. And by organizing this information using the CBOT's Market Profile, you can monitor market

```
M
M
M
M
LMP
LMP
LMP
LMP
CHLMP
CHLMP
CHILMNP
CHILMNP
CHILNP
CHILNP
CGHILNP
BCGHILNP
BCFGHIKLNP
BCFGHIKLNP
BCFGHIKLN
BCEFGHIJKLN
BCEFGHIJKL
BCDEFGIJKL
BCDEFGIJK
BCDEFGIJK
BCDEFGJK
BCDEFJ
BDEFJ
BDEFJ
BDE
BDE
BD
BD
D
D
D
D
D
D
```

FIGURE 1.4 A market profile of a market in balance showing symmetry in market structure.
Source: Copyright © 2006 CQG, Inc. All rights reserved worldwide. www.cqg.com.

structure in real-time context, which enables you to recognize paradigm shifts in equilibrium. When there is symmetry to market structure (as shown in Figure 1.4), which manifests itself in a traditional bell-shaped curve, then there is generally a balance between good opportunities and bad.

```
B
B
B
BC
BC
BC
BC
C
C
C
C
C
C
C
CD
D
D
D
D
D
DJ
DJ
DJ
DJ
DFJ
DEFIJ
DEFIJ
DEFHIJN
DEFHIJKLN
DEFGHIJKLN
DEGHIJKLMN
DEGHIJKLMN
DEGHKLMNP
EGHKLMNP
EGHKLMNP
EGHLMNP
HM
HM
HM
M
M
```

FIGURE 1.5 A market profile of a market moving out of balance, showing asymmetric opportunities.
Source:

When the market profile becomes asymmetric (as shown in Figure 1.5), then there is a lack of balance, which results in opportunities to distinguish favorable (and unfavorable) investment opportunities.

Structuring and reading market-generated information via CBOT's Market Profile is about identifying opportunities where risk is considerably less than the potential reward. Asymmetric opportunities are often caused by irrational human behavior, such as the herd instinct that pushes price away from value. We'll delve more deeply into using the Market Profile tool and behavioral finance (often referred to as *neuroeconomics*) in later chapters. The point is that having a reliable, objective information source becomes more important every day. Markets continue to exhibit overwhelming, ever-increasing complexity, driven by growing diversity, globalization, technological advances, an increasing numbers of participants, and almost limitless outside factors that result in constant change. The remainder of this book is about how you can better understand and interpret the most objective source of information—the market itself.

PEOPLE CHANGE MARKETS, MARKETS CHANGE PEOPLE

Change is the beating heart of this book. *Markets in Profile* addresses the nature of change as it relates to markets and market participants of every type and timeframe, from macro to micro, from large institutions to investors who hold positions for decades and traders who roll with the market's daily vacillations. Everything in this book is equally applicable to individual traders, money management organizations, the proprietary trading units of major financial organizations, and all the newly formed alternative-investment shops.

For all market participants, the financial world has changed dramatically in the last two decades. This change can work to your advantage—most practitioners have either failed to recognize this change, or, more likely, have chosen not to adapt, blinded by the assumption (or the desperate hope) that what has worked in the past will continue to work in the future.

Your second, and more important advantage, is that despite the astonishing rate of change in the investment world, the fundamentals of market activity are just as they have always been: price and volume move over time to facilitate trade in the pursuit of value. It really is that simple.

It is the belief of the authors that in order to better manage risk, you must first understand the ways in which people change markets, and the ways in which markets change people. We will endeavor to investigate the nature of change, starting with a general discussion of perceived paradigms and culminating in a close look at the specifics of securing favorable trade location in the active, endlessly changing market.

On a final note, *Markets in Profile* is also about addressing what could be your greatest adversary: yourself.

CHAPTER 2

Information

There are relatively simple changes in the presentation and structuring of information that can make a big difference in how much of an impact it makes.

—Malcolm Gladwell, *The Tipping Point*

In Chapter 1, we discussed the central role change plays for all market participants. We suggested that people change markets, and markets change people. Let us now turn our attention to *information*—the byproduct of change, the ubiquitous evidence that change is, as they say, the only constant.

Information has no power until someone acts on it. There are as many responses to any given piece of information as there are humans who receive it; we all find ourselves somewhere on the long continuum between "leader" and "follower," in every endeavor. To illustrate the importance of this concept, consider what would happen if you were to simultaneously share a perfect investment idea with five different people. One of those five might act immediately, without requiring further evidence, while each of the remaining four would act in successively later time periods, waiting to see proof that the idea was, in fact, generating profits. *The diffusion model*, made popular by author Malcolm Gladwell in *The Tipping Point: How Little Things Can Make a Big Difference* (Boston: Little, Brown, 2000), would label each of these individuals as innovators, early adopters, early majority, late majority, or laggards. These five archetypes can help us better understand the way the various timeframes' interactions influence the market's auction process. We'll discuss this interplay at length in a later chapter, but first, let's explore the two predominant types of information that affect the behavior of all investors: fundamental and market-generated information.

FUNDAMENTAL INFORMATION

Fundamental information includes a broad array of different types, from the esoteric, like Kondratieff waves and S-curves, to basic demographic data and big picture business cycle research. Fundamental information can also provide insight into the expansion of price earnings multiples during secular bull market cycles, as well as the compression of price earnings during secular bear markets. This kind of information reveals that good earnings don't necessarily lead to higher stock prices—some of the strongest market advances have occurred during periods of relatively poor earnings growth. Then of course there is fundamental information on sectors, industries, and individual companies that shows earnings, sales, margins, growth rates, and the list goes on.

To make matters more complex, there have been numerous studies that reveal that fundamental information *must be viewed in the right context* to have any relevance. For example, a 5 percent yield on the benchmark 10-year Treasury note is viewed from one perspective if the yield has fallen from 7 percent, but viewed from a totally different perspective if the rate has just climbed to 5 percent after having been as low as 3.5 percent. It's all about context.

Let's take a real-world example that illuminates the importance of context in interpreting information. A few years after the markets peaked in early 2000, the economy showed signs of reduced inflation and slower growth for several months running, which caused the experts to begin talking about recession or perhaps "worse" (there were constant references to Japan, which had recently suffered just such a depression). When the market began to shows signs of inflation in late 2004 and early 2005, it was generally considered to be good news, as the moderate inflation indicated that we were not, after all, likely to slip into a recession. Then in late 2005, bonds again rallied on economic news that suggested inflation was well contained and that real returns were in focus. It's all about context. A fish looks pretty silly flopping around on the dock, but that same motion—in the *context* of water—results in graceful, powerful movement.

In addition to the larger economic environment at any given moment, which dictates whether inflation is considered good or bad news, there is also personal context to be considered—that is, information may be viewed differently depending upon an investor's "timeframe" (such as scalper, day trader, short-term trader, intermediate-term trader, and long-term investor). A company's reported earnings may be positive when viewed from a long-run perspective, but short-term traders might take the same news to be negative due to dashed hopes for even higher numbers.

Countless articles have been written that support the value of fundamental research. But articles have also been published that suggest the same research is so flawed and biased that it actually has a negative effect on performance. Because of this common bifurcation, it is important to distinguish between the accuracy of thoughtful research and the ability of that research to predict future securities prices. A piece of fundamental analysis may be absolutely correct—an analyst may have accurately analyzed a company's earnings—but the market may respond to that information in a completely unexpected way. Of course, that doesn't mean the analysis is bad. Firms that produce fundamental research often produce that research for noninvestment purposes, or from the perspective of a different timeframe, or for institutional clients who use the information to generate new business. They're not soothsayers, however, despite what many might wish to believe.

Nobel Prize–laureate Daniel Kahneman sums up context this way: "People don't assign the correct weights to information, and they assign too much weight to information, especially if they have collected it themselves." Due to the information glut available to everyone who trades, it is nearly impossible to view all incoming information in the "correct context," especially considering the short-term focus that seems to be pervasive today. As a result, information can be used to make just about any point, or justify any position one wishes to make.

A much publicized example of the inherent challenges of understanding fundamental information is commonly known as the *Greenspan conundrum*. In 2005, the former chairman of the Federal Reserve, Alan Greenspan, failed to comprehend why fixed income securities didn't react as expected to the multiple rate hikes he initiated during the previous year. Of course, there was no shortage of experts deriding him for this oversight—after the fact. During this same period, the fixed income trading results of many of the largest and most respected financial service firms were negatively affected by the same conundrum. The experts expected the fixed income market to behave a certain predictable way and positioned their books accordingly, but it didn't. One of the primary goals of this book is to explain how market-generated information can help you navigate through "conundrums" like the one that flummoxed Mr. Greenspan and many of his contemporaries.

RATIONAL OR IRRATIONAL?

Kahneman and Tversky demonstrated that investors are not only irrational, but that they're *predictably* irrational. But is "irrational" really the right term for this behavior? Imagine you're at the track. You've gone over all the odds, read the expert's opinions, and completed your own analysis, which is of course influenced by myriad factors, like the fact that one of the horses shares a name with your alma mater, and another happens to have placed in his last three races. You make your wager before the race starts and settle in to watch the horses run.

What if we changed the rules and let you place your bet *after* the race is already under way? A totally different side of human psychology would be revealed. Once again, all information must be placed within its proper context—how will your decision be affected if the horse you had planned to bet on is currently in the lead? What if the horse is losing momentum around the second turn? How will your betting habits be affected by this real-time information?

We should expect, considering a general understanding of human nature, that the larger the horse's lead, the more individuals will place bets on that horse to win, and that bets on the horse in the back of the pack will evaporate. When you extrapolate this behavior in the context of financial markets, is it really so "irrational"? When you think about it, betting on a clear winner is a pretty rational decision, in the immediacy of the moment. This phenomenon is commonly known as "momentum investing," which is often the primary force behind short-term market movement. And just as the payoff odds decrease in a betting pool as more money is placed upon a particular entry, the payoff odds decrease for late-momentum investors as the market explores price extremes.

The racetrack vignette was meant to illustrate the ways in which markets can change people's actions. But there is one important difference between the track and financial markets: The horse race has a specified beginning and end, whereas financial market movements are never ending. In such a continuously evolving environment, the human behavior described above can provide opportunities for both "momentum" and "value" investors. (Value investors, on the long side of the market, seek securities that are undervalued relative to certain criteria, which may mean low price-earning multiples, low price-to-book value, large amounts of cash, etc.). We'll explore these opportunities at length later in the book.

Irrational or not, market behavior is the sum total of the actions of all of its individual participants and disciplines and timeframes. It is influenced by the confluence of innumerable information sources and the whims of human nature. There are very few individual or institutional investors that aren't affected by this fantastically complex convergence, and it is extremely difficult to gain an advantage in today's markets, dominated as they are by a short-term orientation.

MARKET-GENERATED INFORMATION

The premise of this book is that *market-generated information,* when combined with fundamental information, can provide that elusive advantage. Market-generated information is information gained from observing the actual flow of orders within the market's present-tense context. Making sense of this source of information begins by recognizing that markets are constantly moving from low to high and high to low. This two-way auction process enables all market participants to express their opinions—no matter how those opinions were obtained—with real money; the auctions effectively establish a fair price where business can be conducted at any given time. This expression of the market's collective will results in a constant flow of objective market-generated information.

In order to manage this information, as we mentioned in the preface to this book, we employ the Chicago Board of Exchange's trader support tool called *Market Profile.* Market Profile is not a trading system, nor is it predictive. Market Profile simply allows you to observe the structure of the market as it unfolds, enabling a more accurate interpretation of which timeframe is in control of market movement. This concept of *timeframe control* will be a recurring theme throughout *Markets in Profile.*

The market, as we have said, is the manifestation of all possible influences, all news sources, all global and political events, and all market participants. As the market's continuous auctions unfold, a market profile enables us to experience a composite of all available information (and opinions), because it is solely based on real order flow. Market-generated information, when properly organized and understood, can greatly demystify the endless complexity of the market. Such data can uncover vital information about what is driving change by providing clues that help unravel the strength or weakness of market momentum.

To establish the significance of an objective means of interpreting market activity, let's revisit the potential pitfalls inherent in relying solely on fundamental information. Suppose that an analyst performs methodical, well-informed research on a company and comes to the conclusion that the company is well positioned for strong growth in the next quarter. But what this fundamental information may not reveal is whether the price of that company's stock has already moved to reflect that fact. Or perhaps the industry within which the company operates is on the verge of collapse, and nobody is interested in the sector as a whole. The positive report may be meaningless unless viewed in the proper context. Think of the numerous factors that must all line up to make fundamental information relevant. Even the slightest miscalculation can result over time in serious investment consequences. Of course, investors and money managers must be aware of fundamental indicators, but wouldn't it make sense to employ an objective means of ensuring those indicators are actually resulting in the expected market activity?

Let's say you bought shares of a good company that had an underpriced stock—you bought value—but the price has remained basically flat for an extended period of time. This is not uncommon, and is why many investors wait to invest until price momentum validates their buy decision. By using the Market Profile tool, one can often discover confirming information (positive or negative) in the market structure *before* it is reflected in significant price movement. Securing good trade location—or being able to exit a bad trade earlier—is the advantage we were discussing earlier.

Before we provide a mechanical description of market profile construction, let's first define "trading," which in the context of this discussion is no different than "investing." Trading is the anticipation, timing, and placement of orders to capitalize on change—no matter how short- or long-term the underlying investments.

THE AUCTIONS

Auctions are made up of three fundamental elements: price, time, and volume. *Price* is simply the auction's means of advertising opportunity. *Time* regulates each opportunity, and *volume* measures the degree of success of each auction. As with any auction, there are goods for sale, bidders attempting to buy, and sellers trying to sell. While price is the mechanism used to fairly distribute goods among participants, the skew of volume and prices enables us to see how willing or unwilling the participants were to either acquire or give up their holdings; some will be willing to relinquish their goods at fair value, while others will only enter the auction process if they perceive price to be away from fair value. As in all successful financial endeavors, it quickly becomes clear that not all prices are equal, and that identifying the "fair value" consensus is pivotal in understanding the underlying forces at work in any given market (Warren Buffett has been saying this for years). A market profile, by its very nature, helps identify price in relationship to value.

FAIR VALUE

Fair value is defined as the price levels that are attracting the greatest volume of trade. As you will see as we progress, fair value has different relevance for different timeframes. Markets are generally "fair" only in the day timeframe, and what is considered fair in the day timeframe is often unfair from a longer point of view. As the market's two-way auction process unfolds, there is an ongoing search for information between buyers and sellers (much the same way that manufacturers and distributors continually seek information about each other to maximize profits). Once either party perceives an advantage, they will attempt to move price away from fair value in order to increase profit. This attempted divergence is constant, and the market profile records the resulting auctions via a histogram, or distribution curve.

Historically, scientists have employed the histogram to organize data so that it can be observed and better understood. As Peter Bernstein establishes in his book *Against the Gods: The Remarkable Story of Risk* (New York: John Wiley & Sons, 1998), "The normal curve, or bell curve, enabled the evolution of human civilization" by providing a means of determining, statistically, the potential risk and reward intrinsic in any venture (such as opening a trade route to the West Indies).

A market profile histogram is created through the ongoing development of the market's information-discovery system—its continuous two-way auction process that advertises price in order to distribute volume in a fair and competitive manner. The volume, or bidding activity, determines whether or not divergences from value can be sustained. On one day, sellers are discouraged by prices below value, and buyers are discouraged by prices above value. When both sides have essentially established a "value area," any movement away from value will serve to shut off the flow of auction activity until price returns to equilibrium. This is commonly known as *reversion to the mean.* On another day, the same market may find that divergences from value—higher or lower prices—actually attract *more* volume rather than shutting it off, which forces participants to reassess their idea of value (investors who trade via reversion to the mean will be unable to sustain profitability when divergences from value are successful). We demonstrate how knowledgeable, Profile-experienced traders can perceive both situations while markets are unfolding by observing the Profile's graphic depiction of the relationship between time, price, and volume—the true fundamentals of market behavior.

In the discussion above, we referred to the day timeframe; however, the same theory applies to all timeframes. While we have not yet described these timeframes, we have referred to them as scalpers, day timeframes, short-term timeframes, intermediate-term timeframes, and the long-term timeframe.

MARKET PROFILE FUNDAMENTALS

Authors' Note

The following section contains a very brief discussion of market profile construction. For a detailed discussion on market profile construction and mechanics, please refer to Mind over Markets *and other texts mentioned throughout this book and in the References.*

The construction of a histogram requires a constant and a variable. Market Profile treats time as a constant, placing it on the horizontal axis, with price, the variable, arranged on the vertical axis. You can construct a market profile graphic using any time interval, and any liquid financial market. For demonstration purposes, we've chosen to represent the day-timeframe auction, which we've broken down into 30-minute intervals, each of which is assigned a letter. As the market passes through various price points, the letter designating the current time period appears beside those prices. Over time, the letters (known as *time-price opportunities* or *TPOs*) accumulate, creating a graphic view of the day's distribution curve. Once again, this concept is the same for any of the timeframes mentioned above.

Figure 2.1 shows a relatively balanced market forming a fairly typical bell curve. There is an accumulation of prices (greater volume) at the center of the distribution, and diminishing accumulation (less volume) at the extremes. As you become familiar with the way market profile evolves over time, you can begin to visualize the completion of the histogram—and how best to trade it—prior to the day's completion. To effectively trade the market represented in Figure 2.1, a reversion-to-the-mean strategy would be most appropriate, as it's clear that there is consensus in the market regarding value (highlighted below by the bracket).

Figure 2.2 shows the same profile, only we have kept each time interval distinct, so you can see where the market moved during each period.

In addition to day-timeframe distributions, experienced investors also view profiles that cover longer timeframes in order to maintain a clear long-term perspective of market activity. A longer-term histogram reveals whether the intermediate auction is occurring within the context of a bracketing or trending market. A bracketing market—also referred to as a balancing, range-bound, trading, or sideways market—consists of several days with overlapping ranges. Trending markets show much less tendency to overlap, as price and value areas consistently trend up or down.

```
y
yA
yABL
yzABKL
yzABDK
yzABCDEFK
BCDEFGHJK
BCDEFGHJK
BDEFGHIJ
BDGHIJ
HIJ
HI
H
```

FIGURE 2.1 Balanced market profile showing symmetrical distribution of TPOs.
Source: Copyright © 2006 CQG, Inc. All rights reserved worldwide. www.cqg.com.

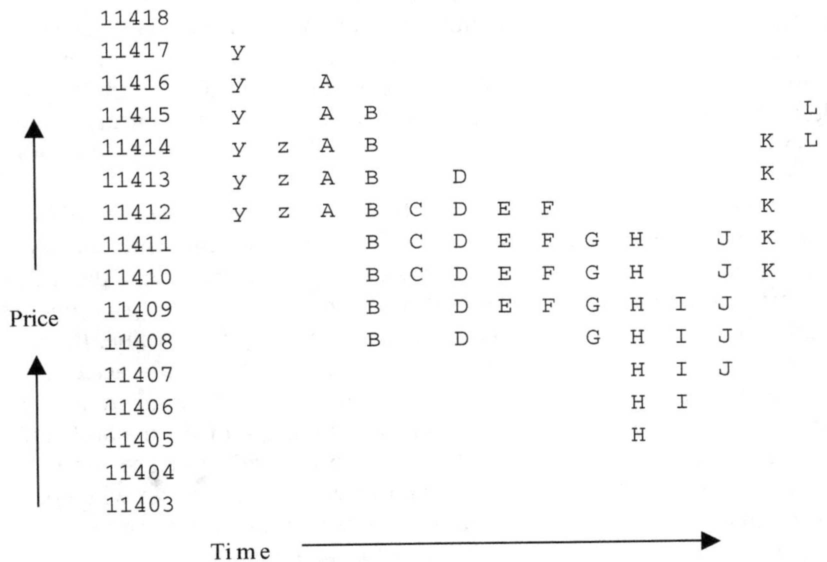

FIGURE 2.2 Market profile from Figure 2.1 separated out according to 30-minute time intervals.
Source: Copyright © 2006 CQG, Inc. All rights reserved worldwide. www.cqg.com.

We will expand on the relationship between price and value as we move forward.

One of the most important, yet challenging market assessments that investors wrestle with is determining whether a market is bracketing or trending. To make this determination even more of a challenge, it is also true that brackets and trends are largely timeframe dependent. A trend to a scalper is of no consequence to the long-term investor. An upward trend to a day-timeframe trader may simply be a series of thirty minute time periods with higher highs and higher lows; however, for the intermediate-term trader this activity is considered non-trending, as the activity remains well contained within the middle quadrants of the intermediate-term bracket or trading range. A trend for the intermediate-term trader may be a move between the extremes of a larger trading rang, with no longer-term trend, as the market remains balanced from a long-term perspective. Context, context, context.

The *value area* mentioned previously, a fundamental element of the market profile, is defined as the range of prices that includes 70 percent of all TPOs in a profile—the prices that saw the most activity, as witnessed by the greatest accumulation of individual time-period letters. The value area is determined by starting with the price that resulted in the greatest volume—the longest horizontal line—then summing the volume occurring at the two prices directly above the high-volume price and comparing it to the sum of the two prices below. The dual-price total with the highest volume becomes part of the value area. This process then continues until 70 percent of the volume is accounted for. Figure 2.3 illustrates this process.

Notice that the value area represents approximately one standard deviation. This distinction enables you to distinguish price from value, the most fundamental principle of investing. When price occurs within the value area, price and value are considered to be the same. When price occurs outside the value area, price is considered to be away from value. Regardless of your timeframe, as price moves away from the value area, there will either be acceptance of the move—witnessed by TPOs accumulating at the new level, which effectively changes the shape of Profile and shifts the value area—or rejection, in which case price will return to the value area with little change in the volume distribution. Trends occur when price movements result in value-area migration. Bracketing markets are revealed when price movements continually revert to a consistent value area, containing price within well-defined parameters that can last for months.

Figure 2.4 (see page 26) shows the S&P 500 futures contract profile from November 21, 2005, through December 29, 2005—a 27-day, intermediate-term trading bracket that ranged from 1257.50 to 1284.70. During this period, the market completed five legs that traversed from low

Price	Volume	TPOs	Selection Order
100-04	A		
100-03	A		
100-02	AL		
100-01	AL		
100-00	AL		
99-31	AL		
99-30	AL		
99-29	AL		
99-28	ACGKL	10	4
99-27	ABCGK		
99-26	ABCGHK	16	2
99-25	ABCDEFGHIK		
99-24[a]	ABCDEFGHIJK	11	1
99-23	BCDEFHIJK	16	3
99-22	BCDEHIJ		
99-21	BCDJ	4	5[b]
99-20	BCD		
99-19	BC		
99-18	B		
99-17	B		

[a] High TPO price
[b] Only the closest price is used since it fulfilled the 70% or better volume requirement.

Notes:
Total TPOs = 78.
70% = 54.6 or 55.
Value area is 99-21 to 99-28 (73%).
For comparison, the volume value area was 99-20 to 99-30.

FIGURE 2.3 Calculation of the Value Area.
Source:

to high; high to low; low to high; high to low; low to high; which was followed by a partial break and rally, and finally a high-to-low break that led to a downward spike on the final trading day of 2005.

Inspection of the profile in Figure 2.4 reveals that the longest horizontal line—which represents the highest volume—occurred in the lower portion of the profile. Recalling how we calculated the value area, by summing the volume both above and below the high volume area (referred to as the point of control, or POC), you will see that the POC was moving lower over the course of the 27 days, which signifies that the value area was being forced lower. Without the multidimensional view (time, price, and volume), what was really occurring in this market might have been masked by hype; the experts, especially the CNN analysts, were all reporting high odds for a *Santa Claus rally*—defined as the trading period between Christmas and New Year's. You couldn't turn on the television without seeing some pundit

```
       128440  JK
       128400  JK
       128360  JKBBE
       128320  JKLBCBCE
       128280  GJLMBCBCE
       128240  GJLMNPBCBCDE
       128200  GJJLMNPBCBCDE
       128160  GHJKLMNPBCBCDEF
       128120  GHIJKLLDJLMNPBCKBCDFG
       128080  GHIJKLLDIJLNBCVJKBCFG
       128040  GIKLLBDIJCHJKBFGHJ
       128000  KGLLMBCDICGHIJKFGHIJK
       127960  KGLMBCDICEFGHIJKFGHIJK
       127920  KGKLMBCDFHICEFGHIJKLNFHIJKB
       127880  KIBDFGMKLMBCDFHICEFGIJKLNPFIJKLBC
       127840  HIBCDFGMKLMBCDFGHCDEFGIJLMNPFIKLCDGBC
       127800  HIBIBCDEFMKLMNBCDEFGHCDEFILMNPILNBCDGBCD
       127760  HBBCDEMKLMNBCEFGHCDELMPLNBCDFGHBCD
       127720  HBBCDEMKLMNPBEFGHCDELMPLMNBCDEFGHBCD
       127680  HPBBCEMKLMNPBEFHCDELMLMNPBCDEFGHIHBLMNPCDE
       127640  HPBBCEMKLMNPBEFCELLMNPBCDEFHIEHBCHIJLMNPDE
       127600  HPEBNBCEMNKLMNPBEFCMNPBCDEIDEFGHNPBCEGHIJKLMNPE
       127560  PBCNBCMNKMNPBCMNPBCDEIDEFGHINPBCFGHIJKLMNPE
       127520  PBIJDFNBCMNKMNBMNPBDIJCDEFGHIMNPBCDFGHJKNE
       127480  EFBIPDFNBCMNKNPIJCDEGIKLMNBDEFGKE
       127440  EFBIPCDEFNPBCNKNPIJCDIKLMNDEFE
       127400  FBIKPDELPBCNPKPIJCIEJKLMDEEF
       127360  BBDIKPDELPNPKPIJCIEFJKLMDEEF
       127320  BCBDIKPBDEKLNPBCDKJBCIJKBEFGIJKLDF
       127280  BDBDGPBDEHKLNPBCDBCKJKBCIJKBDEFGHIJKLDF
       127240  CDBDPBHKBPNBCDFLBCDKJKBCIJKBCDEFGHIJLF
       127200  DDDHIKBHILPNBCDFGKLBCDEKJKBJKLBCDEGHIF
Price  127160  DHIHILNPNBCDFGKLBCDEKJKIBJKLBCDEGHF
       127120  MNCEHFHIHIJLMNBCDEFGKLBCDEFGJKKHIBJKLNBCDEHF
       127080  MNHEEFHLMNBDEFGKLMNBCDEFFGHIJKKLHIJBJKLNBCDEF
       127040  MHIEFCHKBDFEGJKLMNCDEFCFGHIJKKLGHIJJLNPCDFG
       127000  MPILBCDCBDFHEGHJKMNCDEFMNCEFGHIJKKLMGHIJJLNPCDFGH
       126960  BCBCDCDEFGDEHJKMNDEFGMNCDEFIJKKLMBGHJKJLMNPCFGHI
       126920  JMBCDBCDDFGDEFGIDEHJKMNDFGMNPCDEKLMBGHJKLLMNPGHI
       126880  BMPBCDBCDDEGDEFGIDHJKMNGMNPBCDLMBCFGHJKLLMMGHI
       126840  MBCDBCDDEGIDHIJKNPGLMNPBCDLMNPBCEFGKLLMNGHI
       126800  MBCBDDEGIDHIIJNPGLMNPBCMNPBCDEFGKLMPLMNGILM
       126760  PBCBIDHIBEIJNPGHLMBMNPBCDEFGKLMNPLMNILCLMNB
       126720  PBCBIBDIBEHIJPHLMBMNPBCDEFGKLMNPLMIKLMCKLMNB
       126680  KBCIBIBDIBCEFGHIHLNPCDGMNIKLMBCFKLMNBEFHIK
       126640  KCBINPBDIJBCEFGHHIKLCDMNIJKLMNBCFJKLMNBCEFGHIKL
       126600  BINPBDIJBCEFGHHIJKLCDMNIJKLMNBCDEFGJKMNBCDEFGHIJKLM
       126560  GKBJNPBDIJBCDEFGHHIJKLCDMNIJKLMNBCDEFGHIJKNPBCDEGHIJKLM[a]
       126520  PFGKJNPBCDIJKNPCDEFGHIJKCDMNIJKLMNBCDEFGHIJNPBCDEGHJKLM
       126480  NPIFGJKJKLNBCDIJKNPCDEFGIJKCJKMNBDEGHIJNPCDEHM
       126440  NJKKLNBCDIJKMNPCDFGIJKCJKNPBDEGHINPCDM
       126400  GJLKLMNBCDIJKMNPCDFGIJJKNPDHPDM
       126360  LMKLMNBCDKMNCDFGJNPDM
       126320  LMKLMNBCKMNCDJPDM
       126280  CLMKLMKLMNCDPM
       126240  MNKMKLMNPMN
       126200  ELMBMNMKLMNMN
       126160  EBNKLMMN
       126120  DNKLMMNP
       126080  DNKLMNP
       126040  DNPLMNP
       126000  DHNPLP
       125960  HNPLP
       125920  FHNPLP
       125880  FNPP
       125840  BCP
       125800  B

       Time  ------------------------------------------->
```

[a] High TPO price.

FIGURE 2.4 Intermediate-term market profile: March 2006 S&P 500 futures contract, November 21, 2005–December 29, 2005.
Source: Copyright ©2006 CQG, Inc. All rights reserved worldwide. www.cqg.com.

announcing the inevitable rally. But if such a rally were really imminent, the point of control should have been rising, not falling. Volume, as revealed through the Market Profile, was indicating a consensus that said something altogether different than what the "experts" were predicting.

DEMYSTIFYING MARKET BEHAVIOR

The Market Profile is a powerful tool for capturing the structure of the market as it is being built. While Figure 2.1 resembles a normal bell curve, Figure 2.4 reveals a volume that skews toward the bottom of the profile. Price alone cannot distinguish between a market in which movements away from value will be retraced, versus a market that is transitioning from bracketing to trending or from trending to bracketing. Sophisticated traders—defined as those that survive and prosper over the long haul—quickly adapt to different strategies depending on the bracket/trend bifurcation. Investors that incorporate market-generated information effectively increase the odds that they can determine whether the current market action is occurring within the context of an intermediate or longer-term bracket, or as part of a trend. The strategies for each of these two types of markets are quite different, which we will discuss at length in later chapters.

In order to identify change early enough to act, you must be creative, flexible, and innovative when you process information. You have to be able to interpret the fundamentals of market activity in a way that keeps your head clear of the deluge of conflicting information. Any individual or organization that hopes to be consistently successful must continue to learn and develop fresh approaches to investing, always questioning the status quo, reviewing standard practices, and extending their knowledge base.

The Market Profile, which is entirely process driven, provides an objective, visual structure to market activity that reflects the embodiment of the actions of all timeframes and market participants. Once you have learned to read and interpret this profile, it becomes possible to demystify market behavior. You can gain a significant advantage over the competition by better understanding and capitalizing on the market's reaction to fundamental information—before the market reacts and opportunity is lost.

CHAPTER 3

Timeframes

Knowledge is little; to know the right context is much; to know the right spot is everything.

—Hugo von-Hofmannsthal

Change influences market participants of every type, from the day trader to the long-term portfolio manager. Chapter 2 established that we are all affected in varying degrees by the evidence—or lack of evidence—that is revealed as time passes and our decisions are cast in new light. The next step in developing a more holistic market understanding is to explore the significance of market participants' timeframes and the distribution of volume among those timeframes. You are better equipped to assess market risks and opportunities when you understand the ways in which various timeframes coexist and intersect and how this interaction results in volume distribution that reveals the motivation of each timeframe within the evolving market landscape.

To illustrate the importance of volume distribution, we'll look at the automotive and housing industries. General Motors is a "long-timeframe producer" of automobiles, and we, the general public, are "long-timeframe purchasers." (When we use the term *long-timeframe,* we are referring to those market participants whose actions are the result of a long-term commitment.) Of course, we generally don't buy cars directly from GM—rather, we go to our local independent dealer, who operates in the "intermediate timeframe" (those market participants whose motives and commitments are shorter term in nature). Let's examine the role volume plays when these various timeframes interact, as the resulting analysis applies equally well to all markets that are financial in nature.

GM sells a car to the dealer, and the dealer sells the car to an individual. In this perfect scenario, all participants are satisfied. In the real world, however, transactions are never so simple. Let's expand the scope, and say GM sells 50 cars to the dealer, but only 34 of them are purchased by consumers. The dealer's inventory begins to build, and he is forced to offer more aggressive discounts in order to attract sales and balance inventories.

When the dealer sees his lot overflowing, he reduces the orders that he places with General Motors. If dealers all over the country are experiencing the same slowdown in sales, GM will also experience inventory build-up. In order to keep sales and production lines moving, GM will begin to offer incentives to both the dealer and the individual purchaser.

It is worth noting that over the years a substantial number of well-known researchers and economists have failed to recognize the importance of volume distribution among timeframes—as well as the relevance of the very existence of different timeframes. For example, a respected economist recently suggested that it is obvious that there is "a buyer for every seller and a seller for every buyer." While it may be obvious that every sale comes with a corresponding purchase, what many fail to grasp is the relevance of which *timeframes* are behind the buying and selling. This powerful piece of knowledge unlocks key information about the potential for future directional movement.

In our automotive industry example, it is true that overall volume remained constant—for every seller there was, in fact, a buyer. However, *the timeframe that was holding that volume* had everything to do with price movement. Because the dealers and GM were holding the majority of inventory (volume), price had to move lower to attract long-term buyers.

A review of the housing industry over the past five years also serves to highlight the importance of timeframes and volume distribution. As interest rates fell, driving mortgage rates to historic lows, more families (long-timeframe buyers) began to purchase single-family residences. As the real estate market began to heat up, builders like Toll Brothers Inc. (long-timeframe sellers) built both on contract and speculation, confident they could sell into the hot housing market. Talk in the media, among brokers, and in coffee shops consistently described the real estate market as a "seller's market." The combination of a poorly performing equity market, attractive mortgage rates, and rising home prices caused investors to begin to view real estate as an attractive investment alternative. By 2005, following several years of consistently rising home prices, nearly 25 percent of all individuals (intermediate-term timeframes) held second homes.

Let's look a little closer at the different timeframe participants in the housing market and how their actions drove the auction process. Initially, there was a reasonably close balance between the long timeframe buyer and seller. As the market continued to heat up, however, an imbalance developed between them; builders (sellers) couldn't meet demand and so price began to auction higher seeking a new balance. With prices rising (advertising opportunity), more and more local builders entered the market place, building homes both on contract and for speculation. Among the last to enter the foray were the inexperienced individual investors, just as they did at the height of the tech bubble just five years prior. Individuals with no real estate experience whatsoever were buying second, third, and fourth homes with "no money down," hoping to flip them three to six months later at a huge profit. Essentially, a new breed of short-term real estate "traders" was born. But finally, as in all auctions, the imbalance of demand shifted and the housing market became over supplied, which lead to inventory being held by the shortest of timeframes.

The real estate example is similar to the GM example, even though the industries are completely different. Our position has always been that *all markets* that are financial in nature—whether they are comprised of stocks, bonds, commodities, futures, currencies, real estate, automobiles, or any other goods and services—operate in a similar fashion: they all involve an auction process of some form that facilitates the involvement of participants operating under different timeframes.

The market's auction process serves to fairly distribute bids and offers. In Chapter 4, we explore in greater depth how the market's auction process also serves as an important information-discovery mechanism, traveling (via price) up and down to uncover and accommodate the needs of both supply and demand. By observing this auction process unfold via the Market Profile tool, we can begin to assess the attitudes and interactions of the different timeframes. Just as in the GM and real estate examples, imbalances in the securities markets occur among different timeframes and the markets adjust to accommodate. However, unlike the automobile and housing markets with their slow-moving inventories, the securities markets enable extremely fast build-up and liquidation of inventories, which makes it extraordinarily difficult to continually assess market conditions. It is precisely for this reason that market-generated information and the Market Profile are so valuable.

BREAKING DOWN MARKET TIMEFRAMES

The concepts in this book are built on an understanding of the way the various timeframes coexist, intersect, and interact. To establish a foundation for this understanding, we must first define the different market timeframes, as well as the general motivations of each.

Scalper

The scalper lives by the minute hand, continually buying and selling in order to take advantage of fleeting discrepancies in order flow. Scalpers may make as many as several hundred trades a day, comprising thousands of contracts. The classic image of a scalper portrays an individual who shouts, shoves, and survives on the exchange floors. But advances in technology and mobile communication now enable the scalper to conduct his or her business from virtually anywhere.

Scalpers rely on intuition. They buy from and sell to all timeframes, and their ability to respond to the immediate needs of the marketplace provides essential liquidity. As you may have guessed, this, the shortest of timeframes, tends to be utterly detached from longer-term economic thinking; fundamental information is far too slow and cumbersome. The scalper's world is that of bids and asks and order-flow depth. I remember when a friend and comember of the CBOT called to tell me that one of the most successful local traders wanted to come up to my office for a chat. Just before we hung up, my friend said, "Don't mess this guy up with theory—he knows nothing about the inverse relationship between bond prices and yield. He's just a master of reading order flow."

Day Trader

The day trader enters the market with no position and goes home the same way. Day traders process news announcements, reflect on technical analysis, and read order flow in order to make trading decisions. They also have to deal with long- and short-term program buying and selling, brokerage firm margin calls, mortgage banker's duration adjustments, speeches by Federal Reserve governors, and "important pronouncements" by political leaders and influential portfolio managers. Anyone who believes markets are rational should spend a day trying to digest and react to the landslide of conflicting data day traders must wade through to make a decision.

This group focuses on large quantities of technical information; they love numbers and levels and hype. Like scalpers, day traders also provide liquidity for markets, although very often at great personal expense.

Short-Term Traders

Short-term traders often hold trades longer than a day, but usually not longer than three to five days. There is no scientific evidence to support this view, but I observed this timeframe's behavior when I ran a discount brokerage firm in Chicago in the late 1980s. Short-term traders, such as day traders, have to contend with a huge quantity of data. But they tend to pay more attention to technical and economic fundamentals. Short-term traders generally focus on multiple days of overlapping prices, attempting to buy the lows and sell the highs while watching for breakouts. They use market-momentum indicators and monitor trend lines and trading channels to time their buys and sells. They are not out to influence market behavior but to be flexible and adaptable enough to react to and capitalize on events that trigger short-term market movements.

Intermediate Traders/Investors

The difference between intermediate traders/investors and short-term traders is simply that they operate from a longer point of view. Participants of this timeframe are often referred to as "swing traders" because they look to trade the tops and bottoms of intermediate-term ranges such as the one illustrated in Figure 3.1, which illustrates the S&P market from November 11, 2005, through February 16, 2006. Intermediate traders bank on the fact that markets, like pendulums, travel only so far in one direction before changing course.

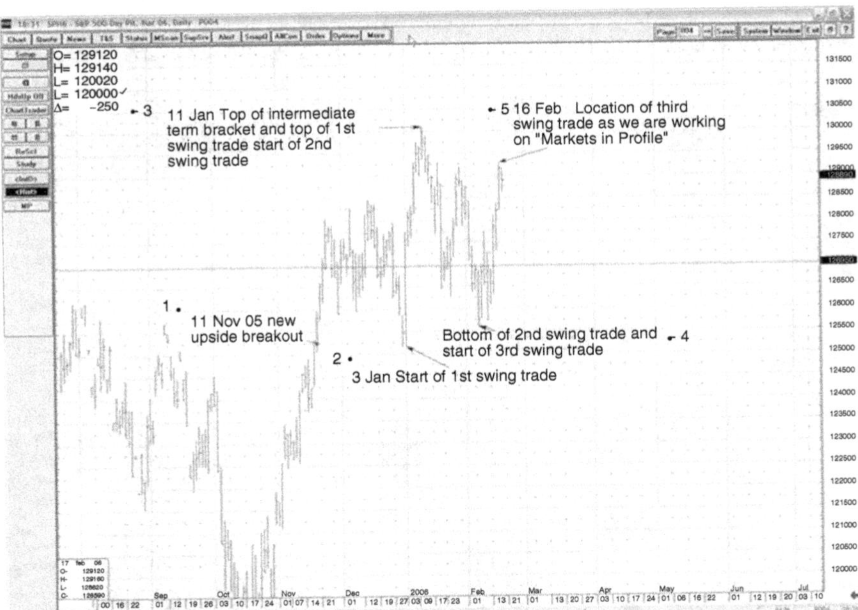

FIGURE 3.1 Intermediate-term trading ranges: S&P 500 daily bar chart, November 11, 2005, through February 16, 2006.
Source:

Within the range defined in Figure 3.1, consolidation areas developed that provided shorter-term traders with fertile fishing grounds. The point here is that the intermediate timeframe relies on distance traveled, not time, to influence trade decisions. Within consolidation areas, volatility can become quite extreme because combinations of these shorter timeframe investors and traders are often active at the same time—and in opposite directions.

The intermediate timeframe uses both fundamental and technical analysis, and normally has no desire to break new ground, choosing instead to operate within historic trading ranges. However, they do pay close attention to momentum and will quickly jump on board a trend when the longest timeframe begins to move prices beyond the containment levels of the intermediate-term market. When this activity occurs, multiple timeframes are acting in concert and longer-term trends often develop.

The weekly bar chart of the S&P 500 in Figure 3.2 shows several intermediate-term trading ranges. Notice that the market tends to spend much more time in overlapping ranges (brackets) than it does trending. This is typical. Notice also that there are several smaller trading ranges within the intermediate-term brackets, and that these brackets (at least

FIGURE 3.2 Shorter-term trading ranges contained within intermediate-term brackets: S&P 500 weekly bar chart, April 2002 through February 2006.
Source: Copyright © 2006 CQG, Inc. All rights reserved worldwide. www.cqg.com.

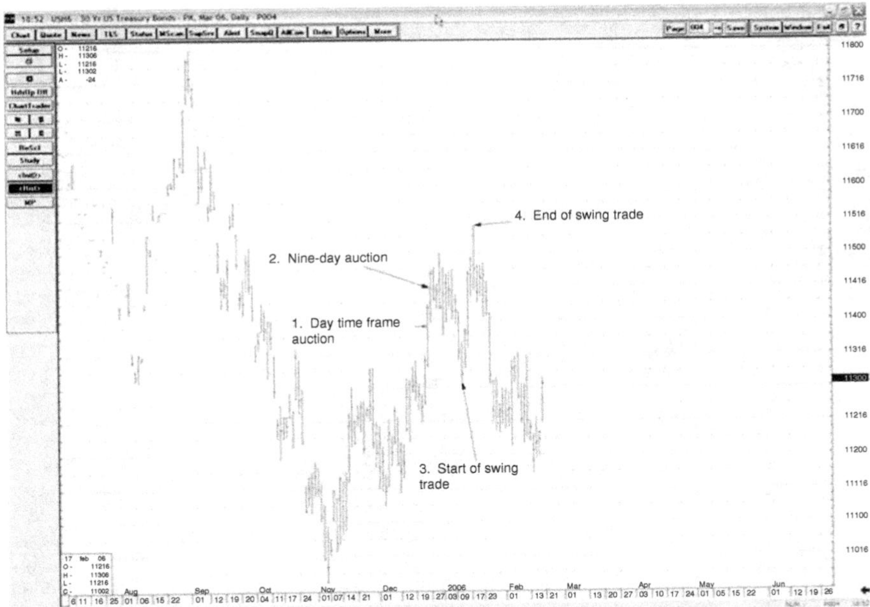

FIGURE 3.3 Day-timeframe auction, shorter-term timeframe and a swing trade: Daily bar chart, 30-year U.S. treasury bonds.

in this case) held for eight months to a year. The shorter-term trading ranges within well-defined, intermediate-term brackets are the focus of the shorter-term traders we discussed earlier. In the last several chapters of this book, we offer tactical trading guidance for day traders, short-term traders, intermediate-term traders, and longer-term investors.

Figure 3.3 shows: (1) a day-timeframe auction; (2) a nine-day, shorter-term auction; and (3) and (4) the start and end of a swing trade occurring in the U.S. Treasury bond market. With the exception of the day timeframe, it is important to understand that the remaining classifications are defined in general terms and vary depending on both market activity and how each individual trader/investor visualizes the market. For example, while some investors see long-term trades in terms of years, others in the money management industry consider "long term" to be a much shorter duration.

Long-Term Investors

Long-term investors are far more attached to the securities they own. They have a stronger tendency to buy securities and put them away for some

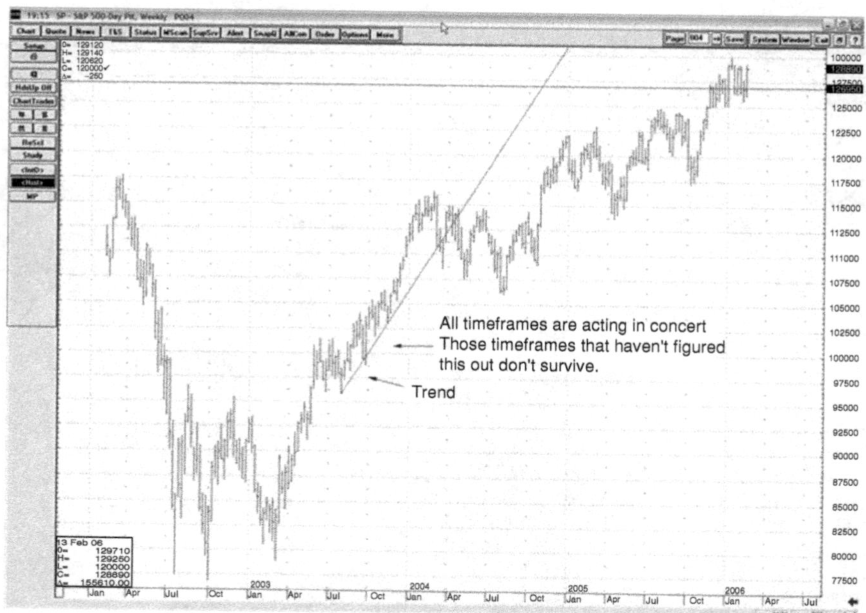

FIGURE 3.4 All timeframes active to produce a strong upward trend: S&P 500 weekly bar chart, January 2002 through February 2006.
Source: Copyright © 2006 CQG, Inc. All rights reserved worldwide. www.cqg.com.

time, with holding periods from months up to several years. When they are active, they tend to deal in large positions that are very visible to the market. Intuitive shorter timeframe participants understand that when the long timeframe enters the market, their purchases are likely to be large and possibly ongoing. With the size of money management firms these days, individual trades—even partial trades—can result in huge orders. In fact, some shorter-timeframe traders research what the long-term investors already hold, so that when they sense them selling they can take advantage of the resulting price movement. When the longest timeframe becomes active, it is not uncommon for all other timeframes to join in a large movement that can result in a major trend. Figure 3.4 shows just such a movement occurring in the S&P 500 during the latter half of 2003. Those traders who fail to grasp transitions of that magnitude will not survive.

When we take an even longer-term perspective, we can more clearly see how the various timeframes coexist, act in concert, and merge over time. Figure 3.5 shows:

1. All timeframes are acting in unison, resulting in a longer-term upward trend.

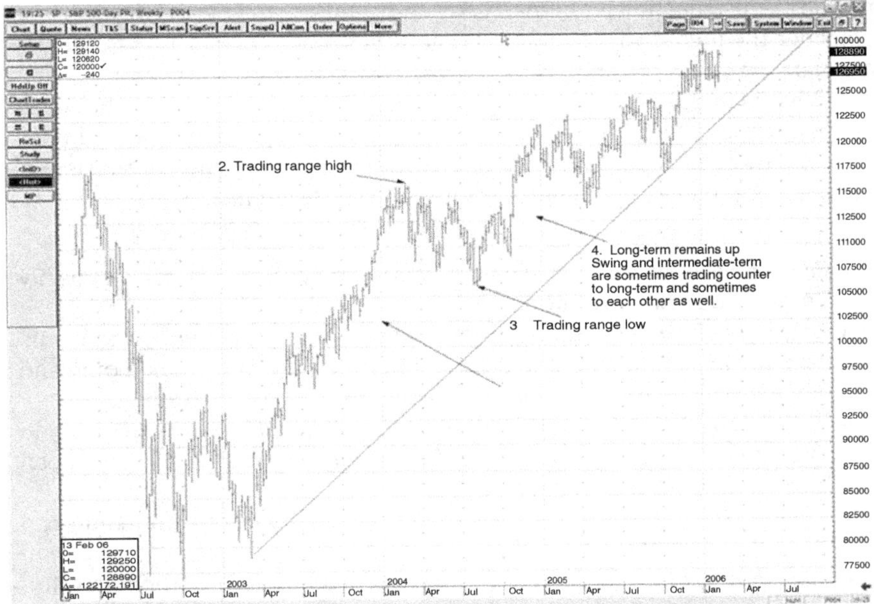

FIGURE 3.5 Coexistence of multiple timeframes: S&P 500 weekly bar chart, January 2002 through February 2006.
Source: Copyright © 2006 CQG, Inc. All rights reserved worldwide. www.cqg.com.

2. The longer-term trend tops out (temporarily) when the market begins a series of intermediate timeframe auctions as it balances and seeks equilibrium. Here, longer timeframe buyers provide support to the market, while the day, shorter-term, and intermediate timeframes facilitate the auction process from both sides of the market. As a result of this auction process, long-term value is established at higher price levels.
3. After the period of balance, the longer-timeframe buyer auctions price above the balance area and the longer-term trend continues.

Long-term investors, as we're defining them here, are responsible for breaking new ground, starting trends, upsetting the status quo. While this investor timeframe doesn't necessarily account for a large portion of market volume, it is generally responsible for large directional moves in the market. Why? Because the shorter timeframes primarily exist to facilitate liquidity, while the long-term investor is placing substantial orders in one direction. In other words, long-term money is much "stickier."

Long-term investors tend to look at the fundamentals of a company, the quality of their earnings, cash flow to book value, P/E multiples, talent, new ideas, pricing power, industry strength, and so on. They might not even consider the technical information that drives many shorter timeframe decisions.

What is important about the preceding discussion is the idea that market activity is influenced by a wide variety of participants operating under a wide variety of timeframes and motivations. The way each of these participants combines and employs information is different:

- *Scalpers* are aware of key market reference points, but rely primarily on intuition and order flow.
- *Day traders* depend almost exclusively on market-generated information, because fundamental information is usually too cumbersome and can actually be counterintuitive for the process of day trading.
- *Short-term traders* supplement market-generated information with an awareness of recent fundamental information and the effects it can have on market movement.
- *Intermediate-term traders* rely on a balanced mix of fundamental and market-generated information.
- *Long-term investors* tend to follow fundamental information first, followed by market valuation, finally looking to market-generated information to supplement their understanding of market activity and individual securities. They also keep an eye out for trims and adds, and inflow and outflow of funds requirement.

It's not easy to comprehend the nature and interaction of the different timeframes. And it's extremely challenging to detect their everchanging influence to implement a successful trading strategy. That's why it's essential that you understand the fundamental nature of each timeframe before we build on that knowledge with new concepts—concepts that may initially appear contradictory. We structured *Mind over Markets* around the five steps of learning (the path from novice to expert), and it is worth noting here that in order to take your market insight to the next level, you'll have to unlearn some of the rules that got you where you were before. But once you have jettisoned concepts that may be limiting the breadth of your knowledge, you'll be better able to comprehend and integrate the myriad relevant pieces necessary to understanding the broader paradigm of market activity.

In real-time trading and investing, the timeframes are far more difficult to distinguish than the neat descriptions above might suggest. While we have identified them separately, all timeframes coexist, intersect, and interact with one another in a constantly shifting tapestry. It is the study of this coexistence, intersection, and interaction that will comprise your real learning. And, in one way or another, it is largely the topic of the balance of this book.

As you continue to observe market activity, you will begin to recognize combinations of timeframe patterns over time. Trading requires a great deal of mental flexibility, because once you have learned to recognize a certain pattern, it may soon be supplanted by another, more-relevant pattern, which itself will eventually perish. The point being that traders who integrate discipline, emotional control, and an agile market understanding are generally able to let go of prior patterns and habits that are no longer working. To be successful, investors must recognize the confluence of evolving factors that will eventually lead to a changing market atmosphere.

YOUR TIMEFRAME IS YOUR STRATEGY CORNERSTONE

If you can correctly identify which timeframe is in control of market activity, and you have a good understanding of how the individual timeframes generally behave, then you are in a stronger position to trade, invest, and effectively control risk.

Throughout the course of this book, you will not only learn how to identify which timeframes are active and in control at any given moment, but you will also begin to learn to identify *your own timeframe*; that is, the timeframe that suits your investment personality best. This is vital, for if you don't have an accurate idea of your timeframe and how it behaves in the context of all other timeframes, you are setting yourself up to be confused and misled by conflicting information. For example, it's easy to be right in the short term but wrong in the long term—a position which can be extraordinarily costly. Once you have clearly defined your timeframe—and how it coexists, intersects, and interacts with the others—you will be more confident and better disciplined, and therefore less likely to break strategy when the market acts contrary to your expectations. You'll also be more cognizant of the larger context, which will enable you to improve your trade location—and good trade location is the key to managing risk, in every timeframe.

CHAPTER 4

Auctions and Indicators

Discovery consists of seeing what everybody has seen and thinking what nobody has thought.
—Albert von Szent-Gyorgyi

In this chapter, we'll discuss how the factors that influence market activity—*information* and the different *timeframes* that process and react to that information—can be observed in a context that promotes *transparency*. We use the term "transparency" here because it means "readily understandable" while also relating to the clarity of your decision-making process. Even when something is utterly clear, if we lose sight of the larger context, we are liable to make significant errors in judgment.

The Market Profile assembles the building blocks of market activity (time, price, and volume) by organizing the auction process into a coherent visual framework. A market profile is an entirely objective organizational tool that incorporates all information in a context that is free of bias, free from the conflicting indicators generated by an overwhelming number of facts, each influenced and surrounded by a diverse set of circumstances. In short, a market profile provides "transparent" information. That is, information that is available to all market participants on an unrestricted basis; information that is easily understood and available in a single coherent mechanism; and information that manifests ongoing market activity in the form of recognizable shapes and patterns.

Let's now assemble the specific elements of market-generated information so that our decision-making process becomes transparent—and you can start to develop an understanding of what key structural patterns may indicate with respect to future market activity.

Historically, price has been the main piece of information that has promoted transparency. The Center for Research in Security Prices (CRSP) at the University of Chicago provides years of price data for indexes, stocks, bonds, and mutual funds. Unfortunately, price without context is just a number—for all intents and purposes a random event. A sequence of prices can be entirely misleading as it leaves vital questions unanswered: Did a particular price occur on higher or lower volume? Was a price sequence the result of new business or old business (short covering and long liquidation are considered old business, as they don't contribute to net new long or short positions)? Which timeframe was primarily responsible for that price? Which direction was the market *attempting* to travel at the time the price occurred? As you will see, a market profile provides answers to these all-important questions by giving *dimension* to price—dimension that is necessary to achieve complete transparency.

In Chapter 2, we identified the three fundamental elements that comprise the market's auctions—time, price, and volume. We stated that *price* is simply the auction's means of advertising opportunity, with *time* regulating each opportunity, and *volume* measuring the success or failure of each auction.

These three auction elements can also be viewed as follows:

- Price is a volatile variable and the fastest moving market element.
- Time is the constant around which all auction data is organized.
- Volume is also a variable, but it changes much more gradually than price (and volume represents the interaction of time and price).

THE SEARCH FOR VALUE

To better understand how price, time, and volume create market-generated information, imagine that you're attending an art auction. Before the first item is introduced, you sit in the audience and ponder a question that has been nagging you, recently: How does auction movement reveal the motivations of the market's participants?

The lights dim, a spotlight reveals a lovely oil painting center stage, and the auctioneer begins his rhythmic pitter-patter banter. The excitement in the room is palpable. "We start the bidding for this remarkable landscape at nine hundred," he says, "nine hundred . . . nine hundred? Do I have nine hundred for this beautiful work?"

You stare at the painting and think it might make a nice addition to your living room. No one has yet bid, and so the auctioneer lowers the price, looking for that first paddle to rise: "Now eight fifty . . . eight fifty? Do

I have eight fifty for this unique oil painting—*I have* eight fifty. Do I have nine? . . . ."

Because no one responded to the initial price, the auctioneer quickly lowered the bid until he found a level at which participants began to respond. Now that the ice is broken and the auction is underway, the bid quickly exceeds the initial, unaccepted $900 bid: "I'm bid *nine hundred*. . . now nine and a quarter nine and a quarter. I'm bid nine and a quarter . . . now *nine fifty*, nine fifty, I'm bid *nine seventy-five*."

The bid races to a thousand dollars, and you feel your adrenaline surge, as you really like the painting. You lift your paddle and the auctioneer nods and his patter speeds on, the price ratcheting rapidly higher as he creates excitement with the intensity of his voice. Once bidding gets underway, it's quite common to have bidding begin to build. Just like in the financial markets, very few individuals want to accept the risk of being first and being wrong, which might be seen as foolish by peers.

The price of the painting climbs past $1,500, and you decide the green of the fields might actually clash with your living-room rug. The auctioneer's rapid-fire delivery continues unabated, sustaining the excitement in the room. But being a careful listener, you note that he is beginning to add quite a lot of "filler" to his patter to make it appear that the auction is still proceeding higher. This process continues until the last bidder bids, and the rant is capped with a hearty: "SOLD at eighteen seventy-five!" You're glad you didn't get caught up in the hype, and you turn your attention to the next piece being unveiled on stage.

In the preceding example, there was only one item to be auctioned. If this were the everflowing process of a financial market, however, the auction would have begun again in the opposite direction once the upward auction had discovered the last bidder. From the price at which the auction finally got under way—$850—there was only a brief price/time relationship because price moved quickly. As price began to climb steadily higher, "value" was established as multiple bidders actively engaged in the auction at prices they believed to be fair. At the level where the price advance began to slow, and the auctioneer began to pad his banter in order to make it seem as if the auction were still healthy, an extended price/time relationship developed; bidders in the top quadrant of the price range were most probably engaged in an overreaction to the momentum of the auction, finally purchasing above the value area.

The *value area*, as we explained in Chapter 2, represents the range in which approximately 70 percent of the volume of activity took place (one standard deviation of the resulting bell curve's distribution). In the art auction, there was a lone bidder at the bottom and a lone buyer at the top, and of course the highest number of bidders in the middle; volume was high in this range because the auction process revealed an area of "fair value"

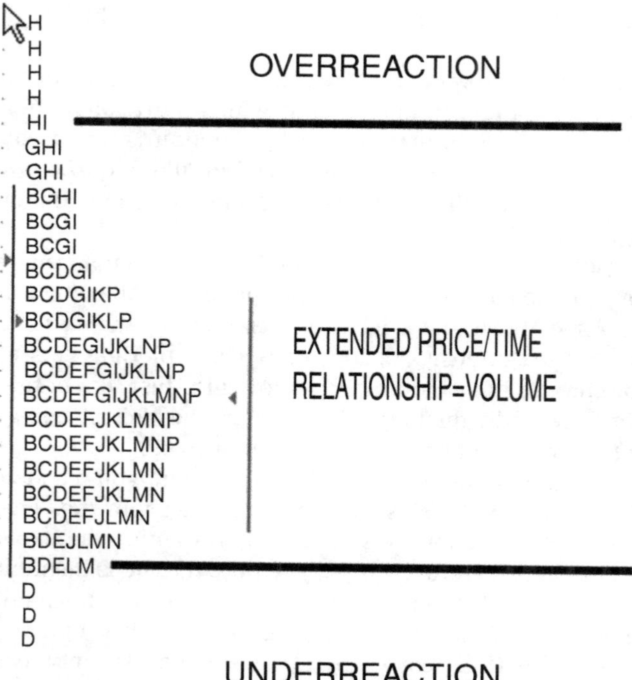

FIGURE 4.1 The value area and its relationship between price, time and volume. Source: Copyright © 2006 CQG, Inc. All rights reserved worldwide. www.cqg.com.

for the painting on the block. In a financial market, the value area at the end of the day represents the range within which most market participants that had day-timeframe business to conduct were willing to enact that business. A review of Figure 4.1 reveals the value area in the center of the market profile. The top end of the profile was where price auctioned too high and buying dried up, and the bottom of the profile was where price auctioned too low, cutting off selling activity.

Our art auction example, of course, doesn't represent the complexity of the auction process in financial markets. Daily markets are comprised of several continuous two-way auctions that establish a range for the day, including a high, low, and value area. These indicators do not occur in any particular order—the high for the day can be established at the opening bell, right at close, or anywhere in between—and are not fully defined until the day's trading is concluded and the market profile is complete. However, with enough training, concentration, and practice, you will be able to visualize which profile patterns are most likely to develop, long before the market close.

As we begin to delve deeper into the confluence of various market variables, it is important to emphasize the value of *a receptive mind*; pattern recognition is only valuable if you can avoid wishful thinking and continually seek to understand market activity in the present tense. The patterns we are about to discuss are not set in stone. It is hoped, however, that they will serve to prepare you to recognize change ahead of your competition—and before opportunity is lost.

If you compare any given day in a market to the previous day, you will observe that some degree of change has occurred. This change may be very slight—almost insignificant, when a market is in balance. Or the change may be pronounced when the market is trending, breaking out of balance, or in the midst of a short-covering rally, liquidating break, or other unusual occurrence.

Each day will also, to some degree, create a divergence between price as it relates to value. As price attempts to move away from value, there are both expected and unexpected responses. As price auctions higher, it is *expected* that demand will dwindle and prices eventually trade back down toward the daily mean. As the prices move lower, supply usually diminishes and prices auction back up toward the daily mean, or value area.

Returning to our art auction example, we can demonstrate another phenomenon. Once the auction is underway, the price quickly surpassed the failed early attempt to open at $900 and then proceeded upward until the auction slowed and the final bid was eventually cast. In some cases, however, higher prices, instead of diminishing demand, have the opposite effect. If this had been the case, the auctioneer would not have needed filler to maintain a feeling of potential and excitement; you would have heard him say (with some enthusiasm): "New bidder!" Higher prices could have served to attract increased demand, rather than shutting it off. This kind of activity tells us that the auction is far from complete. As we have said, all markets that are financial in nature operate in a similar manner, and this same phenomenon occurs in listed markets, as demonstrated in Figure 4.2.

In Figure 4.2, price continued to auction higher throughout the day, with occasional pauses that served to communicate to new buyers that value was being accepted higher.

Concept Review

Before we proceed, let's review the salient concepts we've covered thus far in *Markets in Profile*:

1. Structure, as revealed by the Market Profile, is developed through a two-way auction process, and every day the auctions result

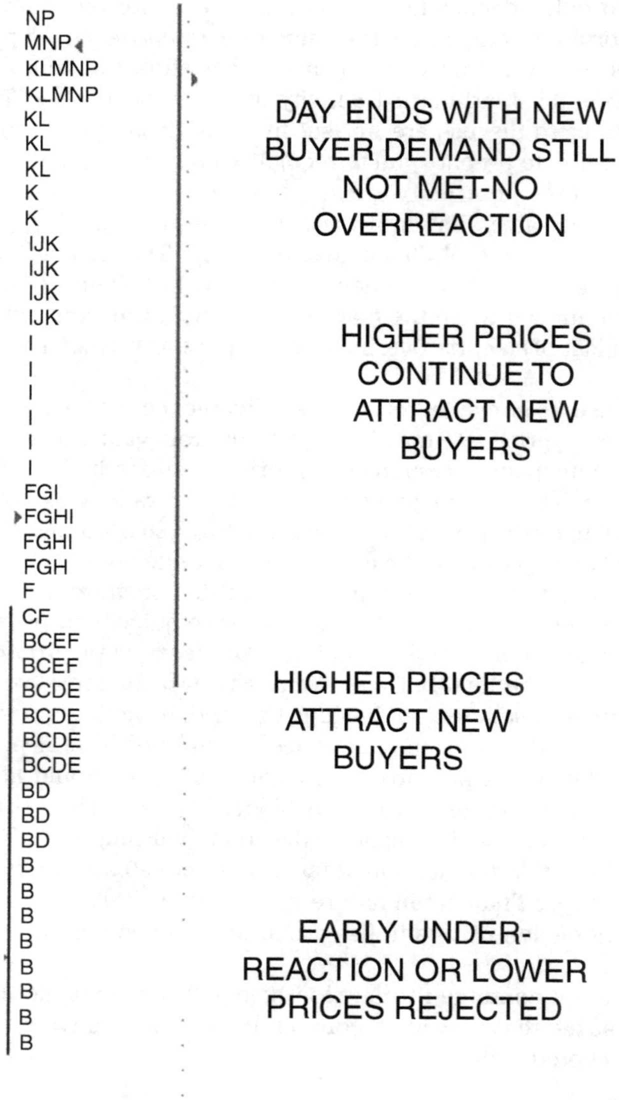

NP
MNP
KLMNP
KLMNP
KL
KL
KL
K
K
IJK
IJK
IJK
IJK
I
I
I
I
I
I
FGI
FGHI
FGHI
FGH
F
CF
BCEF
BCEF
BCDE
BCDE
BCDE
BCDE
BD
BD
BD
B
B
B
B
B
B
B
B

DAY ENDS WITH NEW BUYER DEMAND STILL NOT MET-NO OVERREACTION

HIGHER PRICES CONTINUE TO ATTRACT NEW BUYERS

HIGHER PRICES ATTRACT NEW BUYERS

EARLY UNDER-REACTION OR LOWER PRICES REJECTED

FIGURE 4.2 Price auctioning higher and attracting new buyers.
Source: Copyright © 2006 CQG, Inc. All rights reserved worldwide. www.cqg.com.

in a range, value area, high, low, and comparative amount of change when measured against previous days (and weeks, months, etc.).

2. By reviewing the resulting profile, we are able to observe the difference between price and value, so we can begin to assess whether price might return to value (see Figure 4.1) or might lead to value higher (see Figure 4.2).
3. The auctions, on most days, enable us to quickly see which prices strayed too far from value and were not accompanied by increased volume, resulting in a regression back toward the mean. In Figure 4.2, we saw just the opposite—the auction explored lower prices early in the morning and established an overreaction low, which, after the auction got started, was never challenged again that day. The upward auction continued to attract new bidders each time prices explored upper price levels, as witnessed by higher volume (acceptance of value).
4. A market profile enables us to see structure as it develops in real time. With receptivity, concentration, and practice, you can begin to visualize the final market structure prior to its completion. We will spend time more fully developing this theme in later chapters.

The practical side of what we have seen so far is as follows:

Figure 4.1. The market is in balance in the day timeframe. If you are looking to buy and the auction explores downward with the expected response—lower prices slow down supply—then you buy at those lower prices and so acquire your merchandise below perceived value. Market-generated information reveals that this is your opportunity. If you wait for price to return to value, you can still make your purchase at a "fair price" for the day (within the value area). However, buying as price explores the upper price levels—on a day in which the market is balanced in the day timeframe—means that you have acquired your merchandise at prices *above* value. And as a result, the odds are not in your favor that price will be able to raise value.

Figure 4.2. Again, if you are looking to buy and enter the market during the early downward exploration, you would have successfully purchased your merchandise below value. Waiting for a return to value will, as in the last example, still allow you to purchase merchandise at fair value. Any purchase *above* the value area (on this day) *still allows you to purchase at value* or below, because price is leading value higher. If, however, you had merchandise to sell on this day and you sold at any time, the best you could have hoped for was to sell at value; more than likely you sold at prices below value. Of course profits occur when you purchase below value and sell at or above value, but profits also occur when you buy at value and sell above value.

You should realize by now that not all prices are equal, nor are all opportunities. Buying below value in either of the examples above provided an asymmetric profit opportunity in which opportunity exceeded risk. Selling below value, in either example, also resulted in an asymmetric situation in which risk exceeded potential reward.

The key, of course, is recognizing these developing patterns *before* they're complete. Learning how to extract structural clues early in the day, or early on during an intermediate- or longer-timeframe auction, is what this book is ultimately about. Now, let's continue to explore the ways in which market-generated information enables transparency around the market's everchanging motives.

KEY MARKET-GENERATED INDICATORS

In Chapter 1, we said we would show you how to use market-generated information to identify and adapt to change before your competitors. Let's now turn our attention to several key reference points that make it possible to measure degrees of change. We have established the fact that the developing value area helps us observe the changing relationship between price and value in the day timeframe. Taking a slightly longer viewpoint, *value-area comparison* can reveal important clues about the movement of value across days and weeks. By comparing daily value areas and price ranges, the market's proclivity to change becomes somewhat transparent.

Each day's *initial balance* is also part of the larger contextual understanding that we seek. Nothing more than the range a given security traded within during the first two trading periods, the initial balance represents the market's open and initial auction explorations and can reveal vital clues as to where the day's activity is likely to occur.

Range extension occurs when new auctions lengthen the market profile shape beyond the range established during the initial balance mentioned above. Range extension is an indicator that allows us to gauge buyer/seller strength. If price auctions above the initial balance and results in new buying activity, it becomes clear that there is real buying strength; and when price auctions lower and gains acceptance, then it is apparent that selling strength is materializing. Range extension elongates the profile, allowing us to visualize the aggressiveness of buyers or sellers. Returning to our art auctioneer, if price extends upward and higher prices continue to attract additional buying, then the auctioneer would constantly be announcing "new bids!"

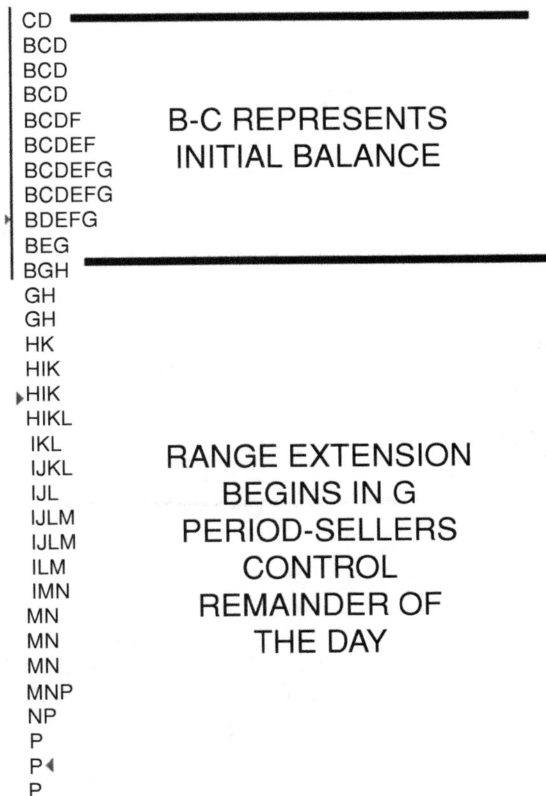

FIGURE 4.3 The initial balance and selling range extension.

Figure 4.3 shows the initial balance—B and C periods—followed by selling range extension beginning in G period and continuing downward through the end of the day.

Let's begin to synthesize these key indicators. If there is a lack of range extension, limited range extension, or range extension in both directions with price returning to the value area, then the structural evidence suggests that the market is balanced—for the time being, at least. In Figure 4.4, price explored above the initial balance (B and C periods) in G and H periods, but new buying did not occur and price returned to the center of the market profile, which reaffirms that the market was indeed balanced.

Now let's further widen our understanding of market-generated indicators by examining a day's value-area placement in relationship to the

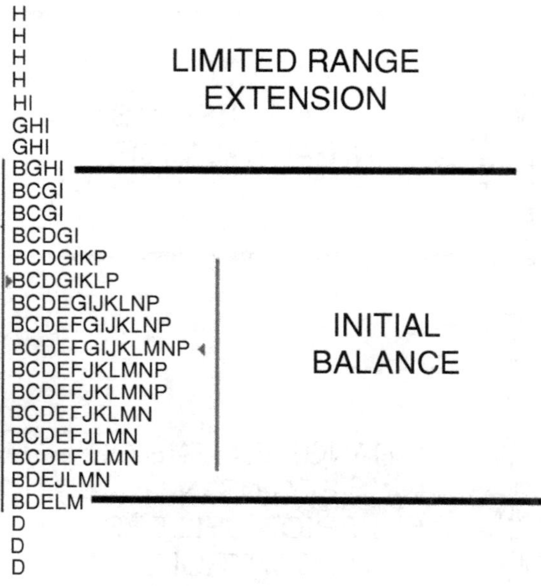

FIGURE 4.4 Range extension during a balanced market (day timeframe).
Source: Copyright © 2006 CQG, Inc. All rights reserved worldwide. www.cqg.com.

previous day's value area. Figure 4.5 graphically displays some of these possible relationships.

Starting with the relationship in the upper left of Figure 4.5, you can see that the new day's value area has developed clearly higher than the previous day's value area. We are far more interested in value than price because value is far more stable and indicative of real market momentum. For example, there are frequently occasions in which price is higher, while value is actually unchanged—or even lower. In the second example, in the upper center, the value area has migrated lower. The following two examples portray overlapping relationships, and the final two exhibit days in which value develops either outside of the previous day's value or, in the last example, totally within the prior value area.

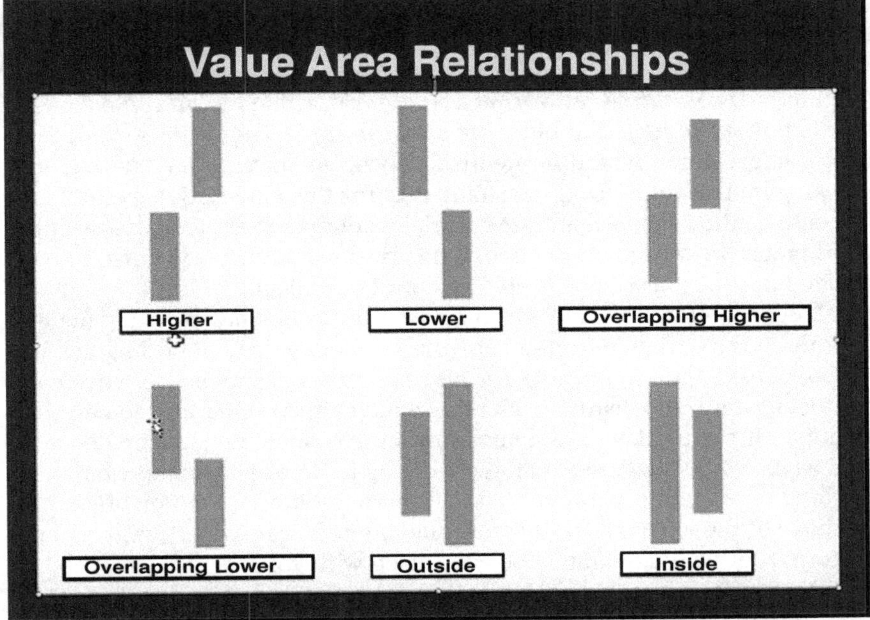

FIGURE 4.5 Value-area relationships.

In Chapter 5, we begin to create a coherent whole out of all the analytic indicators introduced here; however, before we begin that process, you must first understand the significance of volume transparency, attempted direction, and symmetry.

When we first began to employ the Market Profile in the 1980s, we could be exacting with the horizontal axis, which represents *time*, and the vertical axis, which represents *price*, but *volume* had to be estimated by employing the following formula: Price × Times = Volume. This proved to be fairly accurate when compared to the daily volume breakdown at each price level reported after the close. Only a limited number of exchanges such as the Chicago Mercantile Exchange and the Chicago Board of Trade, which fostered the development of the Market Profile, reported volume in this manner. Today, an increasing number of exchanges, both in the United States and overseas, have endorsed electronic trading, which captures volume instantly, greatly increasing transparency for all market participants. With electronic trading, time, price, and volume can be graphed in real-time via Market Profile. Where electronic trading and instant volume reporting is available, transparency is complete, and the playing field is level; all market participants have access to the same timely information on actual order flow.

Rising price on increasing volume reveals the fact that value is rising ("I'm bid *nine hundred*, now *nine and a quarter*. I'm bid nine and a quarter ... now *nine fifty*. I'm bid *nine seventy-five*.") The same scenario on decreasing volume would be neutral at best, indicating that the auction is losing momentum ("Do I hear nine fifty for this superlative example of fifteenth century landscape?"). As markets conduct their business through continuous two-way auctions, declining price on increasing volume is bearish, and decreasing volume is either neutral or bullish.

The final analysis of any given auction or trading day is highly dependent upon the variance-from-mean volume. Remember, the principles we have discussed are applicable for all timeframes. This can be extremely confusing until you learn to identify which timeframes are active. For example, if the markets are demonstrating intermediate-term balance, as well as short-term balance, volume is likely to be of lesser importance to the long-term trader. However, should the market approach or break out of either of the extremes of the intermediate-term range, the long-term investor/trader would definitely be concerned with volume.

Most serious traders and investors are familiar with the term "regression to mean." This simple concept is at the core of the current discussion—attempted breakouts that result in decreasing volume are likely to see price revert back toward the mean. Attempted breakouts that result in increasing volume, however, reveal that new, aggressive participants have entered the market. In these circumstances, new value areas are likely to be established for all timeframes.

We have continually stressed the importance of context. The following examination of *attempted direction* is no exception. The first step in properly assessing the relevance of volume is to determine which direction the market was attempting to auction when that volume was established—an assessment that can often be difficult. If the attempted direction cannot be determined, then it is not wise to make a volume assessment; the market was probably balanced, and the auctions rotated relatively equally between high and low. In Figure 4.6, for example, the market opened near the high of the daily range, traded lower, rotating several times above and below the midpoint, and finally finished near the highs for the day. In this instance, we don't see any clear signs of attempted direction. For those trading very short timeframes, such as 5- and 10-minute bars, there may have been clearly defined attempted direction. As your timeframe lengthens, however, determining attempted direction on this day became non-productive.

In Figure 4.7 (see page 54), it's relatively easy to observe that the day's attempted direction was up as the market opened near the low and closed near the high. But let's consider a more complex example, one in which

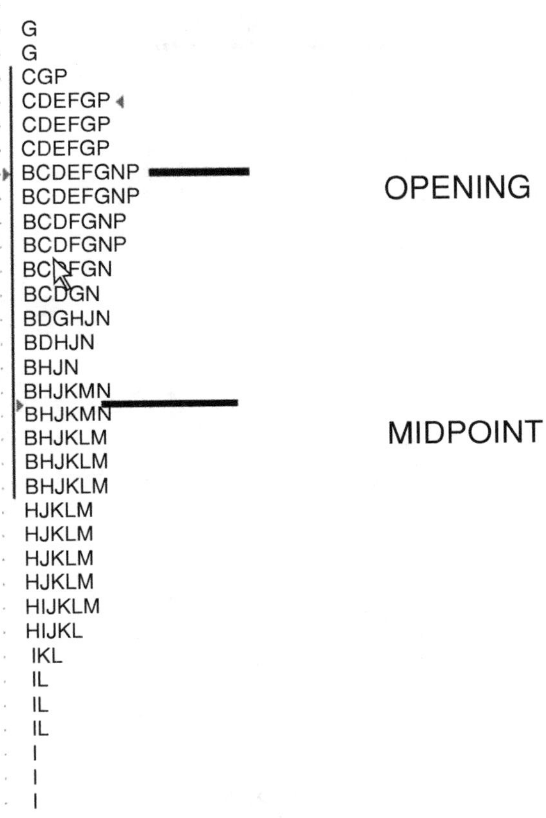

FIGURE 4.6 Attempted direction in a balanced market (day timeframe).
Source: Copyright © 2006 CQG, Inc. All rights reserved worldwide. www.cqg.com.

a stock rallies to new highs, breaking 100 for the first time. Experts go on record saying they'll buy the stock on a correction. Most investors assume that a "correction" in this context would mean a decline in prices after the stock's rally. While such a dip could occur, the "correction" does not necessarily have to result in lower prices—new long-term buyers could enter the market, buying from short-term sellers and keeping the price from falling. This activity effectively relieves holders of old long positions of their merchandise, replacing them with new long-term buyers.

Without a flexible, well-prepared mind, this latter form of correction could take place without your ever having realized it. In fact, the market could exhibit clearly *higher* price and value—but with attempted direction

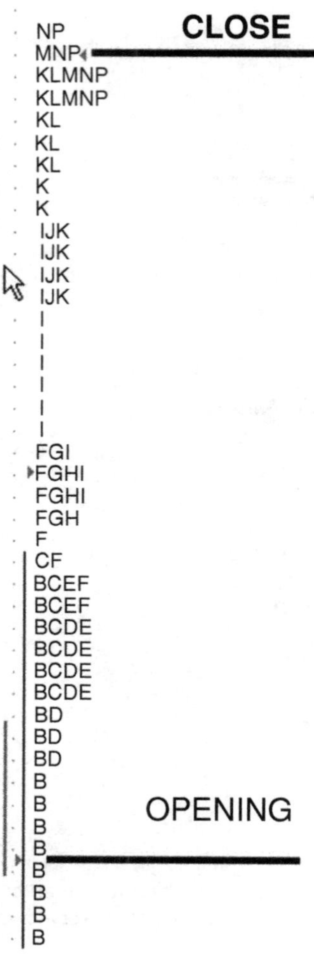

FIGURE 4.7 Attempted direction in an upward trending market.
Source: Copyright © 2006 CQG, Inc. All rights reserved worldwide. www.cqg.com.

down on decreasing volume, with prices closing on the low for the day. Without considering the larger context, price alone could confuse you, so that you completely miss the next bullish move upward. Of course, the same thing can just as easily happen on the downside.

Attempted direction is an important element in compiling a holistic opinion using market-generated information. Like any task that requires skill, however, it takes time and dedicated practice in order to learn to make the correct assessment of attempted direction on any given day.

The final market indicator we'll address in this chapter is *symmetry*. The market profile is not, as you have already surmised, always symmetrical, and that lack of symmetry can have very specific consequences. In his book *The Mature Mind* (New York: Basic Books, 2005), Gene D. Cohen, M.D., Ph.D., discusses the ways in which younger people tend to place more emphasis on the left hemisphere of the brain—that hemisphere that perceives the world analytically—in making decisions, while more mature (older) people tend to merge information from both hemispheres in their decision making. Not surprisingly, Cohen surmises that whole-brained decisions are better decisions. Words and numbers are the language of the left hemisphere, while the right hemisphere is more capable of capturing the world synthetically, parsing the meaning and import of images, models, and feelings.

The market profile captures the market's fundamental building blocks (price, time, and volume) in a visual graphic that enables us to *see* the market's structure. This allows us to evaluate market activity by using both of our information-processing modes—the analytic left hemisphere in conjunction with the synthetic right hemisphere. According to Dr. Cohen (and everybody else), this should result in better decision making.

The profile graphic captures and displays a great deal of data in a simplified form, which enables us to better understand the complex relationships that exist between the multiple economic indicators and timeframes we have discussed. A market profile that is symmetrical, within its timeframe, offers symmetric risk/reward opportunities on both the long and short side of the market. Such a market in balance represents a situation that is as close to the efficient market theory as is possible. A symmetrical market is waiting for new information before it makes its next directional move.

Nonsymmetrical profiles identify markets that are imbalanced. In such out-of-balance situations, the market profile helps identify advantageous investment opportunities, as well as situations that would yield poor odds. Nonsymmetrical markets occur under several conditions. The first develops when the market is trending, and multiple timeframes are acting in concert; the resulting series of profiles will be elongated in the direction of the move. The second is a nonsymmetrical profile with a weighted upper end, which occurs when only limited timeframes are buying the market. A pronounced example of this phenomenon, shown in Figure 4.8, generally signifies short covering that is not accompanied by new long-term buying.

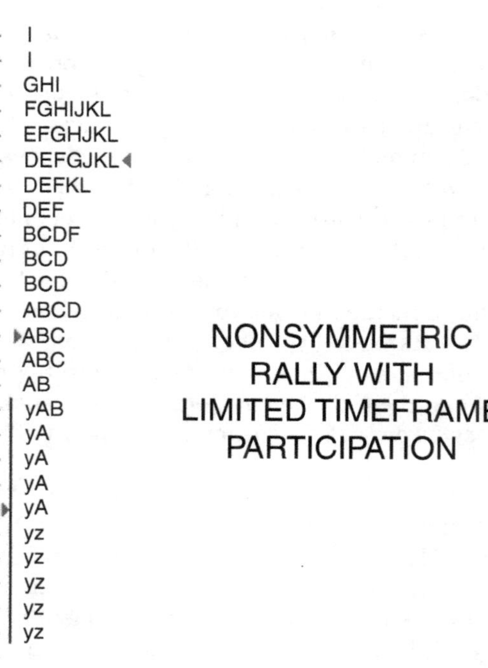

FIGURE 4.8 Nonsymmetrical profile created by short covering.
Source: Copyright © 2006 CQG, Inc. All rights reserved worldwide. www.cqg.com.

Similarly, a nonsymmetrical profile shape that is weighted to the downside represents *selling* by limited timeframes. Figure 4.9 demonstrates this condition.

PERFECTING THE ART OF VISUALIZATION

The Market Profile is a simple tool that builds a graphic out of the market's continuous auction process. As that graphic reveals itself over the course of any given day, there are key market-generated indicators that can reveal what the market is inclined to do—indicators like value area, initial balance, range extension, attempted direction, and symmetry. Any one of these indicators, when taken out of context, can lead you down a blind alley; all market activity must be observed in the light of larger market context. In the following chapters, you will begin to learn how to use the indicators highlighted here to make more effective trading decisions.

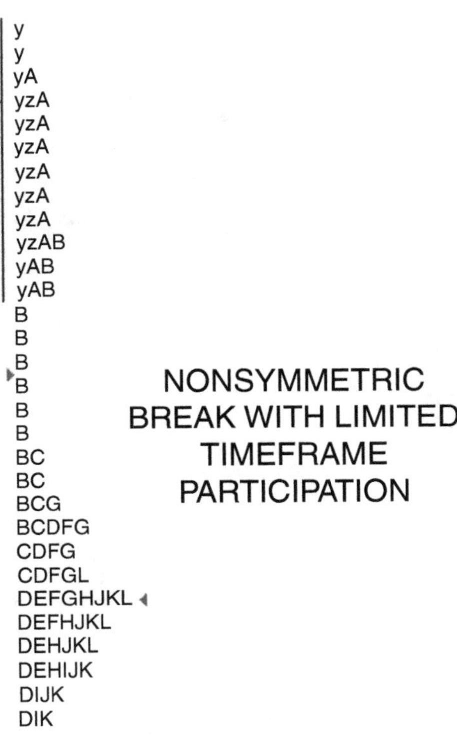

FIGURE 4.9 Nonsymmetrical profile created by long liquidation.
Source: Copyright © 2006 CQG, Inc. All rights reserved worldwide. www.cqg.com.

As in any endeavor that involves complex associations, an actionable understanding of the market's developing auction process can only be perfected through extensive observation and study. The world's top chess players are not merely "intuitive," but have spent considerable time pouring over patterns and potentialities, searching for that elusive advantage over the competition.

CHAPTER 5

Long-Term Auctions

Not everything that counts can be counted, and not everything that can be counted counts.

—Sign hanging in Albert Einstein's Princeton University office

Chapter 4 focused on isolating key indicators revealed by the auction process. The art auction we described was extremely simplified—a one-time event geared only to facilitate the sale of a single item. In the financial markets, this process is continual, with multiple timeframes influencing market behavior and multiple items continually being bought and sold. As a result, the indicators we defined never occur in isolation—they must always be considered within the complex, everchanging context of which they are a part.

To use an everyday analogy, consider the act of picking up a cup of coffee. On the surface, this process may seem so simple it needs no explanation. But the brain must first interpret the reflection of light off the cup's surface, and then send dozens of impulses to a variety of muscle groups that must work in perfect synchrony. Now think about the astounding number of simultaneous processes that must coincide flawlessly to enable a baseball player to hit a fastball moving at 90 miles per hour.

The same is true with trading: the process is complex. Markets are continuously influenced by news, multiple timeframe participants, buying and selling driven by wildly varying objectives, short covering, liquidating breaks, and on and on. When information compounds upon other information, it gets exponentially more difficult to sort out the "net effect" of the current auction and to keep the activity of the different timeframes straight. As we have said before, it takes an incredible amount of practice to become an expert trader, one who is capable of observing, understanding, and deciphering—in the present tense—the flux of constantly evolving market indicators.

AUCTIONS IN ACTION

Now, let's attempt to integrate many of the concepts that we've discussed thus far by reviewing *Treasury refunding*, a relatively short-timeframe auction. Currently, the Treasury sells bills in 3- and 6-month month maturities; notes in 2-, 5-, and 10-year maturities; 30-year bonds; and Treasury inflation-indexed securities. The auction process begins with a public announcement by the U.S. Treasury that includes which security is to be auctioned, the amount of the issuance, maturity of the security, and the amount of cash to be raised, a portion of which will re-fund maturing debt with the remainder funding new debt.

Bids are accepted up to 30 days prior to the auction; however, the primary dealers—the financial institutions that have been recognized by the New York Fed—purchase most of the inventory, generally submitting bids at the last possible moment, often just moments before the auction deadline. There are two kinds of bids that can be submitted: *competitive bids*, normally submitted by primary dealers, and *noncompetitive tenders*, which are generally submitted by small investors and individuals. The primary dealers submit bids for both themselves and their customers, and most of the securities they purchase will later be resold—to other dealers, companies, banks, individuals, and the like. The fixed-income market often "backs up," or "sells off," prior to the Treasury auctions as the dealers attempt to create a spread, so that the securities they buy can be resold at a profit. In this sense, they're similar to the automobile dealers and home builders that we discussed in Chapter 3; the government is the long-timeframe issuer of the securities, and individuals, pension funds, endowments, and foundations are among the long-term holders. If everyone guesses correctly, the newly issued securities pass from the Treasury through the dealers that make their markups and into the hands of other financial institutions that either hold them for their own accounts or resell the securities to long-term, "sticky-money" investors.

Just as we discussed in the automotive example, it doesn't always happen this way. Sometimes the dealers get stuck with inventory that isn't immediately distributed to long-timeframe investors. To balance their inventories, the remaining securities must be priced (auctioned) lower, which increases their yield and makes them more attractive to long-term buyers. The auction continues lower until balance is restored in the market.

Of course, the auction can also be extremely successful when there are more bidders than securities to go around. When this happens, it's not uncommon to see a strong upward auction begin immediately when bidders realize that they're not going to get their hands on the securities that they had hoped to acquire. These bidders may have been short, needing to buy in order to cover, or they might have simply been trying to meet their own quotas or the demands of their clients.

The point of this discussion is that auctions are everywhere—the auction process is the cornerstone of all business transactions. By being a consumer in a market society, you have an intuitive understanding of how this process works. Every time you go to the store you encounter auctions in action. When you decide to pay a higher price for a gourmet frozen pizza, the auction might not be immediately interactive (unless you have to fight through a crowd to get to the freezer), but the long-term effect is the same: if the pizzas fly off the shelf, then prices rise. Conversely, too many pizzas left on the shelf results in prices "auctioning" lower in order to balance inventory. This fundamental understanding—so simple it's taken for granted—will serve as a foundation for developing a more holistic understanding of the financial markets' *compound-auction process.*

THE COMPOUND-AUCTION PROCESS

Market-generated information—data that results from the auction process—is real-time and constantly evolving. The underlying message here is that investment ideas based on *past findings* can often block new insights, which can lead you to favor preconceptions over fresh observations. As a result, you can easily set yourself up to make flawed investment/trading decisions. Combine that tendency with the natural human inclination to focus on solutions rather than the *process* that leads to solutions; and you'll be incapable of understanding the true nature of real-time market activity. In the investment-management business, the tendency by many investment professionals to study only surface indicators has cost legions of investors untold fortunes; if the process is flawed, then you can bet the solution will be flawed as well. If your goal is to be a top-quartile competitor, then you must immerse yourself deeply in the process—the market's compound-auction process.

The art auction we referenced was a useful paradigm to identify and discuss a few individual market indicators, but the same process occurs, with greater complexity and virtually simultaneously, when there are many multiples of an item to be auctioned. For example, once a new auction gets underway, multiple participants bid for supply. At lower prices, only a few bids may be filled—the auction rises quickly if prices are perceived as unfair (below value) for sellers of a certain timeframe. As price auctions higher, more bids are accepted and some bidders drop out as prices exceed their idea of fair value. From there on, only those that must buy to meet demand, or those caught up in the auction frenzy, continue to purchase inventory as price climbs higher. Once market participants sense that prices, for their timeframe, have auctioned above value, and that demand is waning, then offers begin to exceed bids and an auction begins in the opposite direction. Hence, the compound-auction process is an ongoing, multidirectional progression that draws in participants of different timeframes, depending on the direction and significance of each interstitial price movement.

Traders and investors who operate on an intraday basis—which includes short timeframes that can range from minutes to hours—may experience several such rotational auctions in a single day. Shorter-term traders may see their trades last for several days or weeks; intermediate-term participants may find that auctions relevant to their timeframe last months; and long-term auctions can last months or years. *Recognizing where you are in the auction process determines your risk/reward relationship.* You can begin to understand where you are in the current auction process by inspecting bar charts, which enables you to essentially "speed read" the auctions, starting with the longest-term auctions and working toward the daily auctions, where trade location is ultimately secured.

THE EBB AND FLOW OF BALANCE

Through studied observation, you will notice that long-term auctions don't go from bull to bear, or bear to bull. Rather, long-term trends first transition to balancing ranges before either continuing in the original direction or beginning a new long-term auction in the opposite direction. To illustrate this principle, observe Figure 5.1, which displays the S&P 500 market for the period October 1998 through May 2006. (The time period and market are irrelevant, so long as the period is sufficiently long to include a longer-term auction.)

In this case, the S&P 500 trended upward until March 2000 and then balanced through September of that same year. In October 2000, after balancing for seven months, the S&P began a sustained, long-term downward auction that bottomed out and began to balance in October 2002. In May 2003, the market exited this balance area and began a new long-term upward trend that remains intact as this is being written (May 2006). If you look at the two periods marked "Balancing," you will observe that the

FIGURE 5.1 Long-term trends transitioning to and from balance: S&P 500 monthly bar chart, October 1998 through May 2006.
Source: Copyright © 2006 CQG, Inc. All rights reserved worldwide. www.cqg.com.

market began the balancing process several months prior to the completion of the absolute highs and lows for the respective long-term trends. Often, it is not until the balancing process is already underway that you realize the long-term auction is ending and the market is coming into equilibrium.

As you gain experience studying auctions, you will begin to recognize the beginning of this balancing, or bracketing, process. The two balancing periods noted in Figure 5.1 are examples of intermediate-term auctions (which we'll cover in more depth in the next chapter). Long-term auctions are comprised of several such intermediate-term auctions, and provide important context without which trade decisions can get lost in day-to-day information overload.

Figure 5.2 looks more closely at the S&P 500 activity shown in Figure 5.1 by focusing on (1) the start of the balancing process in July 2002, which marked the end of the downward trend that began in March 2000; (2) the upside breakout from the balancing period in May 2003; and (3) two ensuing intermediate-term auctions that are incorporated in the longer-term upward trend that continues as this book is being written.

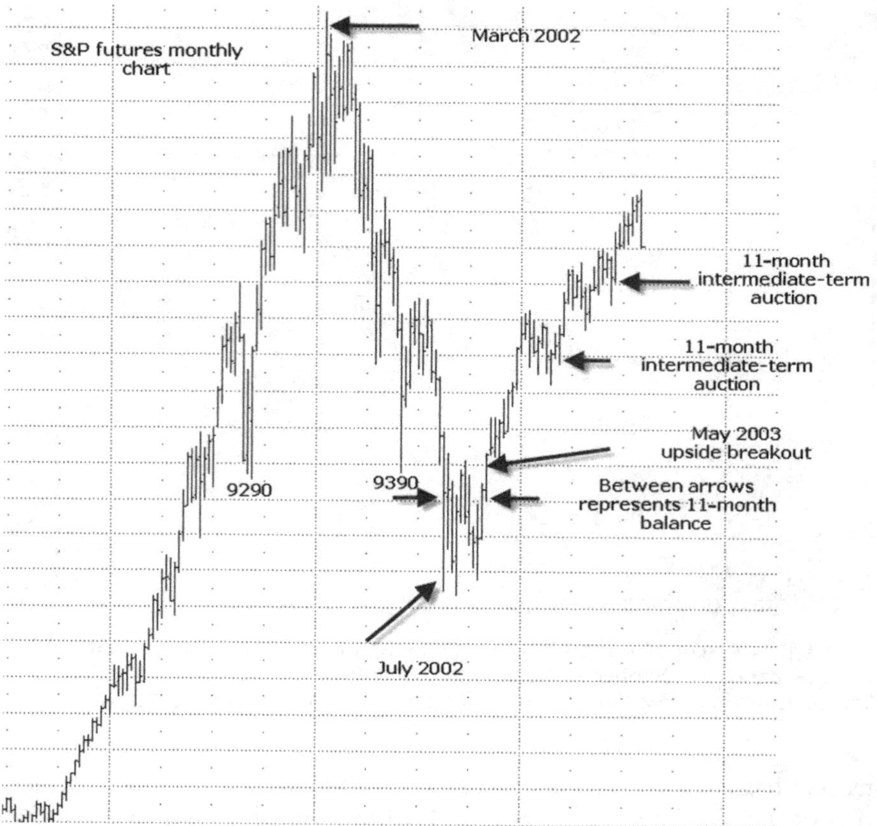

FIGURE 5.2 Breakout from balance as a catalyst for a longer-term trend: S&P 500 monthly bar chart, July 2002 through May 2006.
Source: Copyright © 2006 CQG, Inc. All rights reserved worldwide. www.cqg.com.

WHERE DO TRENDS END AND BRACKETS BEGIN?

(Authors' Note: The following sections are written in the first person to better convey the personal experience of James Dalton.)

The question I'm frequently asked is, "Why did you pick a certain period to designate the beginning or end of a trend or balance area?" I confess that it isn't a science. But after looking at a wide variety of markets over many years, the signs of transition begin to intuitively make sense. For example, Figure 5.2 reveals two distinct lows for the S&P 500, the first at

9,290 and the second a little over three years later at 9,390. May 2003 was chosen as the "upside breakout" because the market had given up probing below these significant reference points. Following the upside breakout, the market again balanced—or "bracketed"—for 11 months before continuing onward.

Brackets arise out of the market's innate need to balance. When price is perceived to be away from value, the market auctions in one direction until a new value level is found. This happens within the day, day-to-day, week-to-week, and longer timeframes. As observers, we only know that a new value level has been found when two-sided trade begins to take place; the market begins to auction in both directions with relatively equal strength, always pulled back to a central value, known in statistical circles as "the mean." The tighter the extremes of the bracket, the closer the perceptions of value between buyers and sellers of all timeframes. The farther apart, the more differing opinions are in play.

Another way to illustrate this concept is to think of a trend as a market that is "unfair" to one side. For example, in an upward trend, the market is telling us that prices are too low—unfair for the seller. In a bracketing period, the market is expressing its belief that prices are once again fair for both the long-term seller as well as the long-term buyer. The resulting activity is a relatively well-defined area of price containment, often characterized by overlapping value areas. As long as the bracket holds, and participants are in agreement regarding value, market activity on the bracket extremes will be met with responsive selling at the top, and responsive buying at the bottom. "Responsive," in this sense, refers to participants *responding* to the advertised opportunity of price above or below value, or the mean.

Auctions that occur near bracket extremes provide significant information about the odds of the bracket holding. For example, if an auction that pushes toward the upper extreme occurs on heavy volume, the odds are high that the bracket will not be able to contain the upward movement. Conversely, if low volume accompanies an auction at a bracket's upper extreme, then it is likely that higher prices are effectively cutting off activity; higher prices are not being accepted as "fair," the bracket's extremes are affirmed, and more balancing activity can be expected.

A common reaction to this definition of brackets is this: Brackets are easy to identify in hindsight. But how do you identify them *as they are developing?* The art of distinguishing real-time bracket activity is more than a matter of drawing neat lines on a chart. It takes time to acquire this skill, just as it takes time to learn to read an X-ray or master chess. With practice, however, you recognize the signs of balance and imbalance—perhaps the most essential element of successful trading. Markets communicate their need to balance via declining volume, thus the same information that reveals the likelihood of bracket containment is also helpful for identifying when a new bracket is beginning to form. One auction isn't enough to make this determination. As you become familiar with the auction process, however, you'll begin to fortify your ability to make this assessment.

From a trading standpoint, accurate bracket identification provides important perspective; not only does it better equip you to take advantage of well-defined moves within the bracket (a trader's paradise), but it also helps you identify when the market is once again coming out of balance, indicating that a new trend may be developing.

CLARITY IN THE MAELSTROM

It's easy to lose yourself in short-term minutia, which can cause you to lose track of the longer-term auction. We recommend that you print out a long-term chart at least once a month and a weekly chart every Sunday. Post them somewhere highly visible to help you keep the "big picture" in mind as you continually assess your long-term strategies. Any time the market departs the boundaries of one of these charts, immediately reprint them.

To illustrate how different market activity appears when viewed in the context of different timeframes, Figure 5.3 displays a weekly bar chart for the S&P 500 for a portion of the same time period shown in Figures 5.1 and 5.2.

I have been amazed over the years by the money managers whom I have reviewed who pride themselves on the fact that they have absolutely no charting capabilities in their research facilities. I recently read a newsletter produced by a top research firm that discussed a vital indicator they missed in their analysis of the Japanese markets over the past several years—they stopped paying attention to what Japanese policymakers were doing. And they weren't alone: Japan's deflationary period simply lasted longer than the attention span of most investors. A periodic review of long-term bar charts could have alerted savvy investors (and investment firms) to the fact that *change* was taking place, and with change comes opportunity.

The attempt to remain as objective and honest with ourselves as possible about what is *actually* occurring in the markets—not what we hope to see or *need* to see in order to justify our positions or past pronouncements—is a natural, ongoing challenge for even the most experienced traders and investors. This may sound obvious; but we know from experience that when multiple people are given the same set of facts, they will invariably arrive at different conclusions. Why? Because our decision-making process is always influenced by our past experiences, and it goes

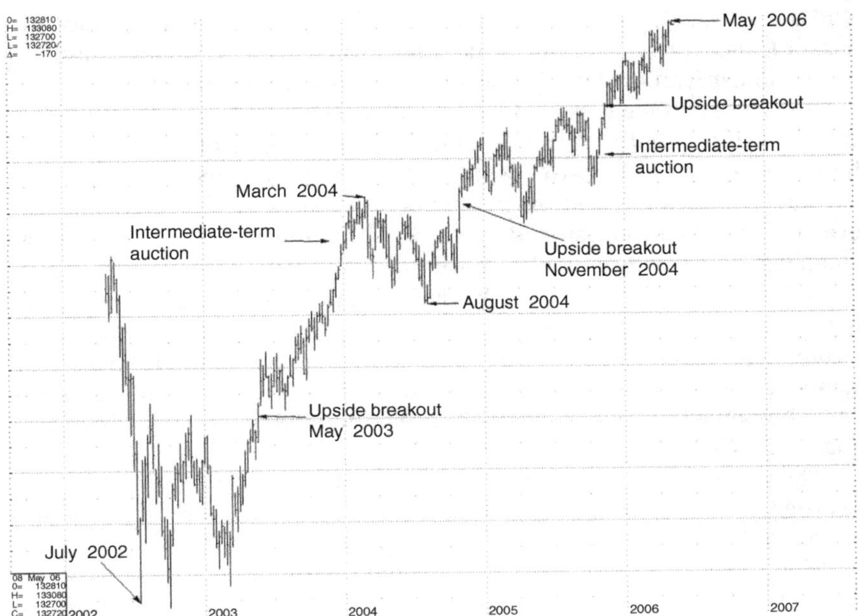

FIGURE 5.3 Shorter-timeframe perspective for a portion of the same time period shown in Figure 5.3: S&P 500 weekly bar chart.
Source: Copyright © 2006 CQG, Inc. All rights reserved worldwide. www.cqg.com.

without saying that everyone has a vastly different background. The point is that it's possible to check your inclinations by frequently referencing the market's long-term auctions, which should support your decisions. For example, the research firm that was negative on Japan should have looked for confirmation of this opinion in the form of lower volume during upward auctions, with no upside breakouts from the long-term balance. A cursory review of the longer-term auction should have revealed—if their conclusions had been correct—that upward movement was not straying far from the lower balance area. Instead, just the opposite was occurring, but the firm's analysts stopped looking and lost sight of the bigger picture.

One way to identify the beginning or end of a longer-term auction is by observing the market's balancing periods. To reiterate, markets rarely perform an "about face," moving from one sustained directional movement to its opposite. For long-term investors who manage large portfolios, learning to recognize when long-term auctions begin and end can be absolutely vital. And fortunately, the balancing process can take several months, for the long-term auction, which allows time to reposition even the largest portfolios. Failure to make use of this time, however, has destroyed many solid track records—track records that can take years to rebuild. Once the market leaves a balance area, price often moves rapidly (at least initially) in a nonlinear fashion, liquidity shrinks and opportunity is lost.

It is worth noting here that a financial market is different than a physical system like a motor. A car's engine eventually wears out, but it remains the same "system" no matter what is done to it. Conversely, a market is constantly evolving based on the actions of its participants; cogent patterns are eventually eliminated by those within the system acting upon it, which explains trends and why they come to an end.

Enter Market Profile, a simple visual manifestation of market activity that changes constantly, objectively reflecting the evolving attitudes of all participants *in the present tense.* Part of the beauty of the profile—its elegance, even—is the simple fact that it records *change.* It is this liquidity-capturing aspect that makes Market Profile such a vital tool for interpreting market activity.

The word *liquidity* generally refers to an individual's ability to execute an order, Here we use the term to address the constant flux of funds into and out of the market.

That's worth reiterating: Market Profile is different than most trading approaches because it is wholly *liquidity driven.* Market fundamentals and technical patterning may be accurate or misleading, may evolve and become anachronistic, but the fact remains: If funds are flowing into a market—whether it's an individual security or a sector or an art auction—then the market eventually auctions higher. If funds are flowing out, the market eventually auctions lower. There's nothing new here, just the primal law of supply and demand made manifest in a simple visual graphic that portrays the developing relationship of price, time, and volume—a graphic that enables whole-brained investors to visualize when a market is both in and out of balance.

The resulting profile enables us to capture complex relationships so that it's possible to better understand what is *actually* happening in the market in the present tense. The long-term bar charts presented in this chapter serve a different function; because they only portray price, they don't capture all the additional complexities and behavioral attributes incorporated by Market Profile. They do, however, provide crucial long-term perspective when reviewed in conjunction with daily profiles, which add the dimensions of time and volume.

THE BIG PICTURE

I use long-term bar charts to speed read the market's "big picture" before I narrow my focus on more granular, daily detail. For example, the bar chart

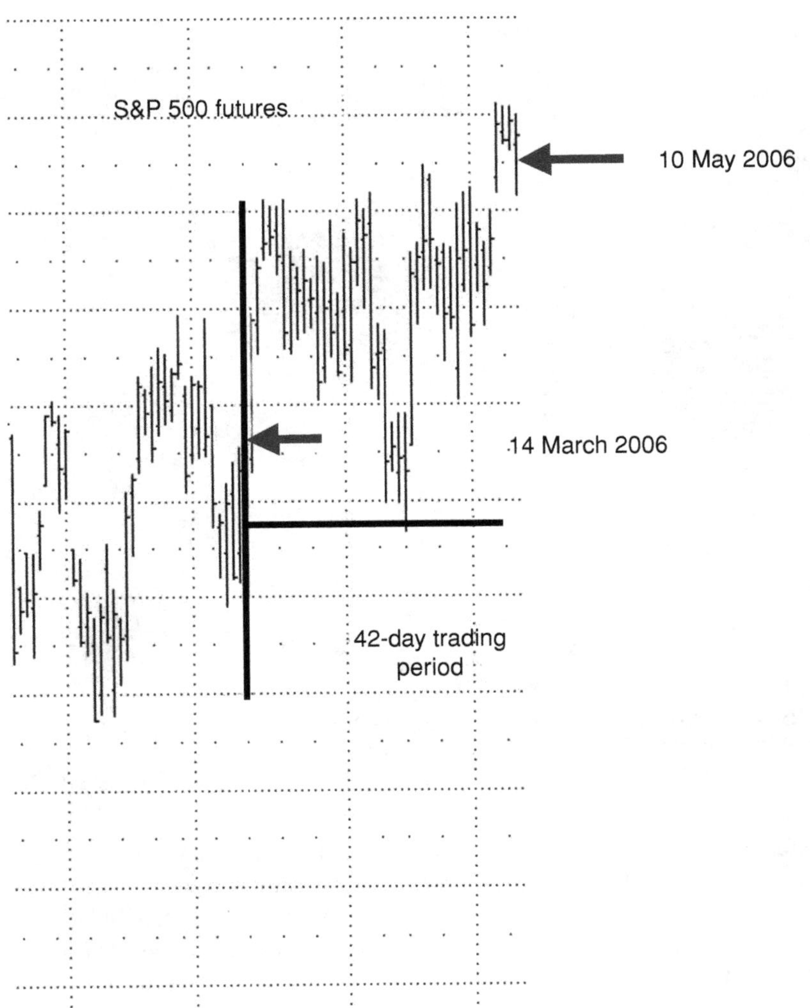

FIGURE 5.4 Longer-term price perspective provided by bar charts: S&P 500 daily bar chart, March 14, 2006, through May 10, 2006.

shown in Figure 5.4 shows price for the identified time period, and Figure 5.5 shows the same period represented in a long-term Profile graphic that displays *time*, *price*, and, by inference (price × time), *volume*—the three essential ingredients to understanding the health of the auction process. With the proper quote system, it is possible to create a Profile that covers

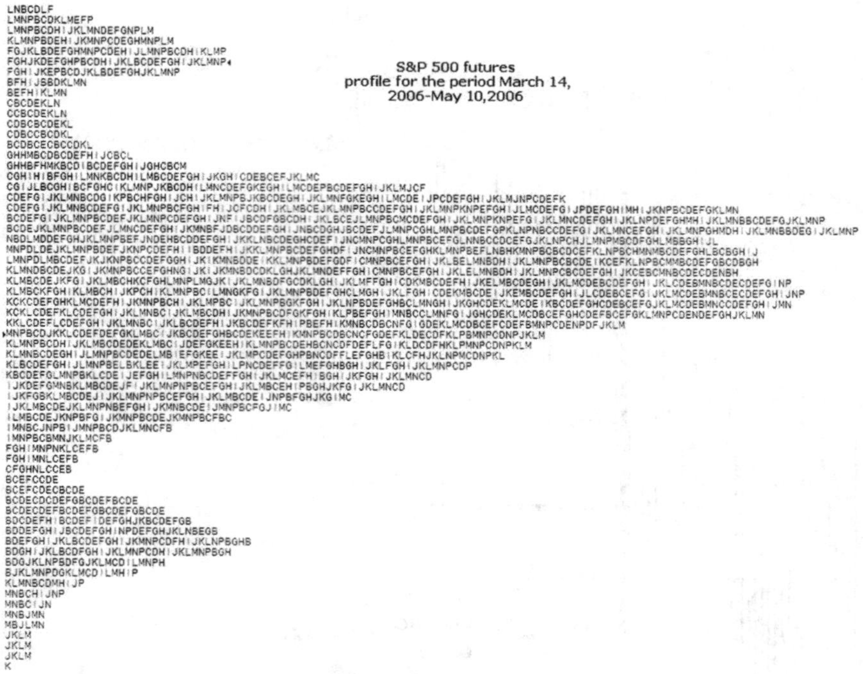

S&P 500 futures
profile for the period March 14,
2006-May 10,2006

FIGURE 5.5 Critical value and volume perspective provided by long-term profiles: S&P 500 long-term profile, March 14, 2006, through May 10, 2006.

any range of days you want to examine. The significance of the longer term Profile graphics will be discussed more fully in Chapter 6.

Figures 5.4 and 5.5 represent the same time period: March 14, 2006—May 10, 2006. Figure 5.4, a daily bar chart, does not enable you to see, at a glance, what is evident in Figure 5.5:

1. The three distributions (the broad areas of the profile, where most trade, i.e., volume, took place).
2. The *mean* of each distribution. Based on the discussion thus far, it should be clear that *volume* measures the success or failure of each auction; higher prices either cut off activity or, in strongly trending markets, attract more activity. When higher prices cut off activity, price generally reverts to the mean.

From another perspective, imagine that volume represents *force*. For a market to successfully auction away from a fully developed distribution area with a well-defined mean (where buyers and sellers have agreed upon value), the auction would need to have excessive *force* to overcome the "gravitational pull" of that value area. If price exploration does not have force—volume—then the expectation is that price will be pulled back to the established distribution value area.

Peter Steidlmayer said that markets are not "efficient," but that they are "effective." By "effective," he means that price has to auction too high before the market realizes it's *too high*, and too low before the market realizes it's *too low*. In effect, what happens is that price auctions higher until there is a lone bidder; when higher prices cut off activity, then the auction has gone too far.

Price is simply an advertising mechanism. Some advertisements are successful and attract new business, while others are unsuccessful, serving to shut down activity. As we observe, via the market profile, a market auctioning away from an established distribution area, the question we're always trying to answer is this: Will a new distribution (value area) be established or will price be pulled back to the prior distribution area? Again, it takes the *force* made manifest in volume for the establishment of a new value area to be successful.

While we have discussed long-term trends for a broader market, the same concepts are applicable for sectors and individual securities as well. Figure 5.6 shows the monthly bar chart of UBS (Union Bank of Switzerland), a global financial services company, from May 2000 to May 2006.

UBS traded within a range of approximately \$35 to \$59 for three years; long-term trends generally begin and end in just such intermediate-term auctions. Notice that UBS traded within a very tight, approximately five-dollar range for four months prior to the upward breakout from the three-year bracket. Figure 5.6 shows this narrow balance area occurring just before the start of an upward trend that, as of this writing (June 2006), carried the stock to a high of \$122. During the four months prior to the breakout, it would have been easy to disregard UBS, as there appeared to be limited trading opportunities and extremely low volatility. Once the trend got under way, however, it exhibited all the characteristics we have previously described—it began to trend, balanced from January to November 2004 and then resumed trending upward, balancing again from December 2004 through October 2005. In November 2005, UBS again began to auction higher.

Any breakout from a balance area signals that a reevaluation of value is occurring. Intermediate- and long-term timeframes may disregard short-term balances; however, traders and investors of *all* timeframes should pay careful attention to long-term breakouts, as they include participants from all timeframes and can result in large momentum shifts. Failure to recognize this principle can result in major losses and missed

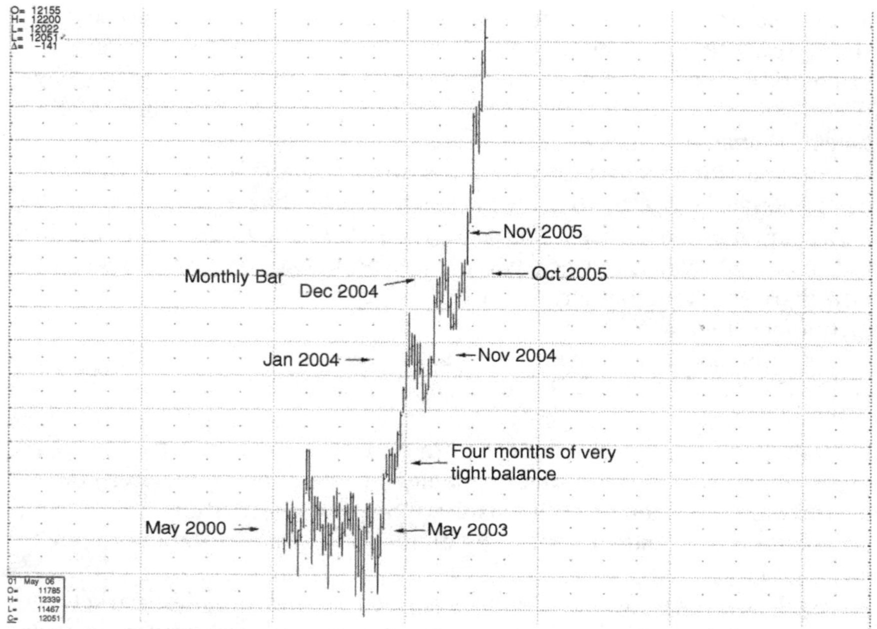

FIGURE 5.6 Long-term trend emerging from intermediate-term balance period: UBS (Union Bank of Switzerland) monthly bar chart, May 2000 through May 2006. Source: Copyright © 2006 CQG, Inc. All rights reserved worldwide. www.cqg.com.

opportunities, some of which can end careers. When a market sea change is in the works, it is absolutely vital that you not only identify the coming change, but that you position yourself correctly in order to weather (or ride) the storm.

ASYMMETRIC OPPORTUNITIES AND RISK

The Efficient Market Hypothesis (EMH) embodies the theory that new information is assimilated into the market so quickly that no single person can consistently outperform the market as a whole. This leads to the theory that the probability of a future price increase is exactly the same as a future price decrease. And, of course, if this is correct, no one could ever consistently forecast the market—a hypothesis supported by convincing research. Carried to its logical conclusion, this line of thought precludes value investing, which is based on the idea that prices travel away from value. If EMH were true, value investing would have no merit, as all prices would be constantly equal, negating the idea of "value" altogether. Growth investing, which is based on continual upward growth, would also have no utility, as it too requires practitioners to be successful at forecasting both higher growth and higher prices.

One of the goals of this book is to provide a logical framework for reconciling these divergent ideas. The discussion of timeframes, along with the idea that price must only be fair in the day timeframe, enables one to argue that the current, tradable price for any given security is, in fact, the true and fair market price—given all the information available at that moment for the shortest of timeframes (the intensely competitive nature of market participants would allow for no other possibility). However, our position is that what is fair for the shortest timeframe participant may, in fact, be viewed as an *opportunity* for a longer timeframe participant.

Most of the investing world desperately wants to believe that there are experts who can accurately forecast, and they are willing to pay dearly for that advice. Obviously, there would be no need for art auctions, auctions for Treasury securities, *or auctions of any kind* if prices could be consistently, accurately forecast. That's why we take a totally different approach—one that is not dependent on forecasting, but on assessing the risk of current auction continuation, stagnation, or reversal. For example, we may say that the risk of holding a given long position is high, and provide an assessment of the odds of continuation—but we never attempt to forecast future prices. The hardest thing to get your arms around is that we don't accomplish this risk analysis with absolute numbers; we employ logical thinking to arrive at a practical assessment of risk asymmetries. We believe that identifying exact numbers and probabilities is not possible for any system that's in a continual state of flux. And furthermore, once people have exact numbers to cling to, their minds tend to immediately close to the present-tense modulations that can utterly belie their long-term leanings.

We have stated that the market is not efficient; however, the mechanism for establishing the current tradable price—the auction process—is the most *effective* mechanism for allocating securities to be traded among those submitting bids and offers. Once the auction is underway, rather than attempting to predict future prices, we instead observe as the market *discovers* future prices. We continually assess the force and health of this auction process in order to identify asymmetrical opportunities that can provide optimal trade location—trade location with less risk. In an upward auction, for example, we assess whether higher prices are cutting off activity or creating increased interest, driving prices higher. If higher prices are increasing the bidding, the risk of holding that security is low. If you are short that same security, however, the odds of suffering a loss are greatly increased. Similarly, if you are long and higher prices are beginning to cut off activity, the risk of remaining long has increased.

We mentioned earlier that a bracket develops when the views of the relevant timeframe buyers and sellers are closely aligned. In a bracket, the odds of the market moving higher or lower around the bracket mean are about equal. If the market auctions to the upper extreme of the bracket and volume decreases significantly, the odds for upward continuation have greatly diminished. This is another way of demonstrating that not all prices are equal. If all *prices* are not equal, then all *opportunities*—and attendant risks—are not equal, either.

Thus the market, through the price discovery process of the auction mechanism, presents us with both symmetric and asymmetric opportunities and risks. Our primary objective, then, is to observe the market's symmetry—or lack of symmetry—and adjust our trading decisions based on an ongoing assessment of the resultant risks.

LONG-TERM STRATEGY DEVELOPMENT

Every reader has his or her own unique opinion about how much stock price movement is a result of overall market conditions, capitalization size, sector performance, or the security itself. We suspect that an acceptable answer is "some or all of the above." It is possible to construct a market profile for each of the above elements through indexes, individual securities, or ETFs. Reviewing each of these market perspectives using the process described in this chapter, and determining the symmetric or asymmetric opportunity/risk of each, will provide you with an objective view of both your overall portfolio and the individual elements that make up your portfolio.

This process is just one step in evaluating the risks and opportunities that affect your profitability. Sometimes the greatest risk is that you are simply wrong in your analysis—like the firm that followed the Japanese market. Perhaps the greatest risk of all is the risk of losing your objectivity to the point that you begin cherry-picking positive information that supports your position, and ignoring negative information that runs counter to your opinion. The greatest investment errors I have made over the years, by far, have resulted from giving in to the tendency to acknowledge only the information that supported my existing beliefs and positions.

Since I first discovered it in 1994, I have kept a chart entitled "Perspective on Performance" on my wall to remind me just how much sector performance can vary. The chart tracks early 1994 performance numbers for 25 different sectors, and reports that the Dow Industrial was—2.13 percent, Wilshire Large Company Growth was –5.01, and the Russell 2000

Growth was –10.09 percent. The company that produces the chart updates and republishes it every year, and while the leaders and laggards change, the basic message remains the same. This kind of variance makes it clear that market opportunities vary greatly—which is why it's vital that you immerse yourself in the same kind of methodical, objective analysis for the overall market, as well as for individual securities and sectors. Without *context*, the most accurate data in the world are worthless.

There aren't very many top-performing money managers—if there were, we couldn't call them "top performers." By improving your performance by only a few percentage points, you can move away from the middle of the pack where performance resembles a money toss. Imagine where you would place in the long-term performance battle if you could even slightly improve the placement and exit of every trade you make. As we have shown, a lot of money is left on the table (lost) because most traders and investors are operating with incomplete information. Like in every endeavor, the greatest reward comes to those who recognize opportunity early; the market profile is the key to being able to act before the opportunity genie is completely out of the bottle.

ASSEMBLING THE BIG PICTURE: CONTEXT WITHIN CONTEXT

This chapter is titled "Long-Term Auctions," but we should note that there is no absolute definition for "long-term," "intermediate-term," or "short-term"—any such definition is specific to the context of each individual investor. There is no set duration for these categories, but they are helpful in the abstract for analyzing market activity through different lenses.

In Chapter 2, we noted that fundamental information must be viewed in the proper *context* to have relevance. The example we used to make this point involved the yield on the 10-year Treasury note, which, depending on your perspective, could be fantastic or disappointing. Market-generated information must also be viewed within the proper context. The market only has to be fair in the day timeframe, which means there could be buying conviction on a given day that will eventually be met with aggressiveness in the opposite direction from the longer-timeframe seller—that's why you must stay focused on the longer-term context when analyzing daily market behavior.

If you consistently employ the long-term bar chart analysis that we covered in this chapter, you will have a much better chance of keeping that "big picture" always in mind. However, as we will experience shortly, at important junctures even the longest of timeframes must closely monitor the day timeframe. We said earlier that there are times when it is more important to be right. Nonlinear market, security, or sector moves can make or break your yearly performance in the blink of an eye.

As we head into Chapter 6, we narrow our focus and examine some telling short-term details for the S&P as it is in the process of making new life-of-contract highs. In Chapters 7 and 8, we then begin to combine theory with tactics—tactics that will help you learn how to monitor the different timeframes in order to identify and capitalize on asymmetric opportunities that reveal themselves in evolving market structure.

CHAPTER 6

Intermediate-Term Auctions

Complexity creates opportunity.

—Jim Dalton

It is May 2006, and events occurring in the U.S. stock market have coincidentally and unexpectedly converged with the topic of this chapter. We couldn't have asked for better examples than those the market is providing right now, in real time. *Convergence* is a term we employ quite often; it comes into play when a market is transitioning from bracket to trend, or from trend to bracket. Such convergence is always accompanied by increased volatility as the various timeframes join the fray, which often leads to the kind of price movement that garners front-page news—such as "Fed Derails Dow Record Reach," which recently appeared in the *Wall Street Journal.*

Before we dissect these unfolding events, however, let us first take a closer look at the bracketing process. In order to successfully navigate intermediate-term auctions, you must first understand the way they begin, develop, and end.

CONVERGENCE AND THE BRACKETING PROCESS

When a trend is coming to an end, the market begins a *bracketing process,* which is the fine-tuning of value beliefs between the long-term sellers and buyers. During this process, the market auctions up and down until a fairly

FIGURE 6.1 Bracket formation in the S&P: S&P 500 daily bar chart, November 2005 through May 2006 (focus area).
Source: Copyright © 2006 CQG, Inc. All rights reserved worldwide. www.cqg.com.

well-defined bracket is eventually formed. From time to time, there may be slight bracket expansions upward and downward. But they generally aren't significant until they occur on increasing volume, when a new trend breaks out of the bracket. The difference between a "bracketing" market and a "bracketed" market is a subtle point and vital to understanding the way shifting forces influence market activity.

The tendency of markets to transition from trending to bracketing recently revealed itself in the U.S. stock market. Through May of 2006, the market had been in a longer-term upward trend for three years. However, Figure 6.1 shows that, after recording new market highs on May 5 for the S&P 500 and on May 10 for the Dow, the long-term buying auction converged with longer-timeframe sellers on May 11, sending the equity markets down sharply and establishing the first leg of a new bracket.

Claiming that a new bracket is being formed is actually a rather **bold statement**, as it is too early at the time of this writing to actually *confirm* that a new bracket is developing. So far, we have observed only a nonlinear, downward auction. For this auction to develop into a traditional bracket, or "consolidating market," we need to see a series of both higher and lower intermediate-term auctions, a process that can expose the convictions of long-term buyers and sellers.

In just a month, from the break after the contract high on May 5 to the low on June 13, both the S&P and the Dow have fallen more than 8 percent, with all indices at a loss for the year. That's a significant move—the kind of move that can make or break one's hard earned track record. What follows is a review of the process that led up to this convergence, this transition from trending to bracketing that became so easily recognizable on May 11 (in addition, we provide an update in Appendix A that summarizes the market activity that occurred between the time this review was written and the book went to press).

DEFINING THE INTERMEDIATE TERM

Earlier, we described five timeframes: scalper, day trader, short-term trader, intermediate-term trader, and long-term trader. We gave general guidelines for each of these timeframes in order to provide some comfort in forming a structure for understanding how markets operate. We said that intermediate-term markets could last for months, and that it isn't always the *time*, but rather the *distance traveled* that determines whether an auction is "intermediate." Consider a bracket that develops over a four-month period. A downward auction is met with the expected responsive buying at the bracket's lower extreme, and then the market auctions higher for four consecutive weeks before reaching the bracket's opposite extreme. We describe this as an "intermediate-term auction" or "swing trade." Likewise, if the market quickly reversed after nearing the upper extreme and fell to the bottom of the bracket in just four days, this would also be considered an intermediate-term auction. It is the distance traveled—not the length of time—that determines the "intermediate-term" classification.

The price range of an intermediate-term auction is generally greater (from the low to the high) than that of a short-term auction. Another distinguishing feature of an intermediate-term auction is that it contains several smaller, well-defined balance areas, which become excellent short-term trading ranges. Regardless of what you ultimately decide to define as either "short-term" or "intermediate-term," the key is that the auction in question begins or occurs within a bracketing period. Once you've identified a bracket, your trading strategy should be to look for swing trades on the bracket's extremes. In such a balancing environment, you should continue to expect a series of two-way, or "swing" auctions.

It is instrumental to acknowledge that money managers who market themselves as "long-term investors," continually advising you to stay fully invested, are in fact trend traders. Failure to distinguish between trending and bracketing markets has historically been extremely costly to trend traders. When the market is trending, of course, trend traders do quite well, but when the market is bracketing—which we have estimated to be in excess of 75 percent of the time—trend traders often give back a healthy portion of what they made during the trend.

THE TRANSITION FROM BRACKET TO TRENDS

It is vital to be able to identify when a market is transitioning to a bracket, and when a new trend has erupted from that balancing range. We begin by reviewing the process that marks the transition from a bracket's intermediate-term auctions to a trend's directional conviction. As you may have already surmised, this is not an exact science.

A *bracketed market* is a market in balance. To reiterate, within a bracket there is likely to be several smaller balance ranges that develop through the shorter-term, two-way action process. When these smaller balance areas (which will be featured in Chapter 7) begin to cluster near the extremes of the larger, intermediate-term bracket, this indicates that the market is coming into tighter and tighter balance. While this isn't *always* the case, it is quite common for this type of clustering activity to represent the final stage in the transition from bracket to trend.

Figure 6.2 illustrates a tight balance range that led to an upside breakout. As a general trading principle, I have found that if the balance range corresponds to your timeframe, you should go with any breakout from that balance and then monitor the trade for signs of continuation. The wider the balance area from which the market transitions, the greater the number of timeframes that are likely to be involved when the breakout finally occurs, and the greater the odds that the ensuing move will be significant.

If price is to remain contained within a bracket, we expect to see responsive action: participants "responding" to the advertised opportunity to sell at the upper end of the bracket, at prices above the mean (value), and to buy at the lower end, responding to price advertised below the mean. However, just the opposite happens when a market is about to transition from a bracket to a bull trend; higher prices generate *more* upward volume, leading to an upside breakout. Likewise, in a nascent bear trend, lower prices actually attract *additional* selling instead of generating the expected action—cutting off selling—which leads to a downside breakout and trending conditions.

Trending markets, at least in their early stages, demonstrate a high degree of confidence that the current price is unfair—for the seller in an upward trend, and for the buyer in a downward trend. With high-confidence

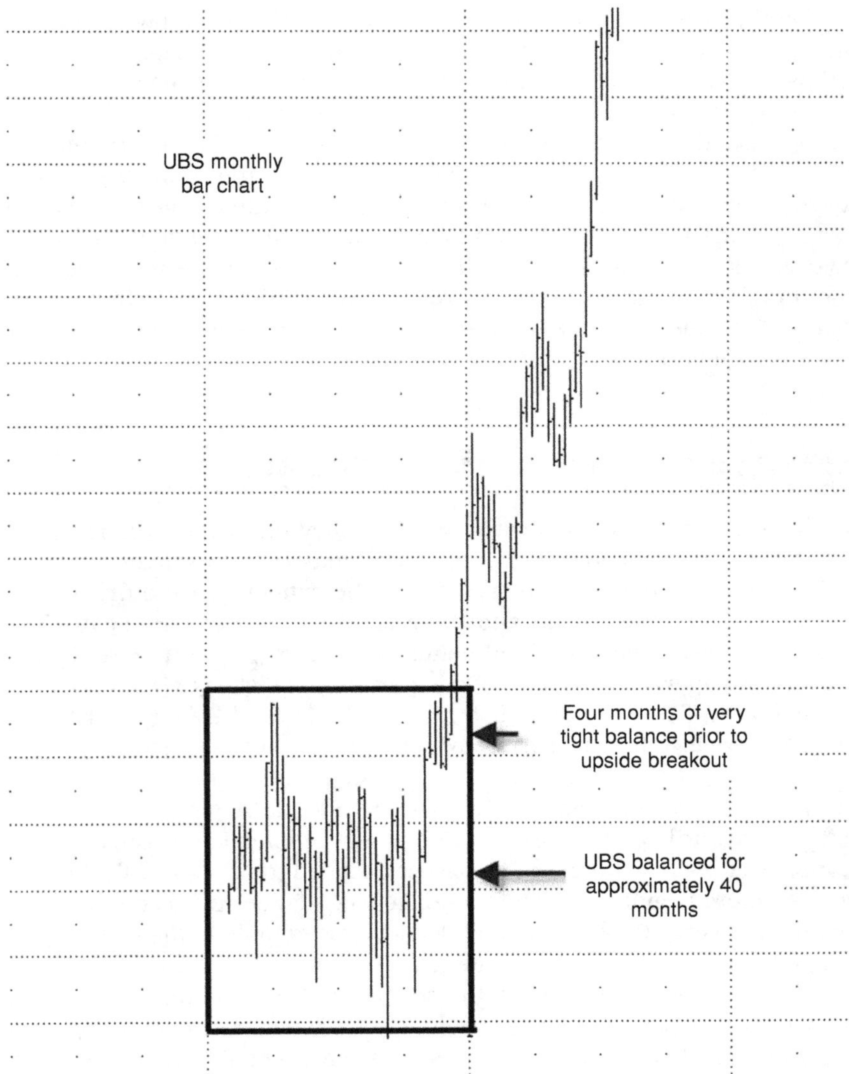

FIGURE 6.2 Upside breakout following extended period of tight balance: UBS monthly bar chart, May 2000 through May 2006.
Source: Copyright © 2006 CQG, Inc. All rights reserved worldwide. www.cqg.com.

markets, news releases that are contrary to the existing trend are likely to cause only temporary setbacks (which can provide good buying opportunities if the trend is up, for example), while releases that support the trend generally serve to accelerate its progress.

Another way to define bracketed markets is that they have absorbed and assimilated all current information, and that the long-term buyers and sellers have basically arrived at an equal sense of value; the market is marking time until new information arrives. In this state, the market closely resembles the textbook "efficient market." It is not uncommon to see a major news announcement, such as the monthly Bureau of Labor Statistics' employment report, have a significant impact on a bracketed market, while having little or no lasting impact in a trending market. A major news release is frequently the final factor that results in a transition from bracket to trend. In other words, a bracketed market is in balance, waiting for substantive new information before it begins its next major directional auction.

THE TRANSITION FROM TREND TO BRACKET

Trends end in either of two ways or a combination of the two. The first, less-frequent type of ending occurs when volume—which is in the direction of the trend—simply dries up, as if the participants that were driving the directional move are "all in" and there is no one left to participate. The transition is relatively quiet and calm; the market just sits there, lulling market participants into a state of complacency and stasis.

In Figure 6.3, S&P futures traded at 1,269.70, 1,269, 1,269.40, and 1,269.90 during four out of five days prior to the intermediate-term auction changing direction. There was less than a full point separating those four highs; the buying had simply dried up, and participants contributing to the downward auction were a combination of long liquidators and new shorts. Over the next 18 days the market declined to 1,223—a 3.62 percent move—before beginning a rally that once again failed to exceed the 1,269 high-water mark. Before the initial decline was complete, the market had dropped to a low of 1,180, a decline of 7 percent.

The creation of "excess" is the second and most common end to a trend. Excess occurs when a market makes a dramatic price high or low on low volume and opposing buyers or sellers react quickly and aggressively by auctioning price in the opposite direction. This type of trend end is often stormy and sudden, which results in a state of near panic as price moves quickly and it becomes increasingly difficult to make a decision that's not influenced by heightened emotion.

Figure 6.4 (on the following page) shows both types of auction-ending patterns. In the first two boxes from the left, volume simply dried up, and in the next three boxes you see the second, more violent type of transition marked by excess.

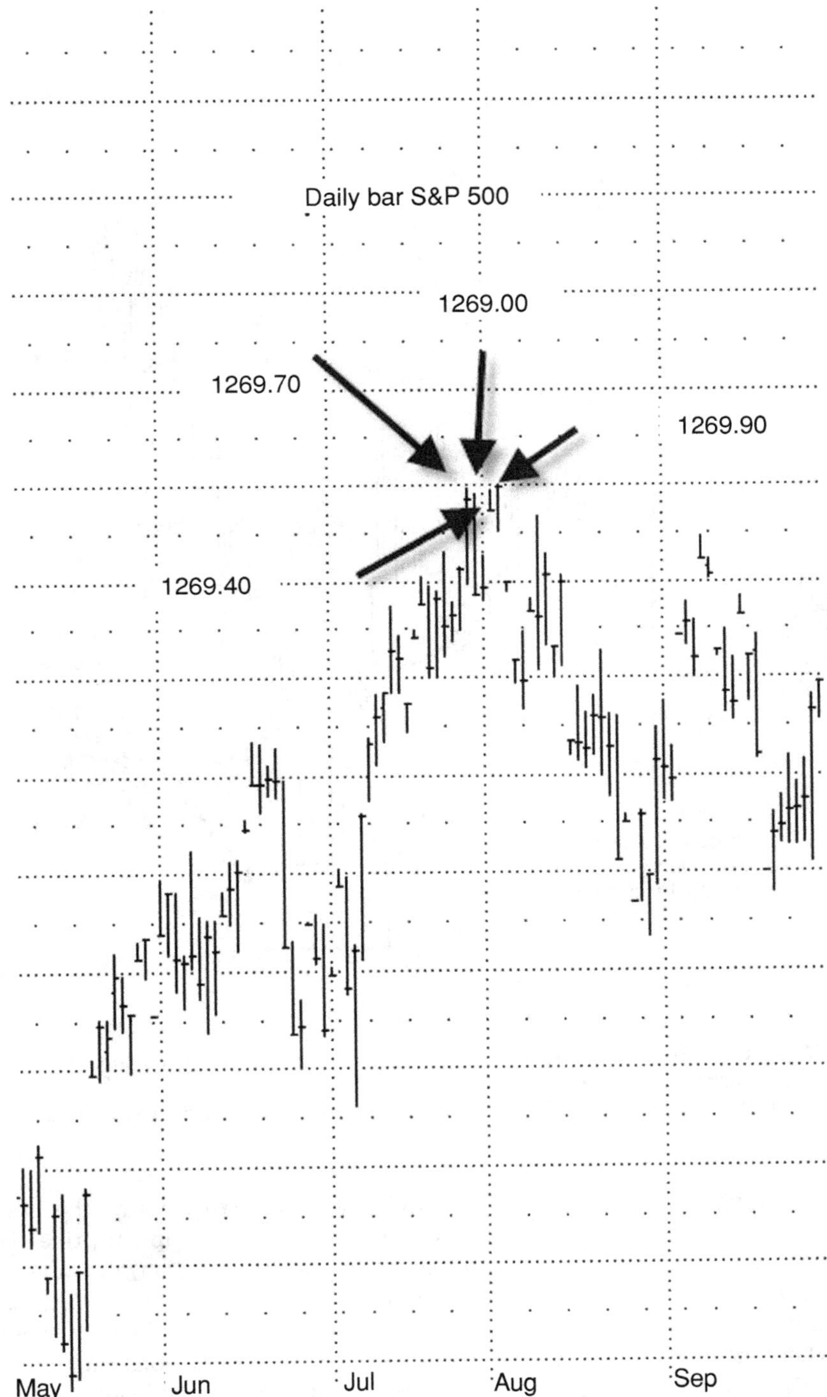

FIGURE 6.3 Buying exhaustion, triggering intermediate-term selling auction. S&P 500 daily bar chart, July–August 2005 (focus area).
Source: Copyright ©2006 CQG, Inc. All rights reserved worldwide. www.cqg.com.

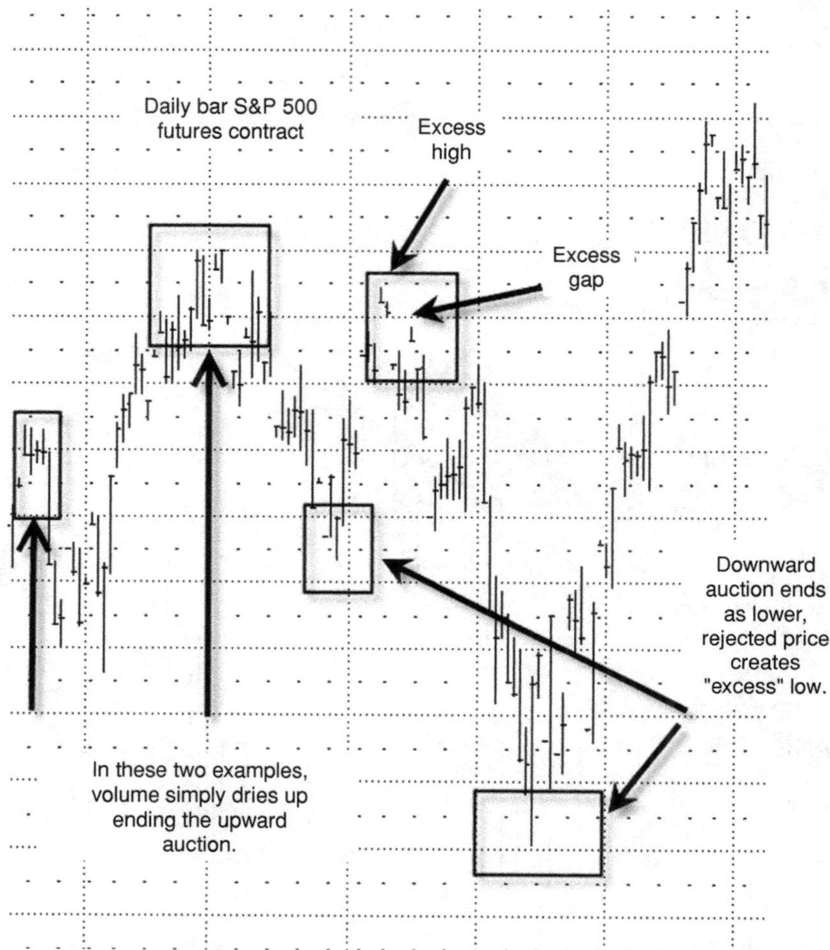

FIGURE 6.4 Selling excess, triggering intermediate-term buying auction: S&P 500 daily bar chart, October 2005 (focus area).
Source: Copyright © 2006 CQG, Inc. All rights reserved worldwide. www.cqg.com.

Following the excess high (identified in Figure 6.4), notice the creation of an extreme form of excess known as a *gap*. A gap (in price) is created when the market does not have an opportunity (time) to trade at certain prices. This happens in one of two ways: when the market auctions so quickly in one directions that prices are skipped altogether, or when market participants have changed their perception of value so dramatically that they simply begin trading at a completely different price level.

In Figure 6.4, the S&P auction ended with an excess high, indicating that price auctioned so high that it was deemed unfair for the buyer. The excess gap on the following day provided further acknowledgment that prices were indeed too high. A gap at the end of an auction that occurs in the direction opposite the most recent trend signals a reorganization of beliefs. As educational psychologist Frank Pajares summarizes Thomas S. Kuhn's groundbreaking work in *The Structure of Scientific Revolutions*:

> *Transition from a paradigm in crisis to a new one from which a new tradition . . . can emerge is not a cumulative process. It is a reconstruction of the field from new fundamentals . . . It changes methods and applications. It alters the rules.*

In short, the laggards are finally "all in," and the market moves with real conviction.

An excess high or low occurs on light or low volume. Most of the investing world, however, thinks the opposite is true. For example, many investors believe that *capitulation* at the end of a downward auction—when all the sellers finally sell—occurs on heavy volume. But this would go against all the principles we've talked about. For example, a market may experience a period of healthy volume as the stragglers (Gladwell's "late majority" or "laggards") get rid of their inventory, but the final prices, manifest in the excess spike, are not made on heavy volume. The volume most people incorrectly ascribe to capitulation is actually a result of the action *in the other direction*, when buyers show up in force and the price spike down is quickly rejected. Confusion occurs due to the fact that after the excess high or low is in place, there is often a dramatic pickup in volume as part of the counterauction.

THE CONVERGENCE OF INTELLECT AND EMOTION

The most common true end to a trend—which also signals when a bracket begins—occurs as a result of both a reduction in volume in the direction of the trend *and* an excess high or low. The ending of an auction offers the moment of greatest opportunity, as well as the moment of greatest risk; both risk and reward are asymmetric at this pivotal point. If the trend is downward and an auction low has been established, the investor who correctly recognizes the low and buys has a low risk/high reward position. Sounds easy, but imagine the emotions that these "innovators" must endure when they buy against what has been universally acknowledged as a bear trend. The market has been auctioning fairly consistently one way—down—for an extended period of time, and thus a decision to buy utterly flies in the face of common (as well as expert) wisdom. It's not easy to go against the crowd. As someone once said, being a contrarian is like committing social suicide. To be a successful trader/investor, your intellect and emotion must work as a team, which is easier said than done.

On a tick chart, this kind of trend-end reversal looks elongated, with a final price spike that is quickly rejected. If you've done your homework and recognize that this spike is on *low volume*, your intellect can be saying "now would be a low risk/high reward time to buy," but when the speed of the reaction takes your breath away, your emotions won't always be in agreement. This cognitive dissonance can freeze your trigger finger while opportunity slips away.

The investor who is short in this example (for a long-only money manager, "short" would mean holding cash, or being under committed to the market), and who fails to recognize that the auction is ending, must endure high risk and low reward; the ensuing rally is often sharp and fast. If you are a large money manager and your analysis hasn't revealed the weakening auction, then once the reversal begins there is generally limited liquidity, which can severely compromise your performance.

ACCELERATE THE LEARNING PROCESS

I had always marveled at the *Apollo 12* moon mission, which was reported to have landed within 15 meters of its target. I thought it was accomplished by a room full of incredibly smart people who created an algorithm, fired the rocket into space, and waited until it landed on the moon. I was surprised to read that the mission was off course 80 percent of the time, which required continual course corrections. Without these on-the-fly computations, the *Apollo* would have been lost in space.

When working with the natural sciences, there is comfort and stability in the reproducibility of results, born of the constants inherent in scientific inquiry. There is a genuine feeling of delight when the mind stumbles across the "correct answer." The human mind is hardwired to seek concrete answers. Moreover, our tendency is to acknowledge only those answers that support our presupposed beliefs, which can lead to tunnel vision, short-sightedness and, ultimately, plunging profits.

The difference between the natural sciences and market-generated analysis is that the elements we employ to conduct our analysis are constantly evolving; the only constant we have at our disposal is *change*. Of course, without change there would be no opportunity, and so we gladly welcome change. But as a result, it takes an extraordinary amount of time and dedication to become familiar with the type of analysis we're describing in this chapter. There is no substitute for experience in any field, of course, but because of the many complexities and subtitles inherent in trading, there is no quick way to gain that essential experience. It may appear to be misleadingly simple to move from novice to proficient, as the ideas we're purporting in this book are not unfathomable. However, it takes an incredible amount of dedication to elevate your trading level from proficient to expert—and that's what differentiates the all-stars from the herd. Think of the difference between an average professional basketball player and the elegance with which Michael Jordan could dominate a game. And it is well documented that Jordan trained relentlessly, studying tapes, staying late in the gym, shooting free throws *after* he was totally fatigued to simulate game scenarios.

To become a truly skilled investor or trader, you must immerse yourself deeply in the market's auction process, experiencing a variety of similar situations until you begin to understand how that process works in a real-time, present-tense perspective. If you observe only long-term markets, it will take years before you will have seen and recorded enough patterns to competently recognize transitioning activity, let alone be able to act on that information while balancing intellect and emotion. However, recall that everything we've discussed thus far is applicable to *all timeframes*; to accelerate the learning process, we suggest that you also study short-term markets, analyzing the shorter-timeframe balances that occur within intermediate-term brackets. This will give you increased confidence about the entire auction process, as well as further insight into the actions and motivations of the various timeframes.

PRELUDE TO A SEA CHANGE

Having examined how trends begin and end, let's now look at the securities markets as they converged with our writing *Markets in Profile* in May 2006, when the U.S. equity market was entering its fourth year of an extended longer-term up trend. After the markets closed on Friday, May 5, I commented to a long-time friend and Chicago-based trader, William Kennedy, that everything we look at to analyze auction strength and confidence was leading me to assess the risk—from the long side of the market—as being very high. The upward auction, despite accomplishing higher price movement, was accompanied by continually decreasing volume, and the volume was not well distributed throughout the market profile. As a result I had refused to trade from the long side for the previous two weeks. Additionally, I commented to Bill that trading from the short side was also risky, as there had been no sign of sellers—only marginal buying activity. *The greatest point of market opportunity is when you feel alone.* Given the high risk of being outright long, and the fact that longer timeframe sellers had yet to surface, I purchased out-of-the-money puts with extended time, feeling that the market would at least have to auction lower to determine if buyers remained present under the current price levels.

Remember the subtlety in what we do: we don't forecast, we assess the risk of our positions. We seek to exit positions that have above-average risk, and to establish positions that provide favorable risk/reward characteristics. Once a position has been established, we then monitor the auction process for continuation. There was no expectation that the May 2006 decline would develop as it did; an auction continues until it is completed.

Let's further this discussion by reviewing a strong upward trending market, so that we'll have something against which to compare the May auction.

Figure 6.5 exhibits the pattern of a strong, upward trending market. Notice how the market trends upward, balances, then resumes its upward trend again and again. The stronger the trend, the greater the distance between successive balance areas. As the auction ages, this distance decreases. In the late stages of the trend, price may continue to rise but the next balance area will often be resting on top of or within the prior, lower balance area.

Long-term trends often resemble stairs, with each balancing area representing a step. Downward auctions appear as if they are descending a staircase, as you can see in the daily bar chart of Figure 6.6 . Figure 6.5, a rising trend, reveals an ascending staircase pattern. Note that the same security, displayed via a different time interval, looks entirely different. That's why we suggest that you review each security you trade using monthly, weekly, and daily bars—it broadens your perspective and assist, you in identifying your own timeframe.

As the downward auction becomes exhausted in Figure 6.6, note that the lower balance area overlaps the previous, higher balance area. This doesn't mean that the downward auction is over; rather, that it is late in the process, and so the corresponding risk of holding short positions has increased. If you're a long-term portfolio manager, at this late point in a downward auction the risk of holding defensive securities or cash has risen, and you would want to begin to commit to new positions or add to favorable positions. Long-term returns are greatly enhanced by committing cash at lower levels, as long as the auction is ending.

Trends that are growing "tired" will begin to exhibit increased volatility without producing much further directional progress. Additionally, volume will begin to decrease and, in some cases, auctions that are in the direction

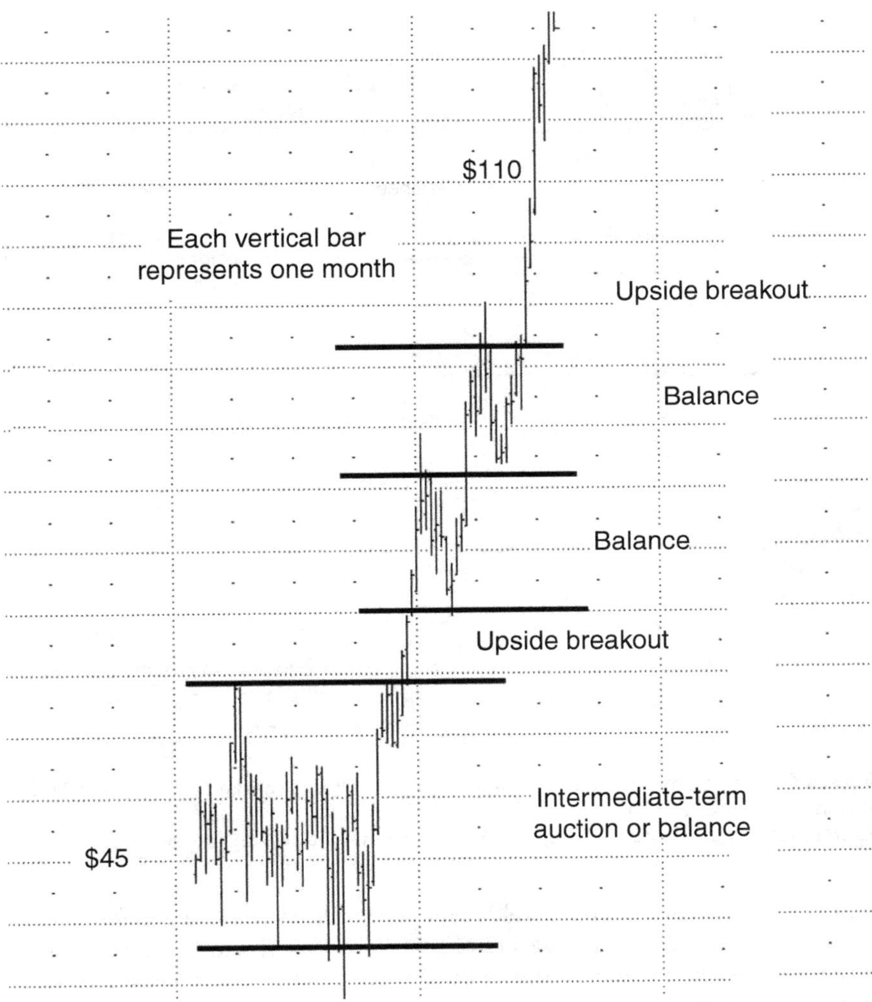

FIGURE 6.5 Common pattern of an upward-trending market: UBS weekly bar chart, January 2004 through May 2006.

of the trend will be accompanied by less volume than on days the market auctions against the trend.

Having reviewed these two auction patterns, let's look at the monthly bar chart for the S&P 500 prior to the May 2006, nonlinear break.

We have labeled the trend in Figure 6.7 a "long-term" trend. However, one could easily argue that the market is continuing to consolidate

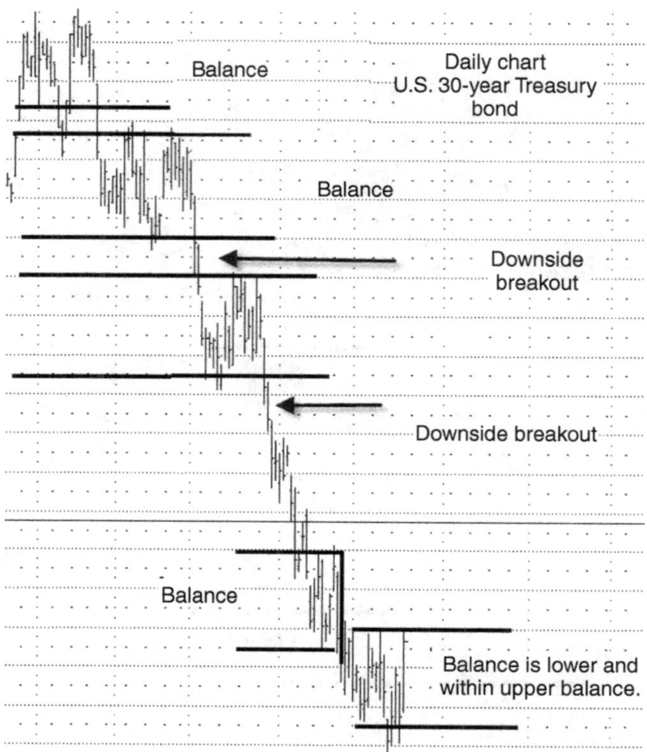

FIGURE 6.6 Common pattern of a downward-trending market: U.S. 30-year Treasury bonds daily bar chart.

(balance) between the high established in March 2000 and the low created in October 2002. While the market has, in fact, stayed within an extremely broad bracket between the March 2000 high and the October 2002 low, it has steadily risen since an upside breakout in March 2003, a period exceeding three years. Few have the patience or perspective to say that a three-year rally is not a bull market; even though it remains contained within the longer-term bracket. (The practical thing for a money manager to do is to treat it like a bull trend, because if he doesn't, he won't retain any clients.) John Mauldin, in *Bull's Eye Investing: Targeting Real Returns in a Smoke and Mirrors Market* (New York: John Wiley & Sons, 2004), tells us that it is not uncommon for markets to consolidate for years. In fact, he writes that the shortest period of consolidation following a bear market is eight years. We are now in year six, and when we finally break out of the March

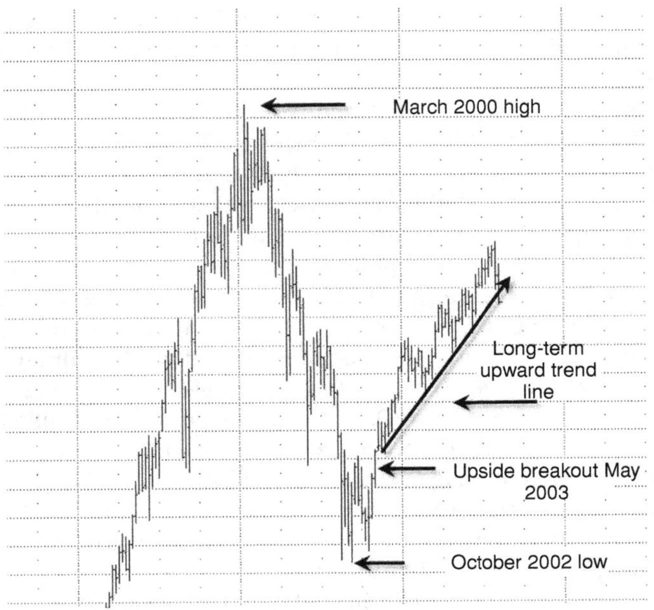

FIGURE 6.7 Longer-term upward trend developing in the S&P: S&P 500 weekly bar chart.
Source: Copyright © 2006 CQG, Inc. All rights reserved worldwide. www.cqg.com.

2000 through October 2002 bracket, we would expect an extremely active market.

The strategies you employ for a trend and a bracket are quite different, but there are times when the market is tricky, exhibiting elements of both. The "final answer," as it were, is to remain flexible and open-minded, and if you want to excel as a money manager, don't be a trend trader, sticking only to long positions—there is a big difference between buying and holding and staying fully invested. The last report I saw on money managers' holdings revealed that the average position was held for less than a year. For the most part, it seems, money managers aren't really "buying and holding" as much as they are staying fully invested. While I was at UBS Financial Services, the team that researched money managers reported to me, and I have monitored the rate of money manager turnover for years, and while there have been a few managers that did exclusively buy and hold securities for extended periods, I have observed that this practice is certainly not the norm. In other words, being more *market sensitive* than dogmatic is not unheard of—which is the core of what we're trying to impart. Even while money managers are selling customers on the idea of buying and holding, there is more nuance to it than that: there is market awareness.

If you measure the price distance from the top to the bottom of the trend line for the S&P 500 shown in Figure 6.7, you will notice that the difference is approximately 5 percent. This distance is commonly referred to as a *channel*. When volatility increases, which expands the channel, it is not uncommon to see a difference of 8 to 10 percent. Common theory would suggest that you buy a pullback to the bottom of the channel in an upward trend, and sell a rally to the top of the channel. The challenge is that if you don't hedge, and instead ride out the decline to the bottom of the channel, and it turns out that there is a downside breakout from there, you've already given back a gain (if you even had one going into the correction). Worse, if you weren't on the plus side as the decline began, it would take a strong rally just to get you to back to the break-even point. This is where money managers can get into big trouble—their emotions say, "I can't sell now; the market's got to turn around." But once you enter that head space, you'll be lucky if you can keep your relative standing, and your absolute performance will be shot.

Now let's view the S&P 500 through a shorter-term lens, a daily bar chart shown in Figure 6.8.

The S&P 500 futures contract broke out to the upside on November 18, 2005 on reported volume in the *Wall Street Journal* of more than 2 billion shares. To provide some reference, typical daily volume during this period ranged from 1.6 to 2 billion shares (although there were certainly a few days above and below these levels). A breakout on high volume, with the close near the daily high, indicated that higher prices were attracting more activity, which means the auction would be expected to continue higher—which it did for three more days.

The world spends a lot of time searching for easy answers, and near the end of 2005 most financial talk show guests were predicting a yearend rally, which then became the "Christmas rally." This talk wasn't enough to actually empower the rally, so hints of a Fed pause were thrown into the mix. Media-generated situations often set up excellent opportunities for diligent investors who can observe the proceedings objectively, without getting emotionally caught up in the media-generated hype.

A review of Figure 6.8 shows that the market first balanced above the November breakout low for approximately six weeks before staging another upside breakout. Following this new upward auction, the market's second balance was established slightly above, but still well within, the first balance—an indication that the trend was aging, but not necessarily over. The second balance occurred over the first two-and-a-half months of 2006.

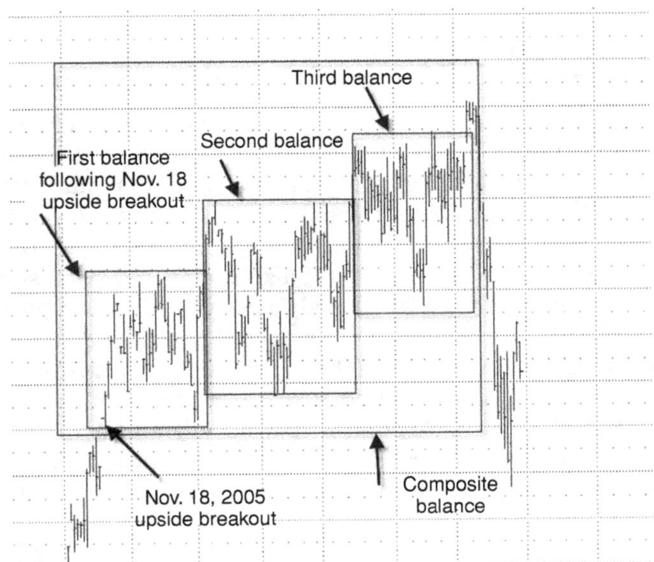

FIGURE 6.8 Balancing marking the aging of a longer-term trend: S&P 500 daily bar chart, November 2005 through May 2006 (focus area).
Source: Copyright © 2006 CQG, Inc. All rights reserved worldwide. www.cqg.com.

On March 15, a third upside breakout took place with resulting balancing action similar to the second balancing period. As new highs were continuing to provide comfort to investors, encouraging complacency, market-generated information (time, price, volume) was revealing that the risk of holding long positions was increasing. For those that focus primarily on earnings, additional comfort arrived in the form of strong reports of individual company and S&P Composite earnings. At the time, a prominent speaker from a money management firm told a daily business show that if investors "keep focusing on earnings, we will be all right." Based on how he addressed the commentator, he probably knew that hype had outstripped reality, but he also understood that if he said anything clearly negative it could hurt his business. I think he was trying to be honest in a diplomatic way, because the will of the herd is a force to be reckoned with, even when it's facing the wrong way.

Opportunities, just like markets, are regulated by time. If you squander that time waiting for confirmation, the consequences can be harsh. Once the investing world recognizes that change is underway, it is usually too late for large money managers to take advantage of it, as liquidity dries up and the "change" becomes the "norm."

HEAR THE BELLS A-RINGING

On May 8, 2006, the *Wall Street Journal's* "Evening Wrap" quoted Merrill Lynch economist David Rosenberg: "There is no question that the quarter earnings season has been superb." The article stated that quarterly results for more than 400 companies in the Standard & Poor's 500 Index are in, and on average their per-share earnings were 14 percent higher than a year ago, according to Thomson Financial. It also referenced Thomson reporting that the quarter was the 11th straight period of double-digit earnings growth for the S&P 500. Mr. Rosenberg, according to the *Journal*, "noted that analysts are already marking up their earnings forecasts for quarters to come." Just three days later, on Thursday, May 11, the stock market began its significant move down. The point is that while earnings are important, *so is market structure* when assessing risk. Unfortunately, articles about weak market structure aren't very sexy, and are easily dismissed as "technical analysis."

When we started writing this chapter in early May, we talked about the market converging. By the time we were in the editing phase it was mid-June and the decline had continued. From the high on May 5 to the close on Tuesday, June 13, the S&P futures contracts were off 8.18 percent and the Dow futures were off 8.58 percent. Still, the "experts" clung to their former beliefs. A typical *Wall Street Journal* quote from a company president said he believed the Dow's pullback was only "temporary," and that the index would close at over 12,000 by the end of the year. Isn't that comforting? Another *Wall Street Journal* headline read: "Fed Derails Dow Record Reach." There always has to be a scapegoat, so everyone can externalize their angst and anger. After all, it would be too esoteric to blame the market's decline on "weak structure." It can't be said often enough: you must develop a holistic understanding based on the market's real-time structure in order to separate yourself from the pack and become a truly competitive money manager.

COUNTERTREND AUCTIONS

Another sign that the upward trend had aged was provided by observing the countertrend auctions—auctions that, in many cases, were stronger than those that occurred *with* the trend. Figure 6.9 shows the final days prior to the nonlinear move that began on May 11, 2006.

On Friday, May 5, S&P futures broke out to the upside, establishing a new life-of-contract high. Volume on this day, as reported in the *Wall*

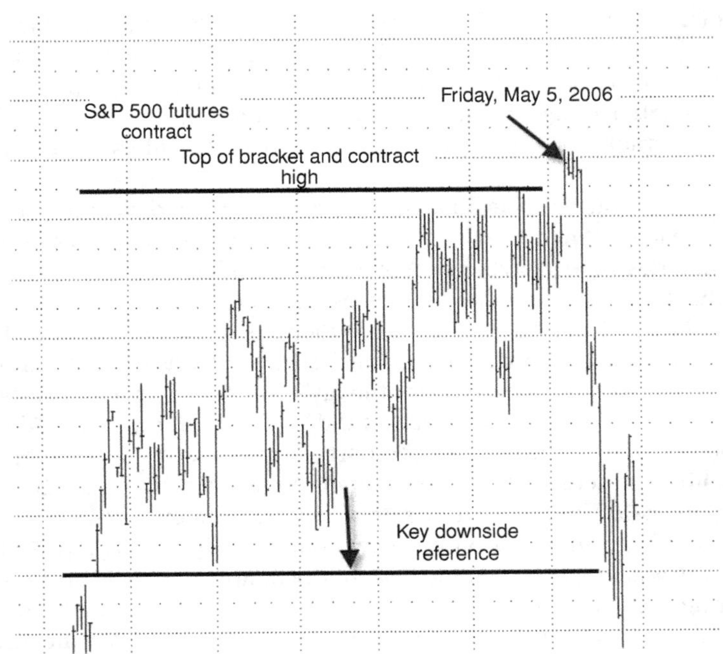

FIGURE 6.9 Strong counter auctions to the upward trend, followed by nonlinear break to the downside. S&P 500 daily bar chart, November 2005 through May 2006 (focus area).

Street Journal following the close, was 1.6 billion shares—at the low end of the range we discussed earlier. If the market was attracting new buyers and had any real underlying strength, an upside breakout to new life-of-contract highs should have *exceeded* the upper end of the volume range. Investors often lament that "No one rings a bell at the top of the market." But in a sense, the low volume that accompanied the upside breakout *was* that bell.

During the first three days of the following week, the S&P high was not exceeded, although the Dow did manage to barely establish a new peak. In terms of assessing the risk of holding a long position, once a market attempts and fails to auction above a bracket high, the odds are good that sellers will emerge and auction price downward and explore the opposite end of the bracket. In other words, the odds were stacked against those holding long positions. If you recall, at the beginning of the chapter we made the statement that a new bracket had been formed once excess was created and the market began a nonlinear move to the downside. When an auction attempt fails to establish value in one direction, and price re-enters a previously accepted value range, the odds are good that the market will auction down and explore the opposite end of the accepted range. Looking back at Figure 6.9, we would define a composite bracket made up of the three previous, interwoven balance ranges.

On May 11, the S&P began its nonlinear descent, and as of the close on June 13 the market had already declined more than 8 percent. Was some of this capital destruction avoidable? We think so. While the world was talking about the Dow being only 80 points from historic highs and analysts were marking up their forecasts, there where many anomalies that should have been raising questions and ringing bells; yet it was not until after the fact that the experts appeared with the answers. Some of the experts said that the drop was because the market didn't like what the new Fed chairman, Ben Bernanke, brought to the party. But obvious clues to the market's eroding structure had been creeping in since early December, long before the world had a look at the new chairman. In our interpretation of market-generated information, we saw continuously overlapping balance ranges, low volume, poor volume distribution among the daily profiles, and counter auctions that were at least equal to auctions with the trend—just to mention a few of the factors that led to our conclusion that the upward trend could not continue. Our question is this: While the talk shows were clearly providing us with a surplus of information and hype, where was the *intellect*?

THE QUEST TO DO BETTER THAN "NORMAL"

In *The Structure of Scientific Revolutions*, Thomas S. Kuhn describes major shifts in scientific theory as occurring when some new set of circumstances—an anomaly—violates "normal" expectations. This change is initially (and fiercely) resisted by all those invested in what was previously considered scientific "fact." Malcolm Gladwell would argue that this dynamic occurs in every type of human endeavor, with the "innovators" first to recognize that a major shift is occurring. These innovators, in both the scientific and financial realms, are generally rebuffed by the majority that have a (literally) vested interest in the status quo. But eventually the change that has taken place is recognized by everyone—even the "late majority" and the "laggards," who get on board long after there is any significant opportunity to take advantage of the change.

The major shift in market sentiment that occurred in May 2006 is a prime example of such a change. The financial media, the columnists, the arm-chair analysts, nearly all of them were in agreement about the fact that the market was going to rip through those historic highs. Unfortunately for them, and anyone else who got long on their advice, the market had other ideas—a new set of circumstances had developed, which were visible for those who knew where, how and when to look. The buyers were finally "all in" (the aforementioned "capitulation"). And while human nature dictates that no one ever wants to be first into the breach, sellers did emerge, and the market did a major about face.

Relative return managers are often caught by moves such as the one just described. (*Relative return* refers to how an asset class performs *relative* to a benchmark.) That is because their clients—which include pension funds, endowments, foundations, and individuals—are quick to penalize managers who miss significant upward market moves. As a result, most managers attempt to stay fully invested during significant rallies (such as the three-year rally preceding the break). Portfolio managers and investment firms don't just risk a little "under performance" at these moments, but rather a significant decline in their business, which sometimes proves to be fatal.

When money managers get too bearish, stay out of the market, and miss the next leg up, their reputation (not to mention their self-confidence) gets damaged. For those that develop an understanding of *market structure*, which provides a strong foundation upon which to build rational decisions, some of the inherent risks in investing can be diminished—which could be the difference between being successful and being a footnote in the history books.

OH, THE DIFFERENCE A FEW POINTS MAKES

We have spent a lot of time demonstrating the difference between trending and bracketing markets, and as you recall, we referred to major trends as *long-term*, and bracketing markets as *intermediate-term*—two distinct timeframes. We have also discussed the distinction between *risk* and *forecasting*. We never know how high or low a market will go (that job is handled expediently by the auction process), but we can assess the resulting risk to existing positions. It is paramount to seek confirmation in the market's unfolding present-tense structure; by observing market movement and volume in relation to the mean, it is possible to monitor auctions for *continuation*. Days in the direction of the auction timeframe you are trading should result in better volume, progressive value-area migration, and more elongated Market Profile shapes.

To recap, if a market is trending upward and higher prices are attracting new buyers *and* additional volume, then the mean is continually rising.

If the opposite is true, and higher prices are attracting *less* volume, then it becomes apparent that the mean has remained well below the current price, which means the odds are high that price will return to those levels.

If you can identify when the odds are changing and then *act* on that knowledge, then you have a meaningful advantage over the majority of investors who wait until proof is incontrovertible before making a move. In the highly competitive investment business, the reward—even if only a few percentage points—can be very significant.

CHAPTER 7

Short-Term Trading

If you can keep your head when all about you
Are losing theirs and blaming it on you;
If you can trust yourself when all men doubt you
But make allowance for their doubting too;
If you can wait and not be tired by waiting . . .

—Rudyard Kipling

Before we plunge into short-term trading, let's take a few steps back and look at a continuum we call the *trader development spectrum.* Understanding the way the different timeframes process and interpret information helps you begin to identify your own unique timeframe:

- Long-term strategy
- Intermediate-term strategy
- Short-term trading
- Day trading
- Scalping

Long-term trades or investment ideas are made from a slower, more logical analytical approach, with little attention paid to short-term details. At the other end of the spectrum, scalpers rely mostly on the unconscious mind, with rote memorization and keen reflexes being paramount skills—long-term information is far too slow and cumbersome to be considered in the frenzy of the daily grind.

Intermediate- and short-term trading requires the most attention and agility because successfully trading in these timeframes requires retaining, recalling, and managing large quantities of information, some of which are part of a long and complex series of events and indicators. Real-time data, culled from present tense market structure, often reveal additional significance in data that we've already seen and processed. When old information is bombarded with a constant flow of new data, it takes an agile mind to continually assess and reassess both the big picture and the minutia of the daily auctions.

Longer-term trading is often enhanced by *not* looking too closely at the smaller pieces of information, while day trading requires that you immerse yourself in short-term market conditions so you can react quickly and intuitively to the day's evolving data. We're in no way suggesting that day trading is "easier," rather, that it requires parsing data that may not be as complex and interrelated as the information germane to longer-term investing.

Take a moment to think about your own thought processes as they relate to the different phases of the Trader Development Spectrum described above. Are you beginning to understand where your individual strengths (and weaknesses) would ideally place you on the timeframe continuum? The "analyst" will likely be frustrated attempting to day trade, while the intuitive trader, with strong reflex skills, will probably be equally frustrated with the prospect of trading the longer timeframes. It's simple in theory, but difficult in practice: *in addition to knowing the market, you've got to know yourself.*

No matter what timeframe you ultimately trade, the market profile provides you with a visual manifestation of market activity—the unfolding patterns that capture complex information in a manner consistent with the brain's mechanism for understanding complex information. Having access to a tool that so cohesively sums the actions of all market participants is simply indispensable for keeping your head about you, especially during times of crisis when your blood pressure soars and opportunity is fleeting.

One last thought before we begin to explicate short-term market activity: *Perhaps the most important skill you must master to become a successful trader is the ability to distinguish "price" from "value."* This is something expert traders do intuitively, and Market Profile does by its very nature, organizing information from the entire timeframe spectrum in a way that enables you to visualize how value is building and migrating. While separating price from value is the hardest concept to internalize, it is absolutely essential to understanding and effectively employing market-generated information.

Remember, the auction's fundamental purpose is to advertise opportunity (price), fairly and efficiently allocating bids and offers among the market's participants. As you gain experience reading market-generated information via a market profile in the "present tense"—as it unfolds—you will learn to interpret *price in context*, which is the key to successfully trading in any timeframe.

ANALYZING SHORT-TERM MARKETS

Short-term trading has no formal definition; a short-term trade can last a day or several days, even weeks. But no matter what timeframe you're operating in, you are a day trader on the day you enter or exit a trade. And good day-timeframe trade location, enhanced by a sound understanding of the auction process, contributes to good performance for all timeframes. Now let's dig in.

We'll begin by analyzing the preceding days' activity in order to determine good trade location for the current day—the day you intend to trade. Like top professionals in any sport, you must analyze past action in order to be truly competitive; tennis star Andre Agassi analyzed endless match films before he ever faced an opponent. The same holds true in the investing realm: securing good trade location has as much to do with understanding the market's prior behavior as it does with effectively analyzing activity on the day you trade.

On Day 3 in Figure 7.1, notice where the market opened—well above the previous day's close and accepted value. This will serve as an early important reference point, along with the previous day's high and the fact that that the previous day's market profile shape is broad, or "fat." Remember, for the market to find acceptance away from a well-established mean it needs *power*, manifest in volume. The more pronounced the mean—such as the wide center point of Day 2 in Figure 7.1—the more significance you should attach to it; a wide mean essentially acts as an anchor, because a large number of market participants have agreed that price was fair to both sides at that level. When a day exhibits a broad market profile, unless the following day's auctions occur on high volume, the odds are good that price will revisit the gravitational center of that mean.

On Day 3—the day we're going to "trade"—the market opens just below the high of day two. After exploring above this reference point, responsive sellers quickly return price to the center of the previous day's value area, where the pronounced mean from Day 2 exerts its pull. In order to secure good execution for trades to be entered or exited on this day, you should have started by reviewing the previous day's activity, followed by a review of overnight activity, in order to get an idea of where the opening was expected to occur. As we have stated in previous chapters, you should have also determined if the market was balancing or trending. If balancing, you should have carefully noted balance area highs and lows, as well as longer-term reference points. If trending, you should have noted the

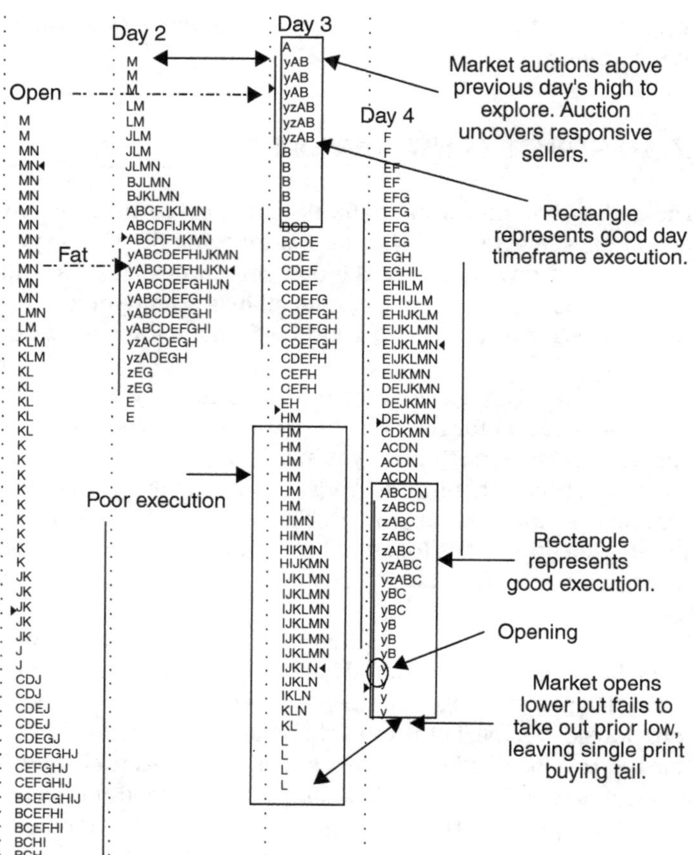

FIGURE 7.1 Analyzing the previous day's activity: Multiple daily profiles.
Source: Copyright © 2006 CQG, Inc. All rights reserved worldwide. www.cqg.com.

direction and conviction of the trend. All of this information should be known but kept in the background; too much attention to specific details can blur your short-term analysis. After the market opens, you should be looking for a place to sell above value relative to the previous day if you're looking to short, or buy at or below value if you're looking to buy.

Markets are much more understandable if you think of price as simply an advertising mechanism; you want to learn how to gauge the market's collective response to each ad, as it were. Unfortunately, most traders focus solely on price, not its qualifications, and it's no secret how "most" traders perform, in the long run.

On Day 4 in Figure 7.1, the market opened by advertising price below the value area for the previous day. This price was quickly accepted by responsive buyers, as evidenced by the single print buying tail in *y* period. Buyers would need to act quickly on this day, while sellers would probably have time on their side. Which brings up an important (and oft-mentioned) point: probability and intelligent risk/reward are not the same thing. It is not unusual, for example, for me to correctly assess that a market has extremely high odds of auctioning upward, yet I'll be in the process of shorting that same market. Why? Because the current, short-term auction, while bullish, may ultimately be providing a greater, lower risk opportunity to place a short. This is applicable to all timeframes. What we're saying, in this case, is that while the odds of the market continuing higher in the very short term are good, the amount of price appreciation remaining is relatively small in relation to the risk of price destruction, once the current auction ends.

For example, let's estimate the odds of the market moving higher at 75 percent with the potential to earn an additional 3 percent. However, because the upward price movement is occurring very late in the overall auction, a break from this level could easily produce a 20 percent loss. As this is being written, the *New York Times* is reporting that small caps are down more than 10 percent and emerging markets more than 20 percent since the beginning of May. There was clearly a point, while these markets were topping out, when late investors were buying and still seeing gains. However, the potential reward—relative to the risk—was not acceptable. In fact, an auction usually isn't over until we see one last upward spike that draws in the remaining buyers (Gladwell's *laggards*).

When we use the term *odds*, we're not referring to odds calculated via prescribed rules of mathematics, but odds based upon logic. If higher prices are causing investors to become less aggressive in their buying, then logic says that the auction is likely to stall and eventually reverse. If higher prices are causing investors to become more aggressive, then logic says that the auction is likely to continue, perhaps even accelerate. What we're describing is a process based on how we observe investors' actions as they are manifest in a multidimensional graphic that combines price, time, and volume—the market profile.

As we move deeper into our discussion of short-term trading, we will continually examine how trade location determines the risk of change inherent in each trade. We are always in search of asymmetric opportunities—which simply means that the odds of success are greater than 50 percent, and that the potential win would be greater than the potential loss. In fact, if we were to rank the importance of the information we have shared with you here in *Markets in Profile*, the concept of *asymmetric opportunities* would rank right at the top—it's the theme of successful investing.

COMMON MIND TRAPS

An important element of successful short-term trading is understanding—and avoiding—some of the common traps your brain can set for you. The first is a natural tendency to believe that if something has been occurring for some time—a trend relevant to your timeframe—then it is likely to continue. You believe that repetition is effectively predicting future events, and with this insight into the future you establish a trade in the direction of the trend. We have provided ample material to support a case for making better judgments, but memories are short, and the longer something has been reiterating, the less risk is involved (or so we imagine). We recently experienced this in the emerging markets, which rose by approximately 20 percent in the first four months of 2006; gold increased in value by approximately 40 percent and copper prices doubled. But of course investors didn't concern themselves with risk, choosing instead to focus solely on return. Was there a way for short-term traders to participate in these advances, as well as the ensuing breaks that carried these markets sharply lower? Yes, indeed—by applying the same auction logic we've discussed throughout the book, and not caving in to the immediacy of emotional wish fulfillment. As long as higher prices continue to attract more volume and the consecutive balance areas are distinctly higher, then the odds of the auction continuing upward are high. Similarly, as long as lower prices continue to attract more volume and the balance areas are distinctly lower, then the odds of the auction continuing downward are high.

The second trap investors fall prey to is over-simplifying the data, which can have the effect of providing a view directly opposite of what is actually occurring, which can of course lead to the mismanagement of opportunities and risks. For example, since Market Profile was first formally introduced by the Chicago Board of Trade in 1982, numerous services have sprung up that attempt to offer trading services based on this innovative tool. These services claim to provide you with hard and fast rules about what to do with each market profile pattern, such as buying and selling tails, range extension, etc. They will also attempt to predict the range of each time period, based on the "average" of these time periods in the past. There's an old adage about the man with his head in the freezer and his feet in the oven who says "Well, my average temperature is just right."

But there is always the hope that *this time it's different.*

It is human to crave predictability. Unfortunately, predictability—like being average—can be the end of your trading life. *Everything is always different,* to some degree. Context is always changing. You can't be successful over the long haul by applying formulated solutions to a market in constant flux.

We believe that success relies heavily on one of two things: being in the right market at the right time, and/or having the right skills for the current market cycle. There are great bull-market traders and there are great bear-market traders, but how often are they one and the same? There are phenomenal volatility traders and there are those traders who fold when the market heats up. In short, we realize that different skills are better adapted to certain types of markets, but the way to increase your odds of long-term success is to become a whole-brained trader, with skills that apply to any type of market. It all starts with looking at the right information in the right context and developing an objective, probability-based approach to trading.

WHEN AND WHERE TO LOOK FOR SHORT-TERM TRADES

We can teach and study endless details, but never make the markets come to life. The market profile enables us to see these details in their proper context by giving *form* to market activity. To make sense of this information, it's important to be involved in the process that forms the profile. Those who stay with it will soon begin to visualize the completed profile before the day is over. When this first happens, you will experience the joy of creativity, just as you're making a nonlinear leap in your learning process.

It should be clear by now that the one thing the market is not is *predictable.* It would be comforting to describe specific patterns to look for, as well as hard rules on what to do when those patterns occur. Unfortunately, it's not that simple—every day the market opens and is influenced by new circumstances, new participants, new contributing factors. In short: everything is always *different.* This is especially true in short-term trading where every piece of new information is important, and may or may not influence market behavior. Thus, for much of the balance of this chapter, we will take you through a series of short-term trading opportunities—as they unfolded—providing you with access to the thinking, analytical framework, and play-by-play commentary of real-life scenarios.

OPPORTUNITIES AROUND INTERMEDIATE-TERM BRACKETS

Good short-term trades often occur within, or on the fringes of, intermediate-term brackets, and might include the following . . .

- *Breakouts from balance.* Figure 7.2 shows a breakout from a balance area following an inside day (an inside day occurs when the most recent day's range is entirely contained within the previous day's range). This scenario can be a high-probability trade. As Figure 7.2 shows, the key is to monitor the auction closely for continuation once the breakout occurs.
- *Fading bracket extremes.* Nonsymmetric trading opportunities—those that offer significantly higher potential return than risk—are often afforded by fading (going against) a recent auction in which price "hangs" at one of the extremes of a range defined by multiple days of overlapping value. It is the opposite of a breakout trade, when price auctions to one extreme of the balance on *decreasing* volume.
- In Figure 7.3, the market rallied to new recent highs and then bids simply dried up. Because it often takes traders some time to get over the influence of price, the market will just hang around like this until the realization grows that the rally is over. And once this realization sinks in, you have limited time to act. Homework is a beautiful thing.
- *Bracket breakouts.* Figure 7.4 shows a breakout from an intermediate-term bracket—an identical trade for intermediate and long-term traders (versus breakouts from balance areas); at major breakouts, multiple timeframes converge and volatility increases.

I don't have hard and fast definitions for "intermediate term" or "long term," but I'm willing to go with nearly any breakout from balance. Likewise, *I will fade a balance area extreme if volume doesn't support the auction's advertisement at that price level.* And then there are those occasions where the market is in total balance and volume doesn't disclose any meaningful information, in which case I simply wait for a new auction to begin.

TECHNICAL INDICATORS

We observe the market's behavior around key technical indicators (rather than rely on the technical indicators themselves) as yet another piece of

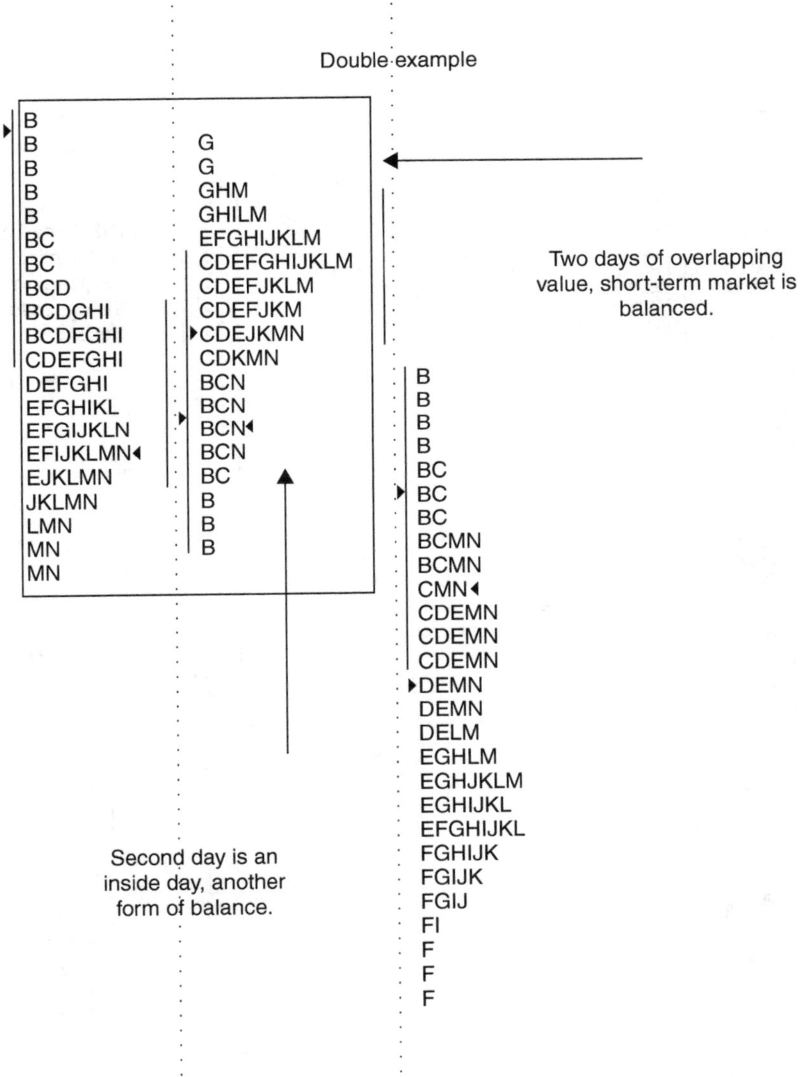

FIGURE 7.2 Breakout from balance following an inside day: Multiple daily profiles.

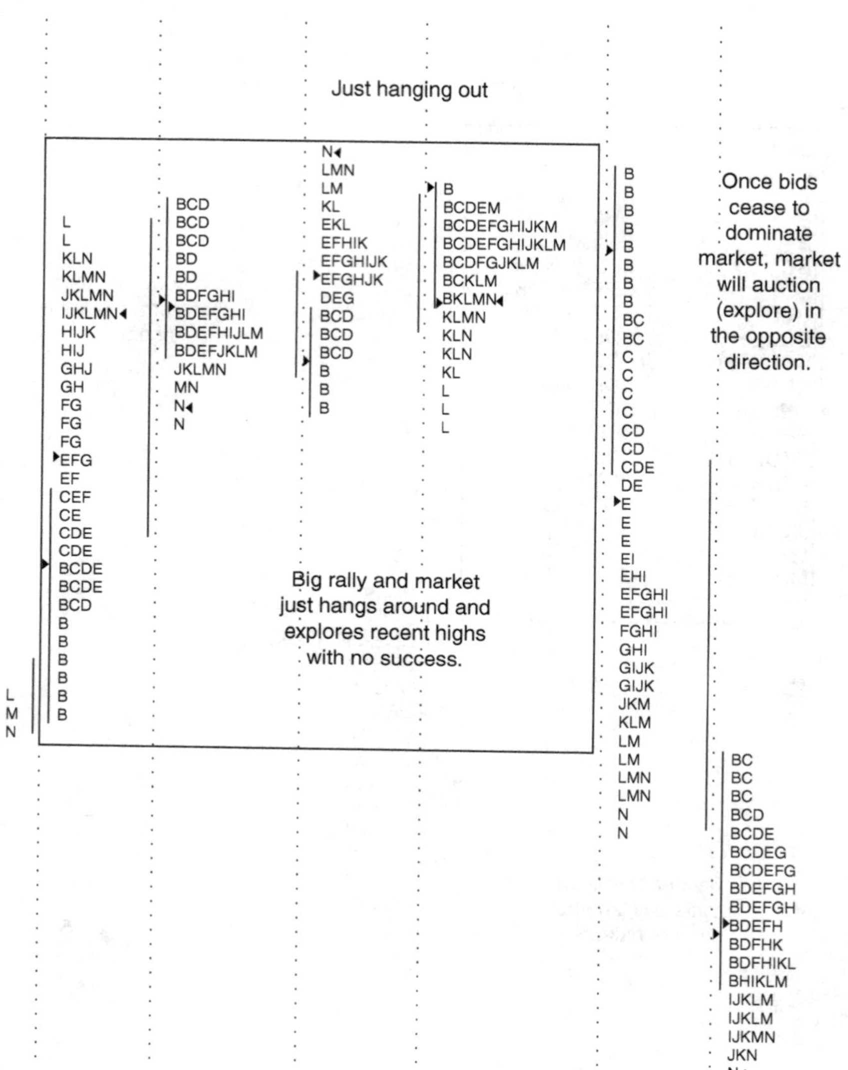

FIGURE 7.3 Bracket extreme in the S&P 500: Multiple daily profiles.
Source: Copyright © 2006 CQG, Inc. All rights reserved worldwide. www.cqg.com.

market-generated information. In many ways, technical analysis is the antithesis of how we approach markets and trading because it fails to include time and volume, which enable the visualization of market structure. A classic example would be a moving average, which is one of the most

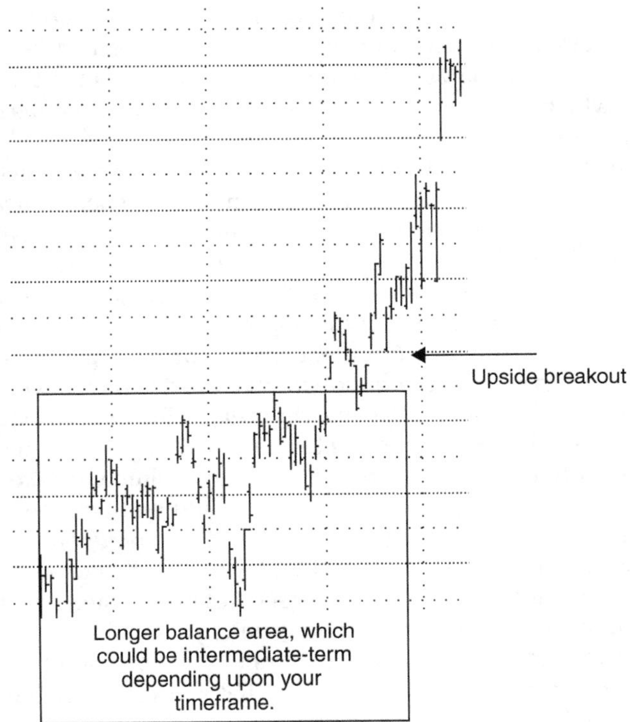
Upside breakout
Longer balance area, which could be intermediate-term depending upon your timeframe.

FIGURE 7.4 Breakout from an intermediate-term bracket: Daily bar chart.
Source: Copyright © 2006 CQG, Inc. All rights reserved worldwide. www.cqg.com.

popular technical tools. A simple moving average is constructed by using the average price of a tradable security over a defined period of time. A five-day moving average, for example, would be calculated by adding the closing prices for the past five days and dividing by five. Our aversion to moving averages is based on the fact that they treat all prices as equal; they fail to distinguish between prices made on low or high volume and what direction the market was attempting to auction that day, which can result in very misleading information.

Let's expand on moving averages by examining Bollinger Bands, which are based on the classic idea that price will revert to the mean. The bands consist of two channels and a center line, which represents an exponential moving average. The bands represent a standard deviation above and below the moving average, which is considered the *true value*, or mean. The upper and lower bands then become price targets. In an upward trend, for example, when price rotates to the lower band, the security is thought to be oversold, which indicates a buying opportunity. Our concern is that the moving average is based on price alone, which doesn't give a true picture of how the mean migrates. The market profile is based on time, price, and volume, which provides a more comprehensive means of observing the mean's progression.

We have similar concerns about mathematically derived technical indicators like Fibonacci numbers. This doesn't mean such indicators are invalid; in fact, we follow many of them closely because they can provide solid trading information. For example, recently the S&P 500 was trading around its 200 day moving average, and as a result there was increased volatility due to the fact that this moving average is widely followed by investors, traders, and hedge fund managers. For example, in May–June 2006, many of the market experts thought that the 200-day moving average would support the May–June 2006 market break. What we saw via market-generated information and the market profile was that as the market auctioned lower, volume *increased*, while on rallies volume *decreased*—data that suggested the 200-day moving average would be taken out, which is exactly what happened (and quickly). The fact that a large number of market participants are focusing on a certain level or indicator increases the odds that we will at least witness increased volatility when that indicator is in play, and with volatility comes opportunity.

There were certainly successful traders in the world long before Market Profile arrived. We maintain, however, that successful traders have always understood that higher prices on decreasing volume will eventually spell trouble. It doesn't require studying a profile to realize that as you approach any market reference point—whether it be a long-standing high or low or a standard technical indicator—it is more likely to be taken out if volume is increasing, and more likely to appear to be a meaningful support or resistance level if volume is decreasing.

YOUR OWN WORST ENEMY: YOUR BRAIN

Shortly after I began trading, I began to understand that I was often my own biggest adversary. I took the standard path and began to read a lot about psychology, which eventually led me to neuroeconomics—which combines psychology, economics, and neuroscience—to discover how we make choices. This study helped me better understand how humans learn and evaluate, and how the chemistry of the brain affects our decision-making process. It is well beyond the scope of this book to provide real depth to these subjects. However, we will suggest that your success in the markets can be highly dependent on your understanding of how your brain processes information; the more you comprehend the brain's workings, the more you'll be able to understand the true nature of your trading decisions. You might also come to learn when it might be necessary to rewire your brain to get past unproductive tendencies. We bring this up here because we suspect that distinguishing between price and value may be extremely difficult for some, requiring not only learning something new, but also *unlearning* modes of thinking that have become second nature.

In *Mozart's Brain and the Fighter Pilot: Unleashing Your Brain's Potential* (New York: Harmony Books, 2001), a book we highly recommend, Richard Restak, M.D. writes, "[C]ognition refers to the ability of the brain to attend, identify, and act." He includes among the components of cognition: perceptual speed, learning, memory, problem solving, and creativity—all of which, in our opinion, are utterly necessary to successful investing/trading.

We have discussed the importance of maintaining a balanced perspective, and how monitoring market profile structure helps maintain that perspective, especially when viewing both daily and multiday profiles. "Experts are not only better at putting things into perspective," Dr. Restak points out, "but quicker at detecting when they are starting to lose the big picture." We have talked a lot about timeframes that coexist, occasionally merging together and causing large, nonlinear moves. I have been well served by continually making sure that I can mentally keep the timeframes separate; significant losses are often a result of allowing the timeframes to blur together—losing the big picture.

When I first heard the phrase *cognitive dissonance*, a condition of conflict or anxiety that results from inconsistency between one's beliefs and one's actions, I paid it little heed. I considered it nothing but a psychological term that clearly didn't apply to me. However, following several periods of extremely shaky trading, I realized that several of the trades that had caused me the most harm clearly went against my analysis. I had seen the opportunity correctly and my timing had been good, but when the time came to act, I couldn't pull the trigger. On more than one occasion, I did pull the trigger, but in direct opposition to what my research was telling me to do. Delving into behavioral science literature and neuroeconomics helped me greatly reduce the negative effects of cognitive dissonance.

For example, once I began to understand what neuronal networks are and how they're formed, I made several trading breakthroughs. Neuronal networks begin to form as the brain encodes our repeated experiences. This occurs as the result of practice over time. As I correctly viewed and acted on market-generated information, it became better encoded in my brain and assisted me in overcoming cognitive dissonance. "Over several games," to quote Dr. Restak again, "but not necessarily in a single game, these networks will prove superior to the trial-and-error approach of the novice."

Some may take issue with referring to investing and trading as a game. However, we agree with the idea of *game* as defined by Sid Meir, designer of the classic "Civilization" computer games, that is, "a series of meaningful choices." Meir's definition also helped me develop a better understanding of how stress impacts performance. Today, because I've learned to handle stress (only occasionally do I now swear at the computer screen), it's difficult for someone in the same room with me to know if I'm "doing well" or not. The point I'm trying to make is that learning must begin with understanding—to play any game, you have to *understand* the game. To be successful, you have to become a lifelong student of the game, immersed in the markets with an open mind and an inquisitive spirit. Of course, you can also choose to be a spectator, someone who knows a lot of interesting facts, able to recite all kinds of impressive statistics. But the fact remains: spectators can't play the game.

SEEKING THE "EXCEPTIONALLY TASTY PATTERNS"

Many of the really good trades require that you place your trade responsively, fading the most recent move—which makes you a contrarian. As a contrarian, you are no longer part of the crowd. You may have to stand alone, occasionally incurring the doubt or even rancor of your friends and associates. By reading extensively about the brain and the way our decision-making process works, I have managed to increase my confidence to a level that enables me to place trades with less stress and cognitive dissonance, particularly those trades that fade the most recent market direction. Self-control is mandatory when markets begin to run hard; in the past, when I wasn't operating from a place of calm self-control, I would have trouble accepting the fact that I had missed a big move, sometimes getting in late with poor trade location and excessive risk.

Let's look at some real examples of market structure that provided excellent trading opportunities, as well as the emotional complexities each engenders. First, we'll examine the development of countertrend auctions.

Prior to the start of the countertrend rally, just one full-size S&P 500 futures contract had declined $21,000 (see boxed area in Figure 7.5). If you have never traded, it will be difficult to relate to the emotions that this kind of volatility inspires. Even experienced traders will suffer the pulse-pounding effects of an adrenaline surge when the market travels that kind of distance in such a short period of time, making it increasingly difficult to maintain emotional control and objectivity. Understanding this natural human reaction, I seldom trade the first countertrend auction following a significant directional move. The emotional G-forces are just too intense.

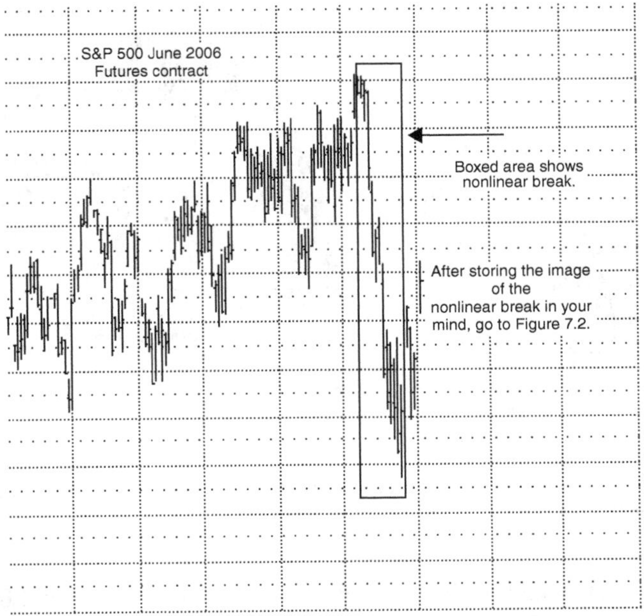

FIGURE 7.5 Countertrend rally occurring in the S&P 500 (after the nonlinear break): Daily bar chart, June 2006.

Figure 7.6 serves several purposes. First, it offers a review of the upside breakout that began in November of 2005 and ended in May 2006. (This is the same period shown in Chapter 6, which enables us to maintain thematic continuity.) Second, it allows us to more easily visualize market behavior during the upward auction from November 2005 through May 2006 so that we can better understand how this behavior reverses once it becomes clear that the intermediate-term auction has changed course, turning down. Third, it reveals the first meaningful low that occurred after the nonlinear, downward auction.

The low on May 24 marks the beginning of the first countertrend (upward) auction. After the excess low is established, it is difficult to know how long the countertrend auction will last. In this example, however, it is safe to assume that the first countertrend auction will not carry very far, as the market has just plummeted so sharply that it will most likely take some time for it to come into balance, giving everyone time to catch their breath. I prefer to wait and study the first countertrend auction, extracting as much information from it as possible. If this turns out to be a longer-term low, there will be plenty of good trades down the road. Now let's take a more detailed look at the countertrend auction via the market profile.

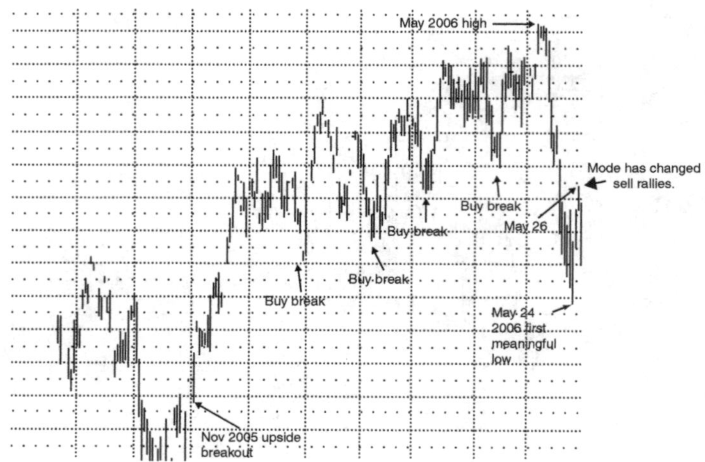

FIGURE 7.6 Longer-term upward auction and subsequent nonlinear break occurring in the S&P 500: Daily bar chart, November 2005 through May 2006.

From the November 2005 upside breakout until the May 2006 high, buying every break eventually rewarded traders with higher prices. Traders—like everyone—have a habit of doing something until it doesn't work anymore. It would follow that once it became clear that the intermediate-term trend had turned down, the expected trader behavior would be to switch to the opposite strategy, selling rallies and repurchasing on breaks. Figure 7.6 shows the first meaningful low, following the May 11 nonlinear break, occurring on May 24—the low that marks the beginning of the first countertrend auction. Let's put the countertrend auction under a microscope by examining the auctions through the market profile.

The low occurred in J period, and the market closed clear back up in the top quarter of the profile. On the following day, the market established clearly higher price and value. (We are always more interested in value than price.) The solid line to the right of each profile marks the day's value area. Notice that Day 2 is fairly elongated, which tells us that prices were auctioning higher with ease. Volume was approximately 1.6 billion, which, from our earlier guidelines (1.6 through 2 billion being the normal range) is light. The light volume should alert you to the fact that the upward auction attempt is weak. However, individual indicators must always be considered within the larger context—the market closed on the high and the day's profile was elongated, which means that the odds would suggest that the rally is not complete. As an investor or trader, you should continually collect and process information as each auction unfolds before you. *It is quite common to observe that some of the information you collect contradicts other information, a phenomenon that is often caused by different timeframes responding to different criteria.* Remember, it is common to have an intermediate-term auction going one way, and either a shorter- or longer-term auction going another direction. Notice in Figure 7.7, on Day 3 of the rally, how the profile becomes squat (from high to low) and wide (from left to right), which suggests that the countertrend rally is ending, or has ended. In addition, the day had light volume—another indication that the rally is coming to an end. This was a three-day, short-term trade that should have been exited on Day 3. Light volume provided an early warning on Day 2, and the shape of the profile and another light-volume report on Day 3 indicated that the odds of continuation were low. Counter-auctions, which by definition are against the trend, generally require quicker exits.

Before and after you place a trade, the most important question to ask is this: *How much confidence is the market exhibiting to support your trading decision?* Some of the factors to monitor in order to better understand the market's confidence are:

- Attempted direction—which way was the market attempting to go?
- Volume associated with the directional move.
- Value area placement—overlapping-to-higher, higher, unchanged, overlapping-to-lower, or lower.
- Shape—was the profile elongated, symmetrical, or squat?

As we have said, the market profile enables you to see the structure of unfolding market activity. And over time, your experience will enable you to recognize partial patterns that enable you to visualize how the day's auctions might unfold. We are always seeking to identify trades that enable an advantageous risk-reward relationship. It is impossible for the human brain to accurately digest, comprehend, and analyze the dense thicket of information that influences the market from moment to moment. But the brain has evolved to be remarkably adept at recognizing patterns, and the market profile captures the complex and everchanging interconnections present in the market in patterns that can be recognized and understood in an intuitive way.

Ralph Koster, author of *A Theory of Fun for Game Design* (Scottsdale, AZ: Paraglyph, 2004) wrote: "Based on my reading, the human brain is mostly a voracious consumer of patterns, a soft pudgy gray Pac-Man of concepts. Games are just exceptionally tasty patterns to eat up." We also believe that one of the problems with patterns is that our minds are also inclined to find patterns that *don't exist.* We seek patterns that support our beliefs—it's just human nature. From an investing standpoint, this tendency becomes nearly inescapable if you also listen to the hype on television and in "expert" newsletters; before too long, the brain begins to actively hide the truth from you.

Koster's enlightening book is about games and game design. The fact is, trading is a game in which there are winners and losers, and score is kept in dollars and cents and those all-important track records that can make or break a money manager (not to mention a personal fortune). That's why we keep reiterating the salient factors—like profile shape, value area, and volume distribution—that enable us to objectively see what the market is really telling us.

ALL PRICES AND OPPORTUNITIES ARE NOT EQUAL

The shorter the timeframe you're trading, the more important the timely placement of your trade; every time you enter or exit a trade, you are, in fact, a day trader. By necessity, day timeframe information will be included in the analysis of Figure 7.8, but note that the day timeframe will be more fully explicated in Chapter 8.

In Figure 7.8, the first three days, reading from left to right, are the same three days that made up the short-term, countertrend auction discussed previously in Figure 7.7. Having seen the initial countertrend rally weaken substantially, we would look to trade from the short side as we come into Day 4. The selling tail—the single set of downward prints in the opening B period—demonstrates a high-confidence opening; longer-term sellers are aggressively selling from the opening bell. Not only are they selling early, but notice that the selling started well below the previous day's close, a clear indication that the prevailing market sentiment is that prices are too high.

With this clear indication of directional conviction, we ask that you consider the profile indicators that provide clues about the collective will of the market. The previous day's close was near the high for the day, which probably gave traders comfort in taking home long positions, thinking that they could get out in the morning if necessary. When the market opened quite a bit lower, however, consider how badly they must have wanted to sell, if they were willing to sell well below the previous day's close, continuing to sell at even lower prices all through the opening B period. Like any game, it is important to continually attempt to figure out what your opponents are thinking and doing, and if they are right—with the larger market movement—or are getting themselves into trouble, which means they'll have to reverse their positions in the near future.

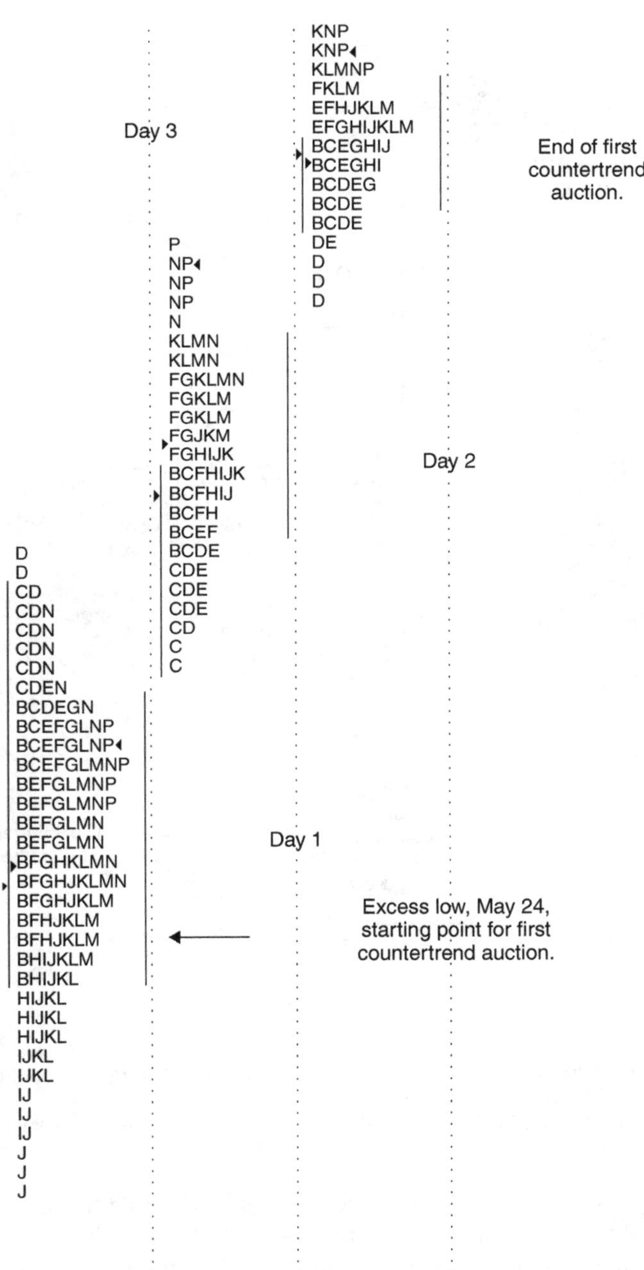

FIGURE 7.7 Countertrend rally following a nonlinear break occurring in the S&P 500 viewed through the lens of the profile: Multiple daily profiles.

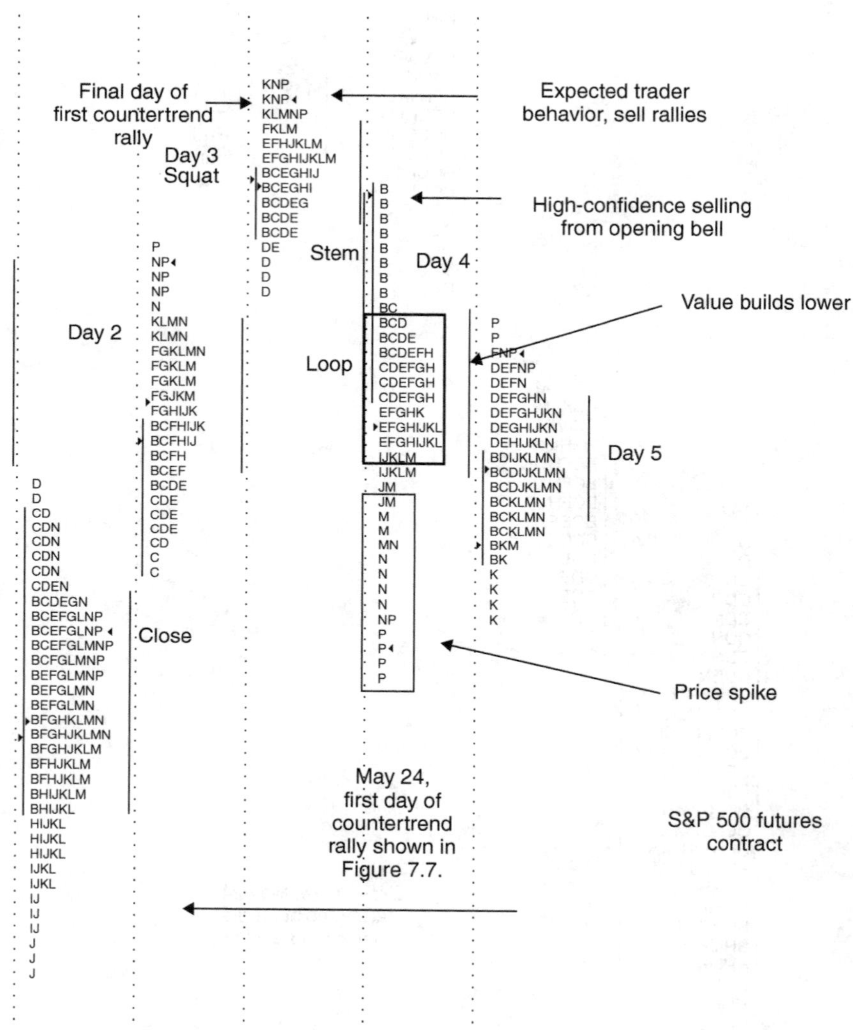

FIGURE 7.8 Fading a countertrend rally following the nonlinear break occurring in the S&P 500: Multiple daily profiles.
Source: Copyright © 2006 CQG, Inc. All rights reserved worldwide. www.cqg.com.

On Day 4 in Figure 7.8, the aggressiveness exhibited in the opening B period should—if the sellers are correct—lead to lower value, an elongated profile, and high volume. Having this as a foundation for your analysis, you now have some parameters with which to monitor the day; your goal is to free yourself from relying solely on the advertising mechanism of price to monitor the market's intentions. Notice that the day's profile shape following the B period sell off starts to resemble the letter b prior to the market making a late-in-the-day sell-off, demonstrated by the M period selling price spike (in the rectangular box). The b-shaped pattern is one that you will see often, and it represents two things: (1) Sellers are primarily liquidating long positions (the opposite of a short-covering rally), rather than a combination of long liquidation and new shorting; and (2) buyers are at least slightly more patient than sellers. This is important to note because these patient buyers are not in it for a "day trade," but rather some longer timeframe—at least overnight. Unlike the day-timeframe trader, these buyers are more patient and may, in fact, be scaling into large positions. You may not see the effects of this type of buying for a few days. Recall that we noted earlier that successful trading requires that you piece together long strings of data, and that you retain your ability to objectively recall that data within the context of constantly evolving market conditions. Not an easy task.

All rallies, at least initially, include a combination of short covering and new buying. For the rally to be sustained, however, new buying must overtake short covering. When this occurs, the profile becomes elongated. When it doesn't, and short covering rules the day, a lack of continued new buying often results in a profile shape that resembles the letter p. The mirror image occurs on market breaks, which start out with longs liquidating existing positions, accompanied by the formation of new shorts. When new shorting is consistent, the market profile becomes elongated, while lack of new shorting often results in a profile shape that resembles the letter b.

Our position, over the years, has consistently been that markets are not efficient. If that is correct, then what has occurred in the past does, in fact, affect the odds of future activity. If the markets were efficient, and all prices and opportunities were equal, the past would have no bearing on later outcomes. Back to Day 4 in Figure 7.8. The b formation serves as an alert that the odds of the market going lower have decreased—but have not gone away. Late in the day the market spikes lower, which should cause you to question the conclusions we've drawn up to this point. Recall, however, that the buying we saw in the center portion of the market profile may have been for a *longer timeframe*. The price spike on Day 4 may also have been the "completion" of what started early in the morning—traders selling what they perceive to be price above value. The question posed by a price spike is this: will value be pulled down to price, or will price revert back to volume? If the spike was on low volume, then the odds favor price reverting back to the mean, which would be the value area from the day the spike occurred; if the spike was on heavy volume, then you would expect value to be lower on the following day as the mean (value) moves toward new price levels.

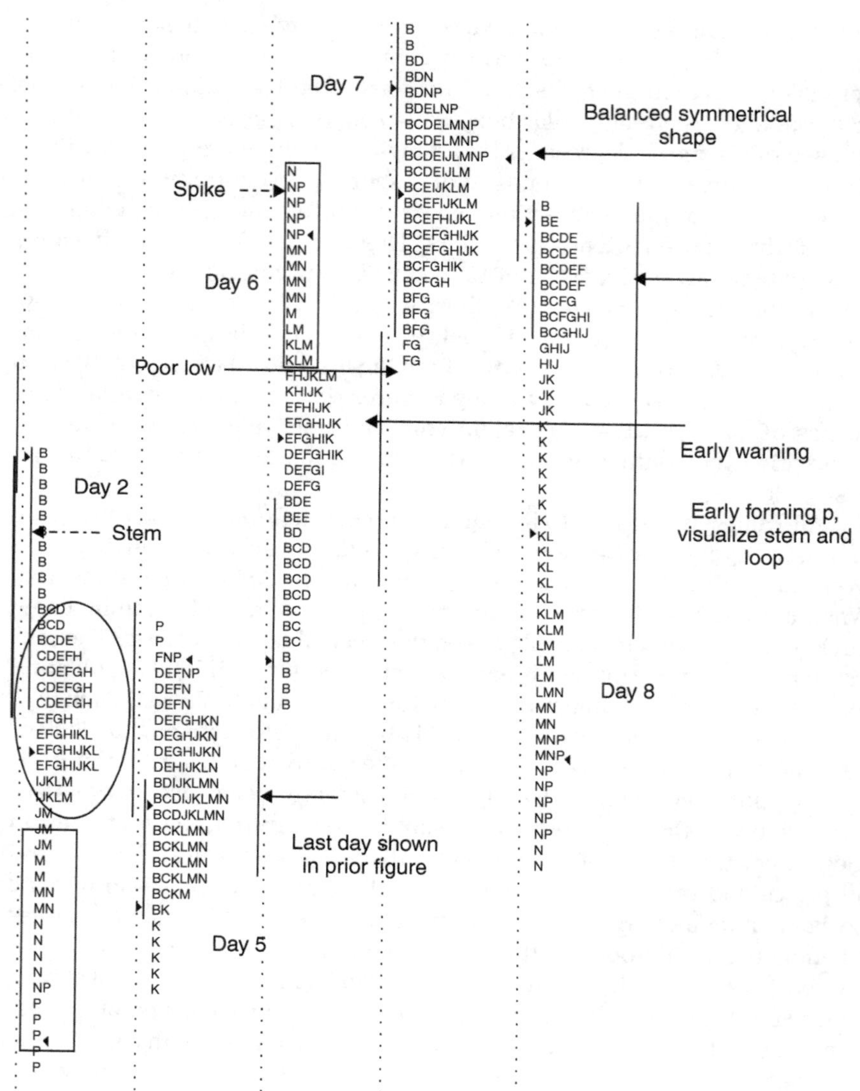

FIGURE 7.9 Further analysis of the countertrend rally following the nonlinear break occurring in the S&P 500: Multiple daily profiles.
Source: Copyright © 2006 CQG, Inc. All rights reserved worldwide. www.cqg.com.

The spike on Day 4 occurred on low volume, as did the whole day. I would have entered this trade—which was *with* the longer-term trend down—looking for conviction to the down side. Because of the b shape of the profile that day, indicating no real seller conviction, the evidence supported closing out such a trade. It takes a great deal of mental discipline to exit a profitable trade that you had been looking for, especially when it is with the trend on a day that closes near the low. But there is a huge difference between closing out a trade and reversing your position. Again, it is important to get inside the head of your opponents. What would most market participants feel about the same trade? Probably that is was a good trade and that the market was weak (because they were focusing on price), so it is unlikely that the market will turn quickly.

Anyone can tell you what the market *did*. But consider looking at things another way—what *didn't* happen? In this last example, the market profile was not elongated; the shape didn't indicate that trade was being facilitated on the down side, and volume didn't validate lower price and value. Because the market was struggling to go lower, the natural reaction is to begin to think about the upside. Remember, the market is a series of two-way auctions, which are the market's means of gaining information—whether we're discussing the day timeframe or any of the longer timeframes, the two-way auction process is ongoing.

ONGOING FORENSIC INVESTIGATION

Turning our attention to Figure 7.9, let's first remember that we had concluded that it would be wise to close out any short positions—despite the fact that price closed near the low of the selling price spike (rectangular box on Day 4), which would tend to make anyone who took home a short feel pretty good. But because of lower volume and the b formation (circled area), the trade should have been exited.

On Day 5, the market opened higher, closed higher, showed overlapping-to-lower value, and never seriously challenged the excess low created by the late spike on Day 4. When a spike occurs, you can't determine if it was, in fact, an excess low until the following day when the market opens; there's simply not enough nighttime volume to enable this determination to be reliably made. Earlier, we talked about the perils of conflicting information, which was evident on this day. Experienced Market Profile users would question going home with a long position on Day 5, as value was overlapping-to-lower. The more important piece of information, however, was that the excess created by the spike on Day 5 was not seriously challenged, as well as the fact that a late rebound closed the market near the daily high. To remain with a long position, I would have needed to see continuation very early on Day 6. The Day 5 range was completely contained within the range of Day 4, which is referred to as an *inside day*, or as a *neutral* or *balancing day*. For short timeframe traders, we recommend that you trade *with* any directional auction following a neutral/balancing day; when markets come out of balance, there is always at least a short-term opportunity to take advantage of the ensuing auction.

The following day (Day 6) was a trend day, which is essentially a day in which the market moves almost continually in a single direction for most of the day. The biggest mistake a short-term trader can make is to refuse to believe a trend day. If you don't want to go with it—that is, trade in the same direction as the trend—then at least don't go against it. The trend day provided early confirmation of our analysis from Day 5. Despite the day timeframe trend day up, the market profile on Day 6 developed a shape that resembles the letter p ("early warning" arrow), which means buying was being met by longer-term sellers, or at least by those who were willing to hold a short position overnight or for a few days. On this day, there was an upward price spike late in the day (the single letter M through the letter N on the high). The p formation—just like its mirror image, the b formation—provides an early warning that the market is struggling to auction higher. It will take some experience to recognize these formations, and the last two examples we discussed were somewhat camouflaged by late spikes, which are often the completion of an auction when they follow the b and p patterns.

On Day 7, value was, in fact, established higher. Notice on this day that the low was made in F period and then matched in G period; if there had been aggressive responsive buyers—those looking for an opportunity as prices sold off—then price would have probably only traded at that level during a single time period. The fact that the market traded on the low during two different time periods suggests that that particular price was not considered to be such a scarce opportunity by longer timeframe buyers, meaning also that it was probably not a very good low (and would be revisited). Some might say that this is just nuance. *It is.* But details matter, and successful short- and intermediate-term traders tuck away these details as part of their ongoing forensic investigation of the developing shape of each day's market profile.

Day 7 is another balancing day (observe how the day is almost completely symmetrical, a sign of balance), and the same rules discussed earlier apply here as well—trade *with* the initial auction away from balance. Remember also that everything must be viewed within its proper context, and in this case the long-term auction remains down, which means that a trade with a break-out to the downside coming out of this inside day is more likely to be significant than one to the upside.

On Day 8 the market broke from balance, auctioning briskly to the downside and creating a trend day capped by a long selling price spike. Take a moment to compare Day 8 to Day 6—both were created by breakouts from balance, but Day 8 was *with* the longer-term down auction, while Day 7 was *against* it. The breakout with the longer-term auction was clearly the more significant of the two.

With this breakout from balance into a selling trend day, we can clearly state that Day 7 marked the high for the market's second countertrend auction following the nonlinear break. Next, we will examine the auctions that followed Day 8, a trend day in the same direction as the major auction that erupted out of a balancing day that had established the high of the second counter-auction. Before we do, however, let's review Figure 7.10, which will help us better understand the two countertrend auctions.

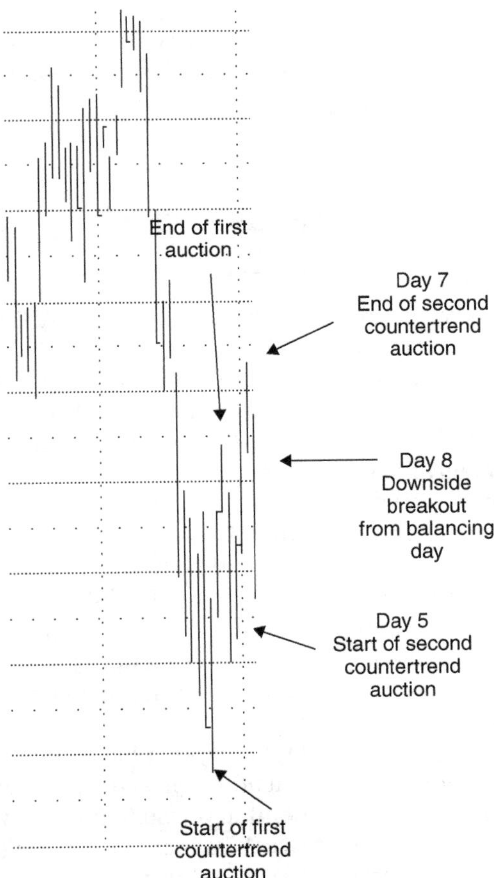

FIGURE 7.10 Further analysis of the countertrend rallies following the nonlinear break occurring in the S&P 500: Daily bar chart.

In the course of examining each day of the two countertrend auctions discussed previously, we have attempted to identify viable short-term trades. With each auction we have learned something new about the shifting responses of the market's participants. For eight days we saw only limited continuation of short-term auctions in both directions, which is consistent with a market attempting to come into balance, to catch its breath after a strong, nonlinear move. Before we push on, take a moment to reflect back on the significance of spikes and trend days, and in particular the significance of trend days that don't result in uniformly elongated shape, such as Day 4 in Figure 7.9—a trend day down that resulted in the b formation, which did not bode well for continuation. Similarly, Day 6 was a trend day up that resulted in a p formation. When spikes occur, you should observe whether price reverts back to value, or value is pulled to price. Finally, Day 8 was a trend day in the direction of the intermediate-term auction.

Now let's review the days that followed, first reviewing them via a daily bar, and then via daily market profiles.

LOOKING FOR THE ALL-IMPORTANT REFERENCE POINTS

Markets by their very nature often provide easily identifiable reference points that can assist in identifying advantageous trade location. In Figure 7.11, for example, you can see a gap that was left at 1,303.50 during the initial nonlinear break. The second countertrend rally (that we just discussed) failed to fill that gap by .50, or half of a point. These are the "tells" that become extremely important to successful short-term and day traders, and they can be best viewed when using futures pit session bar charts, as opposed to cash or electronic futures. While the volume in the futures pit sessions is low relative to daytime electronic trading, I have found that it is more reliable in identifying subtle clues to market intention. The electronic market tends to trade a tic or two both higher and lower than the pit session, which is often on miniscule volume. For example, the gap at 1,303.50 occurred during the pit sessions, and would not have been evident if you were using the electronic contract.

In fact, it's often possible to find compound evidence to help identify asymmetric trading opportunities. In addition to the gap that wasn't filled, you can also observe a reference point in the solid line drawn just beneath the gap that separates the multi-week, upper trading range. This is the line beneath which the market accelerated once price found acceptance, spurring the first nonlinear break. As we have said, the auction continually searches for new activity as part of the information-discovery process. This

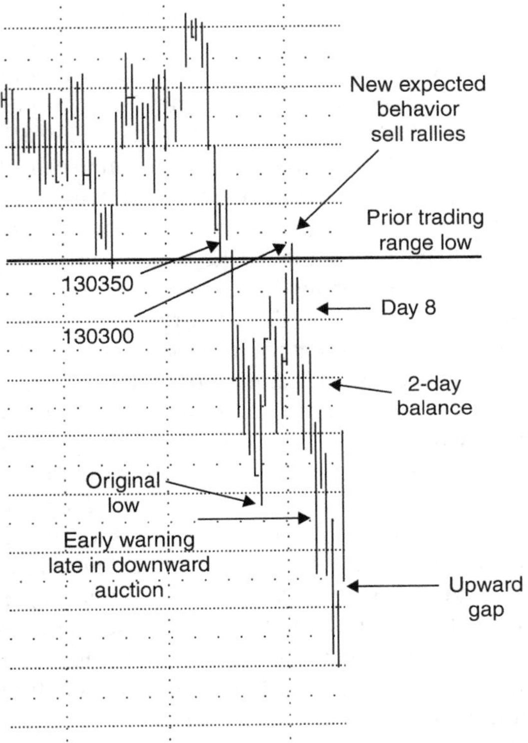

FIGURE 7.11 Key reference points generated by the nonlinear break and countertrend rallies occurring in the S&P 500: Daily bar chart.
Source: Copyright © 2006 CQG, Inc. All rights reserved worldwide. www.cqg.com.

phenomenon is clearly manifest in the second countertrend auction, which peeked up above the solid line into the previous balancing range, where it quickly discovered that higher prices were cutting off activity and attracting sellers; because the intermediate-term auction is down, in this instance, this is the expected behavior. Of the three pieces of information that identified the ideal place for a short-term trade, two were tangible (gap and prior trading range low) and the third, the expected behavior, was more psychological.

Once the downward auction got underway, it continued for eight days. Referring to the arrow marked "early warning" and the arrow pointing to the original low, you will notice how price traded below the original low and then traded back above that reference point for the next two days. Earlier in in this book, we discussed the idea of "clean breaks," which is applicable in this example. The point marked "original low" had managed to contain price on the downside for 15 days after the market broke below the upper trading range and upper gap. After this low was taken out, price quickly returned to the 15-day range for a day and a half before resuming its downside exploration. The "early warning" noted in Figure 7.11 is there because the break was not "clean"—in other words, once price broke through the original low, it didn't immediately continue downward. This provides an early warning that the downside auction is starting to exhaust itself. As you can observe, a few days later the market made a low and gapped higher the following day, quickly returning to the previous 15-day trading range.

Before we review these same days via the market profile, let's consider the heightened emotional state that most traders and investors must often endure. (If you've never traded, hopefully this will provide a glimpse into the mental complexities that must be managed in order to trade successfully; for those who have traded, this may simply add realism to the discourse.) When you see a market analyzed after the fact, like we've just done, it's hard to understand just what it is that's so difficult about trading. Performing this kind of analysis under stress is incredibly challenging, and not just because money is on the line. For several years prior to the nonlinear break we've been discussing, average volatility remained well below its historic average, and individual trader and trading-system strategies operated within a relatively low-volatility environment. Then came the break and volatility rose rapidly. This kind of quick transition is hard to adjust to, both mentally and emotionally. During times of stress and sudden transition, the mind has a tendency to become disoriented, often choosing to focus on worst-case scenarios rather than the bigger picture. After the break, of course the news shows rolled out the "bears," continually focusing on the *declining markets*, how bad things were, and how bad they could get.

Almost all of the experienced traders I talked to during this period were similarly infected with the prevailing sentiment of doom and gloom. No matter how well trained you are, no matter how experienced and confident and calm, it's truly difficult to be objective when everyone around you has lost their grip on objectivity, and price volatility is exhibiting nothing but wide, volatile swings. When the market starts to whipsaw, it's almost impossible to catch your breath. Now the profile in Figure 7.12.

As shown in Figure 7.12, Day 8 was a trend day down, finishing with a late price spike. During the next two days the market balanced from the center of the Day 8 spike downward. This tells us that value was being pulled lower to price, which is a good sign of downward auction continuation. Day 10 also saw a late spike with price probing lower, once again raising the question, will price be pulled back to value or will value migrate

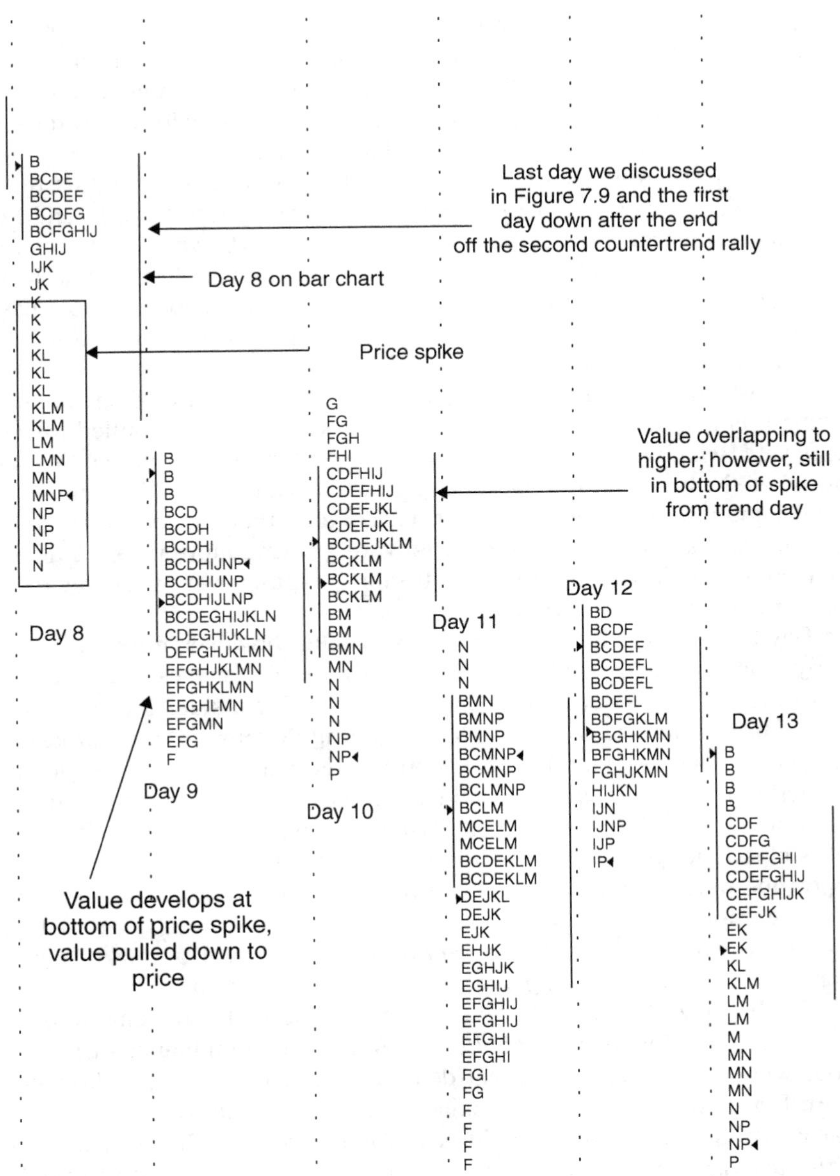

FIGURE 7.12 Further analysis of the nonlinear break and countertrend rallies occurring in the S&P 500: Multiple daily profiles.
Note: The market profiles in this figure have been condensed to fit the page, which changes the scale and can result in slightly misleading profile shapes.
Source: www.cqg.com.

to confirm the lower price probe. As always, *we focus on value, not price.* On Day 11, a value trader saw clearly lower value, while a price trader saw unchanged price. Day 12 exhibited overlapping-to-higher value and lower price. Day 12 was also a balancing day, which positions us for a new directional trade once the market leaves that balance range.

However, there is clearly conflicting information due to the fact that Day 12 resulted in overlapping-to-higher value, while both Days 11 and 12 remained below the average balance of Days 9 and 10, which alerts us to the fact that the intermediate-term auction down may be tiring—but isn't necessarily over. This lets us know that the risk of remaining short has grown substantially; successful trading/investing is based on identifying advantageous probability.

Day 13 was another trend day down with a late downward spike. Following this activity, we again observed to see if value was pulled lower on Day 14, which is exactly what happened. In Figure 7.13, notice the arrow labeled "early warning" in the upper portion of the Day 13 profile. The nonelongated profile shape provided another alert that the auction was tiring. During this day, the news reports were growing more pessimistic as price continued lower, and those with short positions were probably feeling more and more comfortable.

Day 14 provided clearly lower price and value; however, notice another "early warning" arrow—the fat shape of the profile suggests that lower prices are not engendering continuation to the down side. Our evidence shows that while prices are steadily migrating downward, the market is struggling to move lower, laboring step by step without the freewheeling conviction that accompanies sustainable directional movement. But think about how this feels in the moment. When you look only at price, the market is clearly moving lower. How in the world could you *buy*? This is an opportune place to reintroduce Gladwell's diffusion model. At this stage in the auction, it is the late majority and the laggards who are dragging price downward because they focus only on price and because they're scared—*what if I'm missing out on the next major trend?*

On this day, if you could have measured the collective emotions of all market participants, you would have found a predominance of fear in those who were long, and a great deal of confidence in those who were short. But if you considered the balance of market-generated information that we've been discussing, you'd have found evidence that *just the opposite was true.* During this frenzy of market volatility, if you were able to acknowledge your emotions as a product of herd mentality and news hype, instead focusing your empirical mind on the *patterns* being revealed in market structure—revealed by organizing purely market-generated information via the market profile—you would have seen that the market was struggling mightily on the downside.

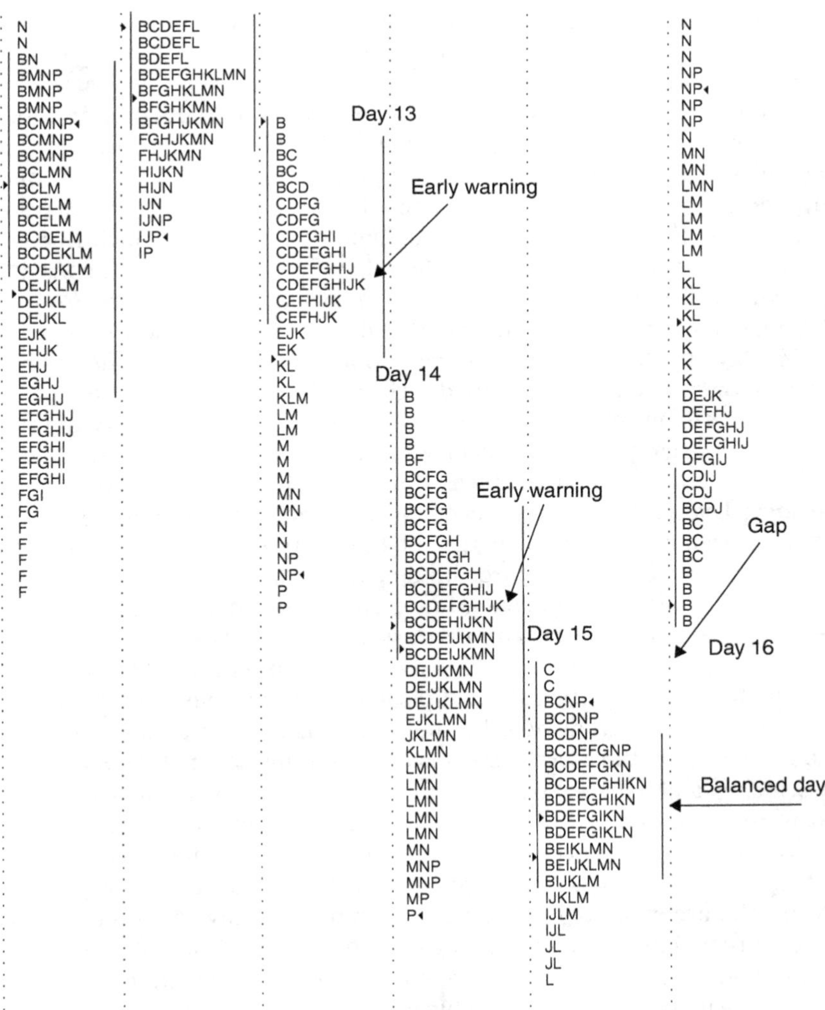

FIGURE 7.13 Further analysis of the nonlinear break and countertrend rallies occurring in the S&P 500: Multiple daily profiles.
Source: Copyright © 2006 CQG, Inc. All rights reserved worldwide. www.cqg.com.

NEVER BE A LAGGARD

We have spent a good deal of time discussing the notion of timeframes and conflicting information. Trading is extremely difficult when you aren't able to separate the actions of the various timeframes; oftentimes, what appears to be "conflicting" information is simply information coming from timeframes with different motives conducting business on the same day. Days 14 and 15, for example, offer excellent day-timeframe opportunities and poor intermediate-term opportunities. For the five days prior, evidence accumulated that suggested intermediate-term shorts were *late* in the auction process, and any new shorts placed during these days had poor trade location. Auctions generally have to complete themselves, which leads to the situation we discussed earlier when the odds are high that the market must continue in the direction of current auction, but that the risk/reward relationship inherent in trading with that direction is extremely poor.

On Day 16, all the conflicting, compounding information finally overwhelmed the market, which gapped higher and nearly took back the previous five days in one elongated trend day. Returning to Kuhn's description of major transitions, such shifts occur when new circumstances violate what has been considered "normal" by all those invested in what was previously considered status quo—in this case, the downward auction. On Day 16, the transition was universally recognized as the market shot upward, leaving the late majority and the laggards holding the bag.

When I'm analyzing any auction for any timeframe, the key issue I focus on is this: *What are my competitors doing?* For example, as the kind of conflicting evidence discussed above begins to mount, I try to discern how much money is getting short at disadvantageous levels, often referred to as "getting short in the hole." Experience has taught me that that those who get in late are the first to exit—as in accounting, last in first out. This is weak money and unlikely to have staying power. The nonsymmetric shapes that we have been labeling "early warnings" not only tell us that the market is struggling as it goes lower, but should also cause us to ask "*Why is it struggling?*" The answer is often because there are patient, longer-term buyers who are gradually but steadily accumulating inventory—inventory that they're willing to hold for a long time. It's not uncommon, particularly in intermediate-term auctions, to see this process occurring over several days before it becomes unmistakably evident to a broader participant base (the late majority and laggards). These are the conditions that lead to reversals, or at least meaningful corrections.

A GOLDEN OPPORTUNITY

We've made a pretty strong case that a healthy trending market trends, then stops and balances, then trends again. But it doesn't always happen this way, particularly when speculation takes over like it did in gold

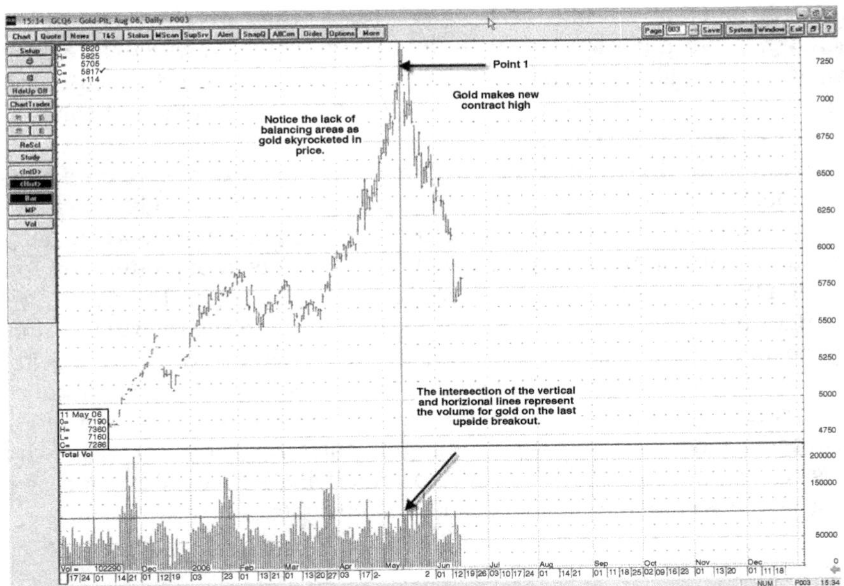

FIGURE 7.14 Upward trend in Gold driven by speculation: Daily bar chart, December 2005 through June 2006.
Source: Copyright © 2006 CQG, Inc. All rights reserved worldwide. www.cqg.com.

during the first half of 2006. Due to extreme speculation, the market neglected to stop and balance along the way; when such speculative trades are unwound, a freefall can result. Let's examine the relatively rare instances in which trades can start out as short-term positions and then evolve into much bigger opportunities.

At Point 1 in Figure 7.14, gold topped out in much the same way the S&Ps did back in May 2006—gold made a new life-of-contract high on substandard volume. The arrow at the bottom of Figure 7.14 points to volume on the day that we're discussing. As you can see, the volume was well below the range that high-volume days can generate in this precious metal.

Notice that gold rose from about $580 an ounce to about $750 without a prolonged balancing period. This is usually a sign of extreme speculation, which can end badly for those who arrive late, or those who get in early but continue to build on their positions, and for momentum players. Balancing periods are healthy and important, in that they allow the market participants to "catch their breath" and reevaluate value before proceeding onward. Balancing periods enable you to judge the structure of the market in order to determine how much more momentum is remaining in the dominant auction. Periods of balance create what are akin to "market memory." Once a market begins to fall (or rise in the converse), previous balance areas will often provide some level of support (or resistance), serving to slow price down as market participants assess whether this area of previously accepted value is still relevant.

Without this balancing process, there is no structure to support a market. Once a market begins to fall, for example, the balance areas act like elevator stops—they may not completely stop the fall, but they will usually provide a pause in the downward auction that offers enough time for you to exit a trade, or at least judge where you are in the larger decline.

Returning to Figure 7.14, anyone who was monitoring the volume during the final run-up in gold at Point 1 and placed a short-term short, quickly discovered that all timeframes had joined in the selling. With no structure to provide support to a downside break, what might have begun as a short-term trade can blossom into a meaningful, long-term trade. For those who insist on buying into markets with no underlying structural support, we suggest you do it with options rather than outrights.

FADE THE EXTREMES, GO WITH BREAKOUTS

Good short-term trades often present themselves when a market has come into balance. Such markets usually provide two opportunities: fading an auction that reaches one of its bracket extremes and fails to continue; and going with a breakout from the balance area. Figure 7.15 demonstrates both of these possibilities.

Day 1 of Figure 7.15 is a trend day that has moved sharply higher. You could reasonably expect that a move of this magnitude should show some additional upward price appreciation. You can also assume that much of the buying that drove the stock higher during the initial trend day occurred late in the day, as that is where the market profile begins to take shape (the circled area); the lower portion of the profile is thin, which indicates price was moving rapidly without much time for volume to attach to it.

Day 2 established a very narrow value area that was totally contained within the upper portion of the value area from Day 1. At this point, you should be thinking about the mindset of the buyers from Days 1 and 2—are they satisfied? Are they frustrated? Know your competitors, and stay one step ahead of the game.

Day 3 opened slightly above the close on Day 2, trending higher all day and closing with a late upward spike. When the day was complete, value only managed to be overlapping-to-higher, and the shape, prior to the late spike, exhibited the familiar p shape of short covering; it's clear that MER

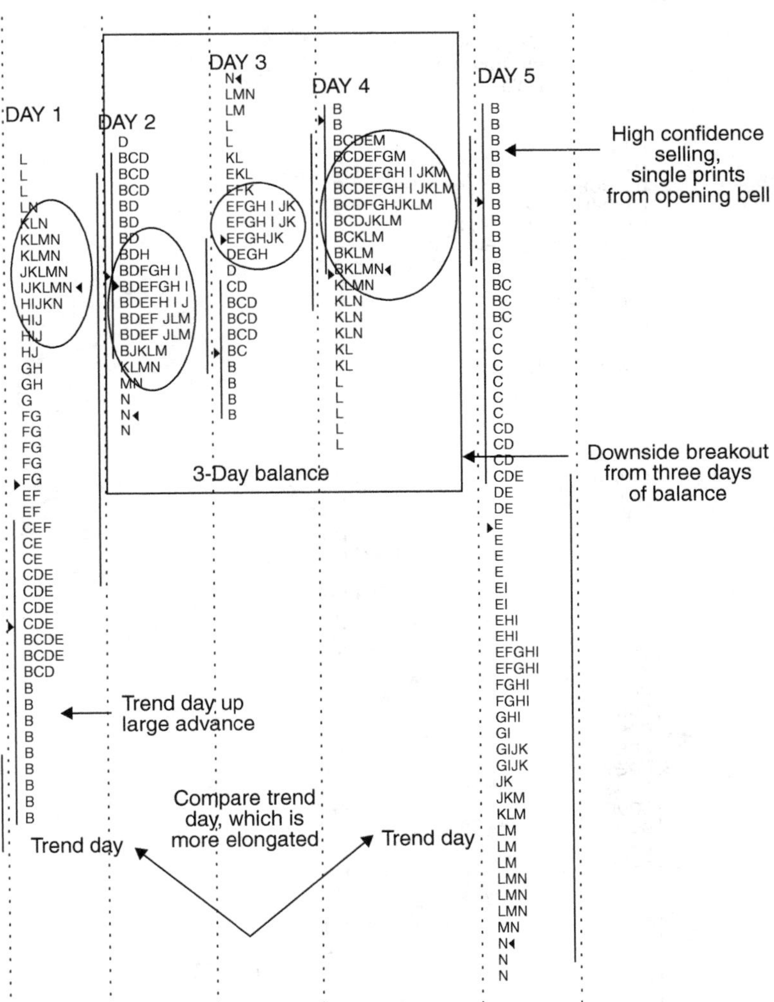

FIGURE 7.15 Bracket extreme and subsequent breakout from balance occurring in the S&P 500: Multiple daily profiles.

(Merrill Lynch) is having difficulty advancing. Price traders probably felt good at this point, as everyone who bought within the past three days has gone home with a profit.

Day 4 opens on the high and establishes inside value, with price closing lower at about the same closing level as the original, upward trend day.

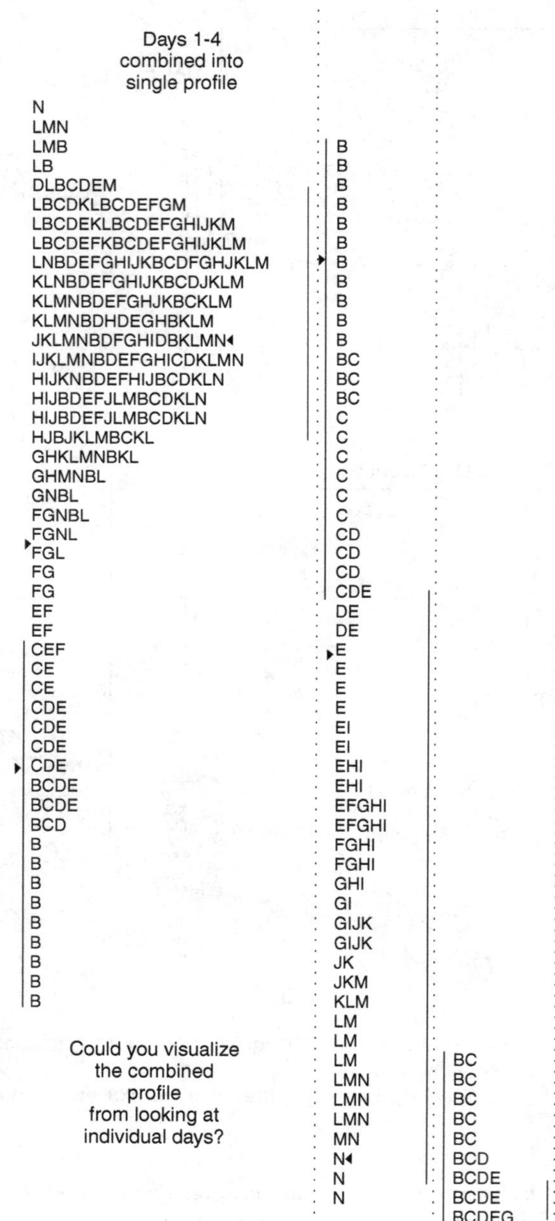

FIGURE 7.16 Multiple-day profile for the Days 1–4 shown in Figure 7.15, followed by the activity on Day 5: S&P 500 profiles.

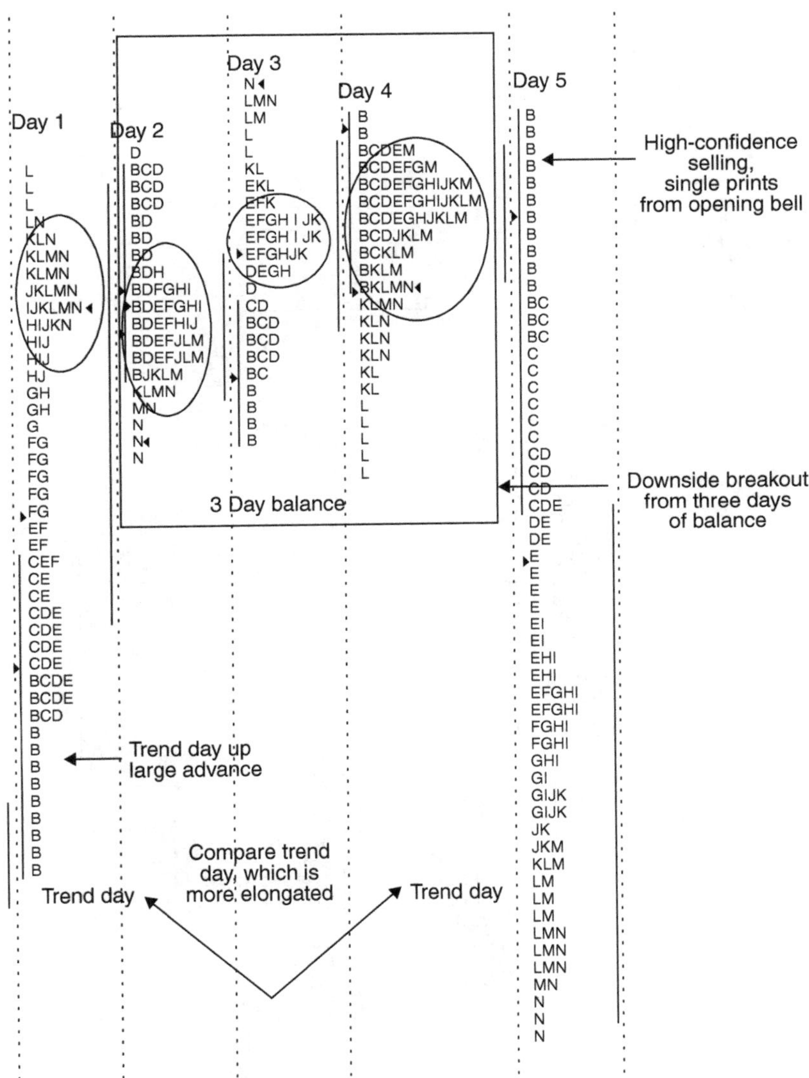

FIGURE 7.17 Bracket extreme and subsequent breakout from balance occurring in the S&P 500: Multiple daily profiles.

How do you think all the price traders who bought during the previous four days are feeling at this point? Before we continue, take a look at Figure 7.16, which combines the four days we have just discussed.

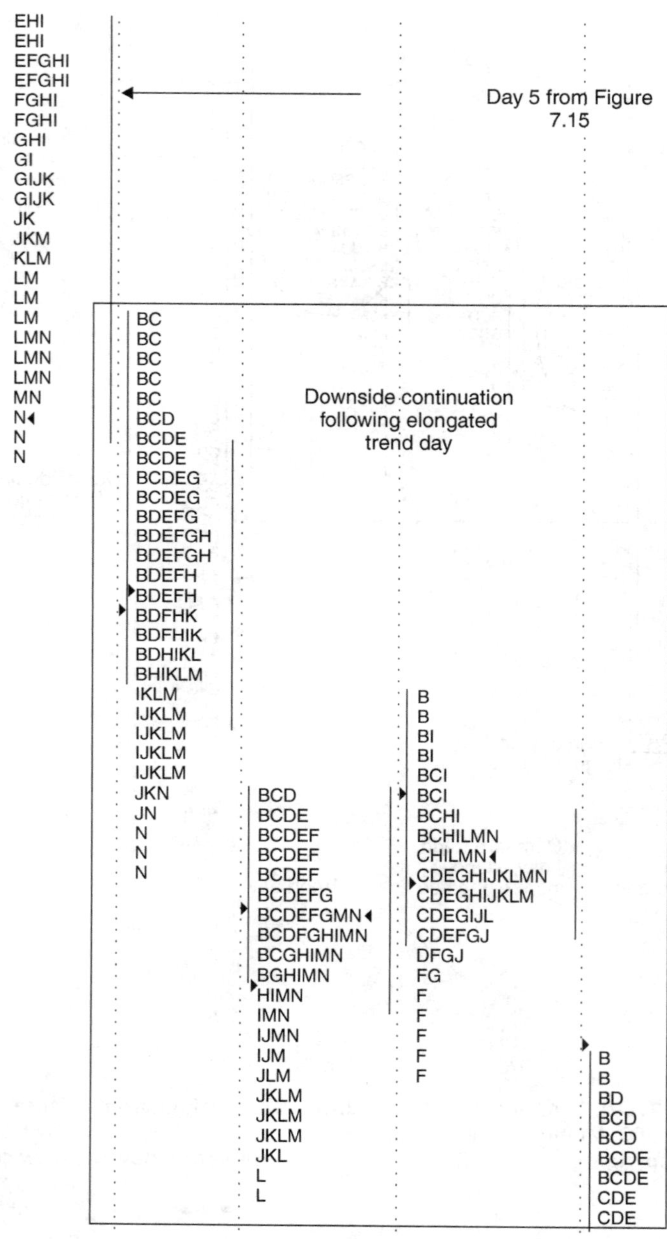

FIGURE 7.18 Subsequent downside continuation in the S&P 500 following Day 5 shown in Figures 7.15 and 7.17: Multiple daily profiles.

The combined profile shows the cumulative p pattern that we have constantly discussed when viewing individual profiles—short covering met by new sellers who are selling for a longer timeframe. As you gain experience, you will begin to visualize different patterns long before they're complete, which will make you feel more comfortable leaning into the wind, placing short-term trades before they are actually under way, which will help you secure advantageous trade location.

In Figure 7.17 (see page 135) (a repeat of Figure 7.15), we see that after four days, more and more market participants have begun to recognize that the upward auction is over; nearly all long positions placed during the previous four days are now under water. Put yourself in their shoes, imagine the stress level climbing. Short-term trading is a game, and they are your opposition.

Notice the notation in Figure 7.17 that suggests you compare the trend day up that started the last rally with the trend day down that reversed that rally. The trend day that started the rally lost its elongation near the upper end of the range, and during the following three days there was very little follow through. The trend day down stayed elongated through the closing bell, which suggests downside continuation. This trade should have been taken home short, and any long positions established during the previous several days should have been exited. While it can be psychologically difficult to take this loss if you're still long, the exit may be one of the best trades you make. Figure 7.18 (see page 136) shows the resulting downside continuation—Day 5 exhibits an elongated profile that tells us that price did not go low enough to cut off the selling.

This type of analysis is what trading is all about, and unless you are fully immersed in the markets, you will simply never learn to assess and amalgamate the many elements—both tangible and intangible—that enable you to place a trade that ameliorates risk without compromising potential reward.

"THE EXPERT REASONS CONTEXTUALLY"

In his book *Enhancing Trader Performance: Proven Strategies From the Cutting Edge of Trading Psychology* (Hoboken, NJ: John Wiley & Sons, 2006)—which should be read and reread by all serious market participants—Brett Steenbarger states:

> *Where the novice thinks concretely, the expert reasons contextually. Instead of thinking A always leads to B, the expert creates a web of possibilities in which A leads to B under conditions X and Y, but leads to C under other conditions.*

In other words, the expert is able to stay flexible, avoiding the natural human tendency to make choices based on available surface information, then to defend that choice come hell or high water—regardless of whether "other conditions" have arisen that invalidate all previous beliefs.

We all face a continuous flow of conflicting information, and it's easy to overweight the *latest* piece of information, or to choose just one of those pieces of information as the basis of a trade decision. History reveals that people aren't very good at reaching accurate conclusions when enormously complex information must be analyzed and weighted correctly. We may be good at looking at each piece of information separately, but when it comes to relating each piece to the larger, cohesive whole—well, let's just say context is an elusive thing. Consider just a few of the myriad divergent information sources that can influence the performance of a market, sector, or single security at any given moment:

- Corporate governance—both good and ill
- Shifting government regulations
- A company's ability (or inability) to innovate
- Earnings—rising, falling, or remaining static
- PE multiples—expanding or contracting
- Sales—expanding or contracting
- Competitors—entering or exiting
- Profit margins—expanding or contracting
- Overall sector growth and acceptance
- Global events
- Analyst upgrades or downgrades
- Money managers long or short on cash
- Redemptions vs. new cash entering
- Commodity prices—rising or falling
- Interest rates—rising or falling
- Trending vs. trading
- Tax selling
- Forced liquidation due to an external event
- Foreign market crises

And of course every element on this list can exist anywhere on the scale of "relevant" to "immaterial," depending on whether the market has correctly anticipated the future implications of that element. The bottom line: We are constantly bombarded with a mind-boggling amount of information, and the brain has a habit of filtering out everything except what is most self-serving. This process may make us temporarily comfortable, but when has comfort ever been associated with profitability?

That's where the market profile proves to be an invaluable tool, keeping us psychologically and intellectually honest. We may not be good at crunching enormously complex data, but we humans are exceptionally adept at spotting patterns and integrating them into workable solutions. Economists claim that you can't understand what markets do without taking into account how people perceive what they do, and that it's virtually impossible to accurately measure the complex patterns of human behavior. We disagree—Market Profile does exactly that by arranging the aggregate result of all these complex actions in a single, simple distribution curve.

CHAPTER 8

Day Trading Is for Everyone

The man who insists upon seeing with perfect clearness before he decides, never decides.

—Henri-Frederic Amiel

Much of the world seems to hold day traders in ill regard. As we have pointed out on multiple occasions, however, *everyone is a day trader on the day they enter or exit a trade.* Every tick, every basis point of performance matters.

Consider this: Everyone who participates in a hedge fund, separately managed account, pension fund, endowment, foundation, or mutual fund is affected by day trading.

Here is a case in point. Over the years I've handled numerous calls from traders with the same question about large institutional orders: "Should I fill it now, or do I have time to work the order over the remainder of the day?" When you're working large orders, the *quality* of the fill affects both the filling broker and the performance of the institution providing the order flow.

Recently, I read *The Mighty and the Almighty: Reflections on America, God, and World Affairs* (New York: HarperCollins, 2006) by Madeleine Albright, a book that delivered one of the messages that we've been reiterating throughout *Markets in Profile.* In reflecting on her daily routine at the State Department, Albright recounted how every morning she would read the President's Daily Brief, after which she would wade through the National Intelligence Daily, which was the longer version of the Daily Brief. This reading was followed by a briefing on terrorist threats. After downloading all this intelligence, she reported one thing missing: "certainty."

What also caught my attention was the following, "[U]nless you were very careful, what you would see often depended more on what you expected or hoped to see than on what was really there."

It is often said that there is "too much noise" to successfully trade in the day timeframe. During the early years of the Chicago Board Options Exchange, I'd occasionally have lunch with Fischer Black, who, along with Myron Scholes, provided us with the Black-Scholes Option Pricing Model. One of our most frequent topics of discussion was "noise." My position, which differed quite a bit from Fischer's at the time, was that there was no such thing. I felt that what people called noise was simply something they didn't yet understand. Peter Steidlmayer best dismissed the concept of noise when he said that *every trade occurs to satisfy some condition of the market.* This remains my belief today. For example, if a market rallies quickly, and just as quickly retreats, it may well have done so because the market got "too short" or, said another way, the market got out of whack in the short-term and inventory had to be rebalanced. The mirror image occurs when the market gets too long and we experience short-term liquidation breaks that serve to correct long inventory imbalances. These rallies or breaks occur for a reason. They satisfy the need to bring inventories back into equilibrium. In this chapter, we demonstrate several techniques for assessing such short-term inventory conditions. Armed with this understanding, you are better equipped to effectively execute your day-timeframe orders.

In *Advances in Behavioral Finance* (New York: Russell Sage Foundation, 1993), edited by Richard Thaler, there is an article reprinted from the *Journal of Finance* in which Fischer wrote:

> *Noise makes financial markets possible, but also makes them imperfect. If there is no noise trading, there will be very little trading in individual assets. People will hold individual assets, directly or indirectly, but they will rarely trade them.*

Imperfection creates opportunity as well as its converse: risk. We bring up noise here because we believe it is vital for traders to accept responsibility for the outcome of every trade and every action, avoiding the tendency to externally assign credit or blame. Let's take the next step and discuss the tactics of day trading.

WHAT'S A DAY TRADER TO DO?

Successful day trading hinges on understanding what your opponents are doing; sometimes you'll want to join them, and other times—especially when either long- or short-term inventories are out of balance—you will want to step aside or even fade (go against) the imbalance. There will also be times when the short-term inventory conditions aren't corrected by the market's close and can be expected to effect the after-hours markets, possibly even carrying over into the following morning's activity.

We begin by discussing the more accepted definition of day trading: trades that begin and end on the same day—a buy and a sell, which can occur in any order. Some complete only a limited number of trades in a single day; others are far more prolific. For a quick recap, let's review the definition of day traders from Chapter 3.

The day trader enters the market with no position and goes home the same way. Day traders process news announcements, reflect on technical analysis, and read order flow in order to make trading decisions. They also have to deal with long- and short-term program buying and selling, brokerage firm margin calls, mortgage banker's duration adjustments, speeches by Federal Reserve governors, and "important pronouncements" by political leaders and influential portfolio managers. Anyone who believes markets are rational should spend a day trying to digest and react to the landslide of conflicting data day traders must wade through to make a decision.

This group focuses on large quantities of technical information. They love numbers and levels and hype. Like scalpers, day traders also provide liquidity for markets, although very often at great personal expense.

The second, nonstandard definition of day trader is one that we have referred to throughout the book: the one-sided buy or sell order placed by other-timeframe participants, including individuals, hedge funds, mutual funds, endowments, foundations, institutionally managed accounts, and so on. In Chapter 7, for example, we discussed short-term trading and stated that the beginning or end of all short-term trades are day trades. However, not all day trades are the beginning or end of short-term trades.

There is endless philosophy surrounding the definition of day trading. Some tell you to study what has happened during previous days and overnight markets; others advise you to do no homework, beginning each day "fresh" with absolutely no opinions. Some suggest that you trade early, as most activity occurs during the first half of the day, and still others advise you not to trade until the market has been open for a couple hours, and you have a better sense of the day's developing structure. Let's begin with the homework debate.

The only group that can consistently profit without doing homework is the pure scalpers—those that execute many trades, often totaling in the hundreds and involving thousands of shares or contracts, that are held for very short periods of time, sometimes only seconds. These scalpers are traders who have become extremely adept at reading market swings; they've developed a purely reflective response to significant changes in order flow. But the truly successful scalpers are few; most have a checkered history in that they've done well in certain types of markets, only to give it all back when conditions change. For example, scalping a low-volatility market is quite different than scalping a high-volatility market. And scalping has become much more competitive due to computer programs that execute via electronic trading and can instantaneously respond to bids and offers.

In a trending market—whether it is a long- or intermediate-term trend—I do a lot of homework (as discussed in Chapter 7) so I can begin the trading day with two or three possible scenarios worked out. This homework consists of analyzing the previous day's volume and identifying past areas of excess (including gaps), beginning with the latest day and working backward. Next, I identify past balance ranges, beginning with shortest time period—the shortest would be an inside day or symmetrical balancing day—and working toward the longest timeframe. (Note that this process is the inverse of what I do for longer term trade identification.) As already discussed, too much detail can blur your focus on longer-term trading, causing you to overreact to short-term information—which is *fuel* for day traders. I also place a high priority on identifying prominent *points of control* (POC) from previous trading sessions. To reiterate, the POC is the longest horizontal line in a day's profile. A "prominent" POC is unusually wide, and tends to create a gravitational center that prevents the day from becoming elongated. Prominent POCs are often revisited, and may provide guidance for placing or exiting the following day's trade. Why? Because they represent a recent area of a widely accepted fair price.

In nontrending markets or markets that are exhibiting a great deal of volatility, I begin with the same analysis described above and then dive into more granular detail by adding short-term references points, such as the previous daily highs and lows, weekly highs and lows, trend lines (not that I necessarily believe in them; however, if markets are trading without direction, traditional technical reference points provide some guidance), and a look at other markets that may affect short-term trading. When markets lack direction or conviction—are nontrending—peripheral influences are far more important. For example, if stocks are in a strong trend, interest rate changes may not have any meaningful short-term effect, while in a nontrending environment interest rate changes may greatly influence market activity.

While I prefer to trade early, there is nothing wrong with waiting for the day to develop. Having said that, I believe you should act as if you were trading the entire day—otherwise you may miss some of the important details that provide harbingers of the structure you're waiting for. In general, I believe that beginning traders would benefit from witnessing the day's structure become more manifest before trading, while experienced traders should be able to gain an advantage from trading early in the day.

I have always maintained that it is unwise for day traders to trade in front of early economic releases; there are simply too many opportunities for chaos that result in unreadable market conditions. If the release has been correctly anticipated, for example, the market may have already incorporated the information beforehand, which can actually result in the market moving in the opposite direction than was expected. Or this month's information may be right on the money, but corrections from past months may end up having a greater impact than was expected. Seasonal adjustments can result in traders reacting to a different spin than you expected, or the market may have been too long or too short coming into the news release, which can trigger a more significant auction to adjust inventory imbalances. If you get in before the release, and the market trades in the opposite direction from your trade, you will find yourself in a losing position that is unfortunate in and of itself, but more importantly, could keep you out of the winning trade that sets up after the market has digested the release. Therefore, it's necessary to maintain maximum flexibility so you can trade after the market settles down and direction becomes somewhat clearer.

It's also a good idea to do your homework and identify significant reference points above or below the current market level, so that you can fade a release-caused spike that auctions sharply in one direction, with salient reference points helping you determine if there will be continuation or rejection following the spike. Using predetermined levels requires the market to come to you, rather than you chasing the market.

WHAT YOU DON'T DO MAY BE MORE IMPORTANT THAN WHAT YOU DO

We stated in the preface to this book that you must understand the way you process and respond to information. That way your ability to act is not blocked or distorted by peripheral influences. In *The Mature Mind* (Basic Books, 2005), Gene Cohen discusses two types of intelligence: crystallized intelligence, which is the intelligence we accumulate in school and from everyday life; and fluid intelligence, which he describes as "on-the-spot reasoning ability—a kind of raw mental agility that doesn't depend completely on prior learning. It includes the speed with which information can be analyzed as well as attention and memory capacity." Many traders constantly listen to business news, visit blogs, talk markets with peers, and read numerous newsletters—all of which provide conflicting opinions for differing timeframes. For those information hounds, by the time the market opens their memory is most likely crammed full, and their attention is accordingly distracted, pulled in multiple directions. In such instances, what do suppose happens to their "fluid intelligence"?

The shorter the timeframe you trade, the more important your fluid intelligence. Intuitively, traders often recognize that they can't effectively process this deluge of information, and so fall back on mechanical approaches or trading systems to decide which trades to execute. But ask yourself this: *What price would you pay for a mechanical system that actually worked over an extended period of time?* There isn't enough money in the world to buy such a system, as it would be priceless. What we're presenting is a more linear thought process that will help you prepare for each day, as well as monitor the day's progress once trading begins. Before we do that, however, let's review the 30-year bond futures for July 5, 2006.

THE REAL WORLD IN ACTION

We have made it clear that the day-timeframe trader must sort through extensive information prior to making a decision. Just like other timeframe traders, *volume analysis* becomes incredibly important in attempting to understand the inventory positions of other day-timeframe traders as well as the actions of the longer timeframes. This is mandatory if you expect to be a viable opponent. Before we delve into the details of volume analysis, let's first understand the context.

In 2006, inflation (or possibly *stagflation*) once again became the buzz in the financial markets, with the experts constantly missing the mark. In the *Wall Street Journal* on July 5, 2006, a headline read: "Sinai Tops Economy Forecasters With Aggressive Inflation View." The article went on to say that in the *Wall Street Journal*'s December 2005 survey, Decision Economics' Chief Global Economist Allen Sinai topped the list with the most aggressive forecast—up 3.5 percent for the 12 months ending May 2006. The article went on to report that the actual number was 4.2 percent. The survey included 56 economists.

Most market participants closely watch the monthly employment report for signs of growth and indications of inflation that can influence Federal Reserve policy decisions. In this case, the next report was due to be made public two days later, on Friday, July 7. Two of the key components of this report, along with hours worked and wage rates, is the number of new jobs lost or created as well as the overall rate of employment. Coming into Wednesday, July 5, the expected number of jobs for the Friday report was approximately 175,000.

Early Wednesday morning, ADP, a firm specializing in payrolls and macroeconomic advisers, predicted that new private sector jobs would equal 386,000—almost double what was anticipated by the market. With

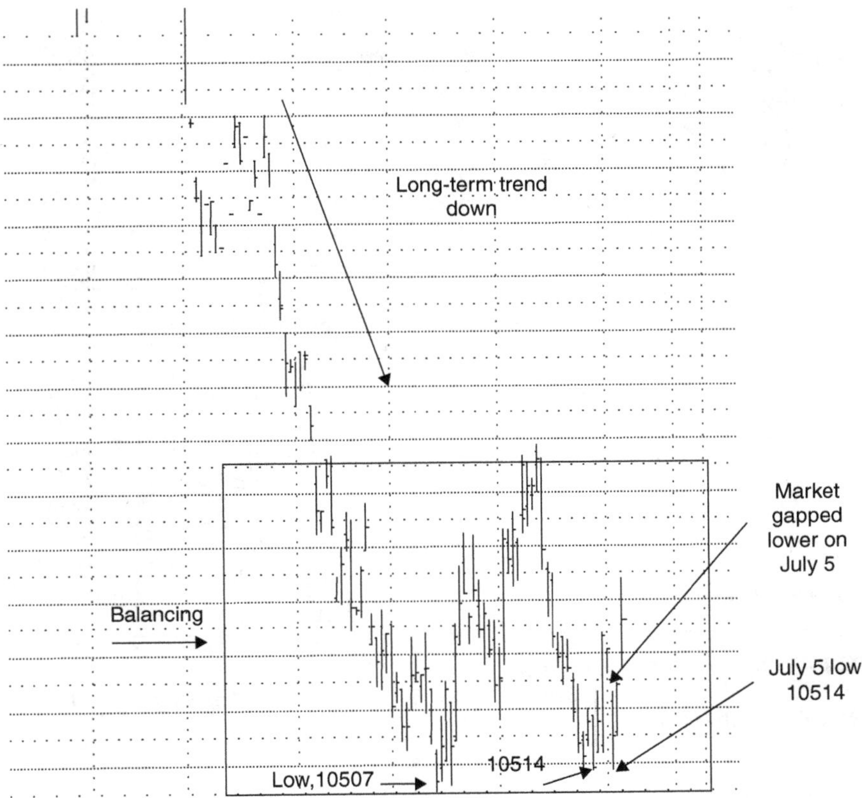

FIGURE 8.1 Intermediate term bracket (focus area) in U.S. Treasury bonds: Daily bar chart ending July 7, 2006.
Source: Copyright © 2006 CQG, Inc. All rights reserved worldwide. www.cqg.com.

this background, we can now examine the trading in the Treasury bond for that fateful Wednesday.

Figure 8.1 revels that the long-term trend is down (at least that is how we view it—longer-term continuation charts might dispute this assessment), with the market in a balancing phase that has developed for roughly three months. This three-month range, as you recall, is an intermediate-term bracket, which calls into play a strategy that suggests buying the lower end of the bracket and selling the upper end, as long as volume analysis supports that decision. (Volume isn't increasing as the market auctions toward the extremes, indicating change is underway.) Now let's expand our analysis to include the individual profile and volume analysis for Wednesday, July 5.

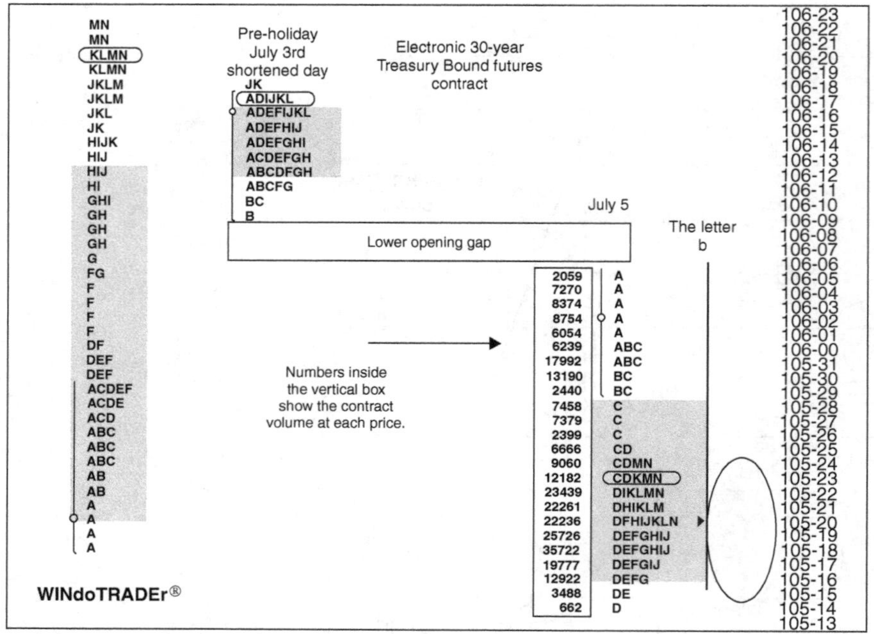

FIGURE 8.2 U.S. Treasury bonds, July 5, 2006.

Viewing Figure 8.2, we see that July 3 was a shortened, preholiday trading session that demonstrated two forms of balance: (1) It was an inside day, as it was totally contained within the previous day's range; and (2) it was also a narrow, balanced day on its own. As you read in Chapter 7, the trading strategy is to go *with* any directional move following a balancing day.

July 5 gapped lower following the ADP report discussed above and sold off sharply for the first four periods (A through D). Once again, we see the b formation that indicates short-term inventory liquidation. The buyers taking the other side of this selling activity are apparently not buying for instant gratification, but rather intend to hold for at least a day, if not longer. It's not uncommon to see an up-trend day following this kind of formation. Now review Figure 8.1 and note that the bracket low is at 105'07, with the low on the 5th at 105'14—only 7 tics from the bracket low. Trade location for shorts, of any timeframe, was very poor on this day. Trading opportunities are created when investors/traders act impulsively and don't consider the risk/reward of their trade. From the profile shape we see here, we have

Contract Volume
89,608 (32%)

Contract Volume
194,141 (68%)

Volume	TPO	Price
		106–07
		106–06
2059	A	106–05
7270	A	106–04
8374	A	106–03
8754	A	106–02
6054	A	106–01
6239	ABC	106–00
17992	ABC	105–31
13190	BC	105–30
2440	BC	105–29
7458	C	105–28
7379	C	105–27
2399	C	105–26
6666	CD	105–25
9060	CDMN	105–24
12182	CDKMN	105–23
23439	DIKLMN	105–22
22261	DHIKLM	105–21
22236	DFHIJKLM	105–20
25726	DEFGHIJ	105–19
35722	DEFGHIJ	105–18
19777	DEFGIJ	105–17
12922	DEFG	105–16
3488	DE	105–15
662	D	105–14
		105–13
		105–12

WINdoTRADEr®

FIGURE 8.3 U.S. Treasury bonds with volume, July 5, 2006.
Source: www.windotrader.com.

evidence that the bonds were not giving up ground easily. Now let's review the actual electronic volume to assess confirmation of these findings.

The settlement, or closing price on the trading day before the one shown in Figure 8.3, was 106'18, with the POC on the 5th at 105'20. After opening approximately 1/2 point lower on the 5th, the market continued to sell off to 105'14, which is approximately $1,100 lower for just one full-size contract. The most important thing to reflect on here is that 68 percent of the daily volume occurred in the lower portion of the range, which is from 105'25 down to 105'14. The circled price at 105'23 indicates the closing price on the 5th. That means almost 68 percent of the short traders from the 5th are going home with a loss. How do you think they feel, with such poor trade location and already upside down? How might this affect overnight and early trading on the 6th? How would your thinking have changed if the profile from the 5th was elongated, volume was more evenly dispersed, and the close or settle was near the daily low?

Figure 8.4 shows the first four periods for the following day, July 6. The market was clearly higher, forcing short covering, or an "unwinding" of the overenthusiastic trades of the 5th. An opportunity for a great long

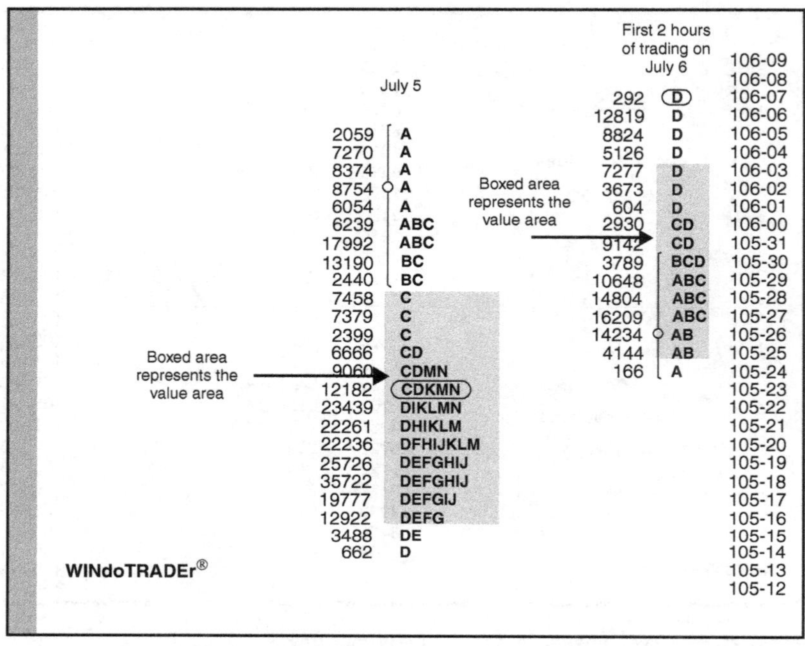

FIGURE 8.4 U.S. Treasury bonds with volume, July 6, 2006.

day trade occurred when price could not find acceptance back within the heavy volume range from the 5th. This could also have been an excellent entry position for short-term traders, which is of course a longer timeframe than a day trade.

As we discussed at the end of Chapter 7, there can be a moat between your intellectual analysis and your emotions. You have seen price decline consistently all day, with the market losing over $1,100 in just two days, and you are expected to feel comfortable *buying* it now? Earlier, we said the brain usually accepts new information at face value, and only gives up this belief after substantial analysis. Truly great opportunities, by definition, only present themselves for a brief period of time. In day trading, there is rarely sufficient time for substantial on-the-spot analysis; the best trades are often those that make you feel the most uncomfortable.

Recall that the original estimate for the employment report due out on the 7th was for approximately 175,000 new jobs. Following the ADP report, several analyses increased their estimate to 200,000. On Friday, when the actual report was released, U.S. employers added just 121,000 nonfarm jobs. The number excluding government jobs was 90,000, versus ADP's prediction of 386,000. The market rallied. All 56 economists missed the inflation numbers by a wide margin, and most of the estimates for the employment report were far too high. Next to these types of pell-mell predictions, market generated-information is an oasis of sanity and objective clarity.

To nurture and maintain that objective clarity, it's vital to keep track of the Big Picture; the following list is meant to get you thinking about your own system for holistic analysis, accounting for all the subtleties that can cloud clear thinking. We'll discuss the ramifications of each in the following sections.

- Top down—preparation analysis. What is currently driving the market?
  - Fundamentals
  - Economics
  - Stock-specific
- Lack of conviction
- Flight-to-safety
- Market condition
  - Trending—early/late
  - Too long
  - Too short
  - Bracketing—where within the bracket
- Inventory imbalances
- Bottom up—preparation analysis
- Intermediate-term bracket
- Define high and low
- Price location within the bracket
  - Upper quadrant
  - Upper middle
  - Lower middle
  - Lower quadrant
- Volume analysis, inventory balanced, imbalanced
- Short-term trading ranges within intermediate-term bracket
  - Identify highs and lows
  - Excess
  - Inventory position
  - Volume analysis
- Yesterday's trade
  - Value area placement
  - Volume analysis
  - Shape
- Current day

- Opening
- Developing value area
- Volume analysis
- Overall confidence
- News announcements
- Projected profile shape
- Possible destinations

TOP DOWN

In the financial business, the term *top down* is generally thought of as the Big Picture, a snapshot of broad economic conditions. To us, however, *top down* refers to an understanding of the key driving forces that are influencing a market—they may be economic factors, but they can be other factors as well. The goal of our top-down approach is to identify these factors because understanding their nature and influence can help us more accurately place all other information into its appropriate context. (There it is again: context, context, context.)

Once you've correctly identified the top down, it's paramount to remain flexible, as conditions constantly change. For example, you may recognize that there is a long-term reassessment of PE ratios underway that is either contracting or expanding PE's on a long-term basis. And while that might be extremely important for positioning long-term portfolios, immediate market activity might be influenced more directly by stock-specific earnings. Identifying the reality of what is most influencing the market *right now* is essential if you want to effectively trade the market in any timeframe, especially if you're trading the day timeframe.

LACK OF CONVICTION

There will be times when the market is directionless. This phase is commonly accompanied by widely gyrating daily price swings, as illustrated by Figure 8.5.

Although directionless markets offer few opportunities for trend and intermediate-term traders, they are often fertile ground for day traders because of their volatility. When markets lack conviction, participants often attach themselves to short-term themes such as yearend rallies or what is occurring as we are writing this book—speculating on whether the Fed pauses in its practice of periodic rate hikes.

Conversely, when markets have intermediate- to longer-term conviction, participants (and therefore the market) will roll right over these short-term themes if they are counter to the directional auction, and will

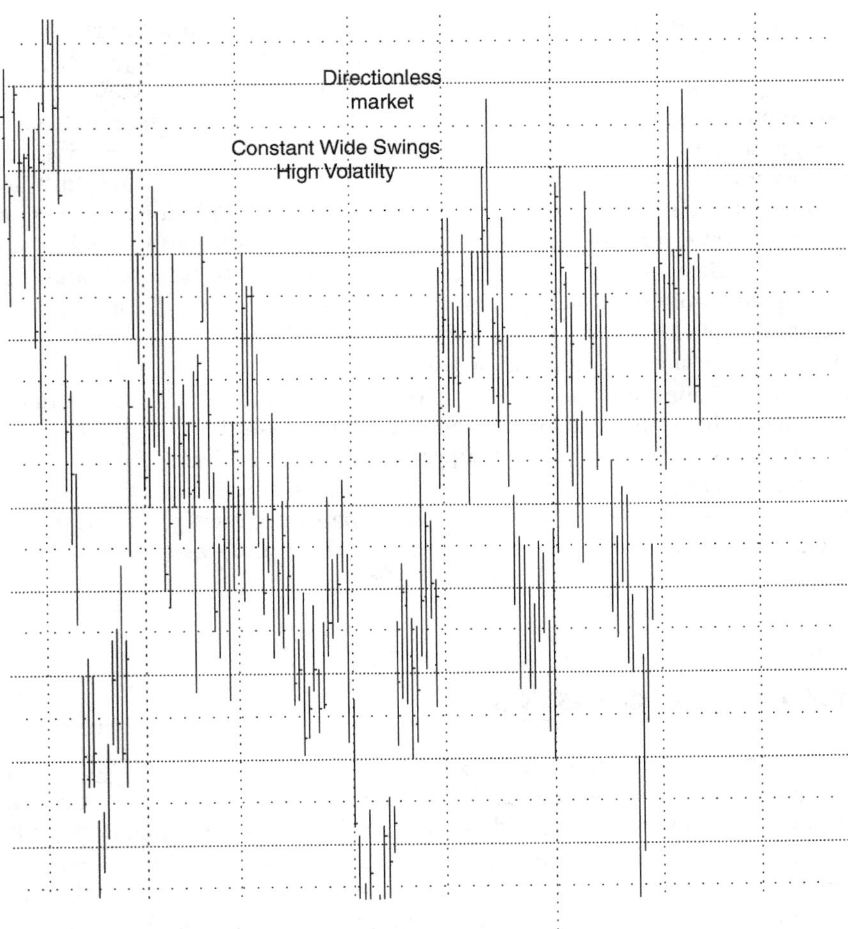

FIGURE 8.5 Directionless market: Daily bar chart.

accelerate if they are facing the same direction. That's why making an accurate assessment of the market's directional conviction is essential to being able to weight the significance—to the market and therefore your wallet—of shorter-term themes and events.

FLIGHT TO SAFETY

Flights to safety can occur when there are natural disasters, terrorist attacks, wars, political imbroglios, large-scale bankruptcies, or meltdowns such as occurred with Long-Term Capital Management and the Asian crisis some years back. Once a flight-to-quality rally is underway, the process for analyzing markets that we have been describing may, in fact, work against you for short-term trading. When markets are being driven by fear and emotion, price and volume simply don't matter. For example, as we are writing this section, the short-term yield in the Treasury market (six-month bills yielding 20 more basis points than three-month bills) only makes sense if you understand that these securities aren't being purchased for yield, but rather for safety because of concerns regarding the international political climate—instability in Iraq, Iran, Israel, Lebanon, and so on. It is imperative to perform this kind of analysis, for when the flight-to-safety trades are ultimately unwound, asymmetric opportunities abound because the market has usually rallied far above value. Once this unwinding begins, the market is likely to return quickly to, and potentially pass through those areas where price movements weren't supported by healthy volume.

During a flight-to-safety rally, previous balance areas and brackets are good visual reference points. Market participants are continually drawn to recent areas of acceptance (value), and once these areas are taken out, the market moves to test the next balance area.

INVENTORY IMBALANCES

From time to time, markets get too short in all timeframes. Hedge funds have contributed to a more realistic employment of investment or trading ideas in that they simultaneously hold both long and short positions, but this doesn't mean that they always get it right. And when hedge fund managers get too short, they too may have to buy to cover, which could add to market volatility and create opportunities for those who are correctly reading the market in the present tense.

On the surface, you might wonder why a chapter on day trading would spend so much time discussing information that is beyond the scope of the day timeframe. The reason is that if markets become extremely active during the day, longer-timeframe information may trump day-timeframe information and take control of the market. On a day that exhibits a narrow price range, for example, it is unlikely that there will be much interest from the longer timeframes. The market may trade in a fairly orderly manner, auctioning back and forth, continually searching for new short-term information. However, on a day in which the trading range continually increases, longer timeframes may be drawn in, and their participation can quickly dominate the activity of shorter-term traders. During situations like this, day traders who have not familiarized themselves with longer-term context are in a precarious position; unaware that the longer timeframe has entered the market, their natural reaction may be to fade what the market is doing, because it conflicts with their day-timeframe analysis. As a result, they can get run over. This often occurs when the market auctions far enough to trigger longer-term short covering.

Staying abreast of the top-down drivers isn't as difficult as it might seem, because once you've completed your long-term analysis, it doesn't change that often. Unfortunately, a nice and neat list of the current top-down drivers will never be found in the newspaper or on the news shows. This understanding must come from being immersed in the markets and paying attention to all relevant information. And as always, the challenge is making sure that you remain objective in your analysis, keeping outside opinions at bay and focusing on what market-generated information—always objective—is telling you.

CORRECTION OF INVENTORY IMBALANCES

Let's focus in on longer-term short covering, as it's one of the more difficult top-down drivers to anticipate and detect.

In Figure 8.6, notice that the two lows marked "Excess." These are considered to be "good lows," in that the market auctioned lower, forced out the final laggards (for this timeframe, at least), and immediately found aggressive buyers that led to a reversal of the downward auction. Remember, excess marks the end of one auction and the beginning of another in the opposite direction.

Now examine the third area noted in Figure 8.6. Here, there are multiple lows at approximately the same price. When a market has repeatedly attempted to auction lower without being able to establish excess, this is usually a sign of inventory imbalance; the market may be too short to go any lower, and so needs a short-covering rally that will allow long-term inventory to come into balance. It's not unusual to hear professional traders say that a market needs to rally before it can continue to break. They're simply expressing the view that there are too many weak sellers in the market—sellers who continue to cover on each small break, which has the effect of stopping any further decline until the covering is over. Shorts are always potential buying power.

Skeptics might point out the ambiguity in this concept, but after years spent observing this phenomenon in all timeframes, I have come to recognize the fact that longer term short covering is a recurring pattern. Long-term investors that take large positions in the market don't wait until the market gets to within a few tics of a prior low to make their purchases. In fact, a lot of them aren't even aware of those levels. Hedge funds and other intermediate-term traders are very much aware of the prior lows, however, and once they start feeling insecure in their positions, they begin to look

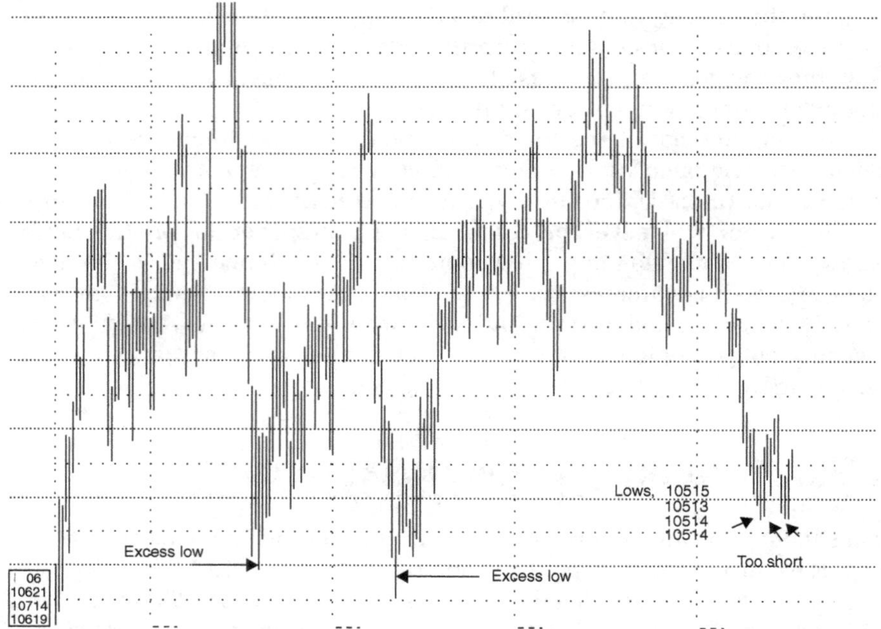

FIGURE 8.6 Longer-term inventory imbalance developing in U.S. Treasury bonds: Daily bar chart.
Source: Copyright © 2006 CQG, Inc. All rights reserved worldwide. www.cqg.com.

for opportune levels to cover their shorts, and prior intermediate-term lows offer a sense of stability.

These are particularly difficult periods for intermediate-term buyers, because they don't believe the long- or intermediate-term low has been established—yet the trade is to go long. Conversely, for sellers, getting stubborn on your short (waiting for more profit) can be extremely painful, as short-covering rallies can be swift. Figure 8.7 illustrates what the beginning of one of these rallies looks like when viewed through the lens of the market profile.

Day 1 and 2 clearly exhibit the familiar p pattern, with Day 3 bringing the market into balance with an inside day. Then Day 4 once again demonstrates the short covering p pattern.

Figure 8.8 (see page 159) combines the individual profile days from Figure 8.7 into a single, multi-day profile. The mirror image of the p pattern, is of course the b formation; just as markets can get too short to go any lower, they can get too long to go any higher, and often have to break before they can rally. Inventory imbalances such as this occur in all timeframes, and under both trending and bracketing conditions.

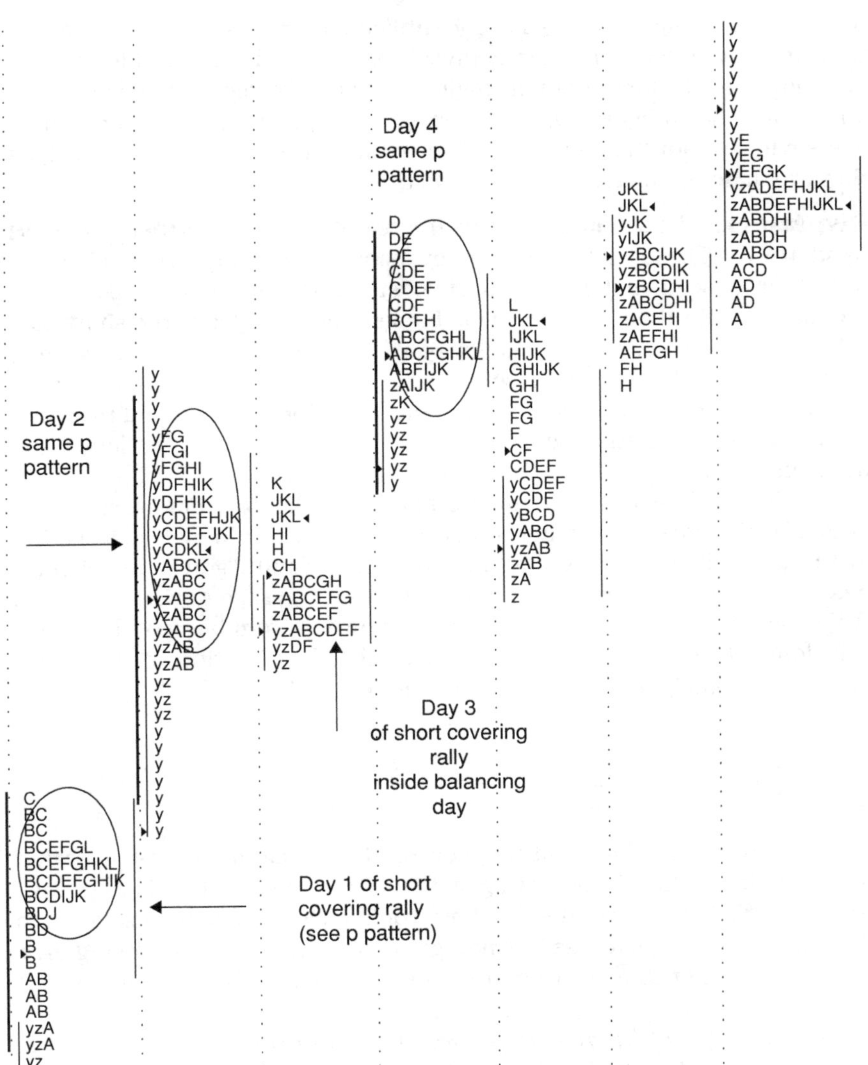

FIGURE 8.7 Longer-term short covering rally occurring in U.S. Treasury bonds: Daily market profiles.
Source: Copyright © 2006 CQG, Inc. All rights reserved worldwide. www.cqg.com.

TREND TRADERS' TRAP

Over the years, I have observed many trend-following systems, as well as trend traders who fail to differentiate between "old business" and "new business," thinking that they have identified a new trend only to have that trade quickly collapse. Long-only investors often feel comfortable as short covering propels their positions higher, failing to recognize this activity as an opportunity to lighten up or rearrange their portfolios. Long-only managers who are not fully invested often consider themselves to be short, as they are under committed to the market.

Remember: "Long only, Fully Invested" Is a Trend-Following Approach These traders and money managers are employing only price to further their understanding. Short covering, once it is completed, leaves the market with reduced underlying buying potential. Once the short covering is over, the market can quickly revert toward the mean, leaving trend traders with big losses. conversely, long liquidation depletes the market of selling potential, which will often set the stage for a meaningful rally that carries price substantially beyond the levels that triggered the liquidation in the first place.

Understanding markets and trading is similar to running any business in which inventory is important; how would you like to be a retailer in the late fall with the wrong merchandise? Think "going out of business sale"—inventory reduction with everything marked down 25 percent. We've spent a lot of time discussing top-down factors because how they can dominate the market—if only for a fairly brief period of time—can have an extremely positive effect on your bottom line.

MARKET CONDITION

After reviewing the dominant force currently driving the market, we want to determine if this is occurring within a trending or bracketing environment. We have covered everything you'll encounter here elsewhere in the book; however, successful trading/investing is about rearranging myriad pieces that enables us to better view the constantly changing market puzzle.

In *The Grace of Great Things: Creativity and Innovation* (New York: Ticknor and Fields, 1990), Robert Grudin uses the phrase "discovery by anomaly" when discussing Thomas Kuhn and his book *The Structure of Scientific Revolution.* Grudin writes that discovery occurs when you notice the anomaly of the uninvited quest (presence of an unexpected factor), the anomaly of the empty chair (discovery that a necessary factor is missing), and the anomaly of rearrangement (all factors are present but strangely rearranged). Going from trending to bracketing or bracketing to trending is an example of the anomaly of rearrangement; once the pieces are rearranged, the expected outcome changes. Those who

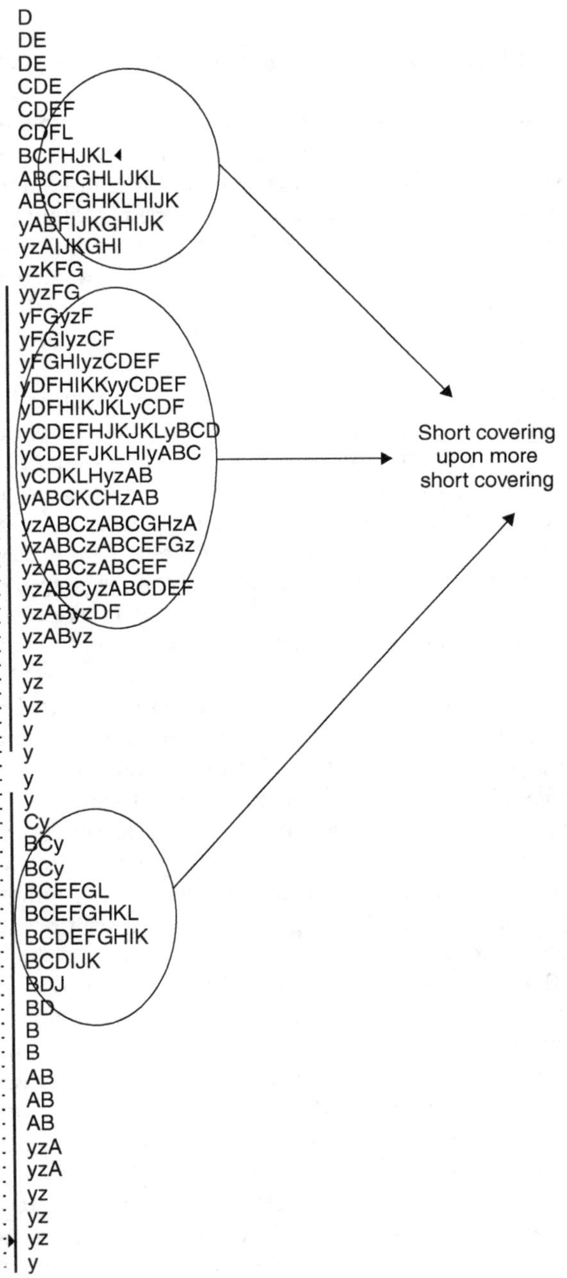

FIGURE 8.8 Longer-term short covering as reflected in a multiday profile (long-term profile) for U.S. treasury bonds.

don't notice the rearrangement are left expecting an outcome that will never occur.

If we determine that the market is trending, the next step is to determine if the trend is young, aging, or old. You will recall that one of the key ways to measure the age of a trend is not by price movement, but by the relationship of successive balance areas: If there is distance between one balance area and the next the trend is young; as the balance areas begin to come closer together or overlap, the trend is aging. Measuring volume on days *with* the intermediate-term auction, and contrasting it with days *against* the same auction will also help reveal the maturity of the larger auction.

If the market is bracketing, then a visual inspection will enable us to determine exactly where within the bracket the market is currently trading. You should write down your observations, recording at least the high, low, and center of the bracket. Next, you should perform and notate volume analysis to determine the nature of market activity near the bracket extremes. The reason we emphasize writing everything down is so you can lean on your notations as the market heats up, as stress narrows your thought processes. Finally, we want to more closely examine the bracket for internal balance areas, or trading ranges, as well as shorter-term trends within the bracket.

Early on we pointed out that the terms *trending* and *bracketing* are applicable to all timeframes. For example, there can be a single trend day as well as a single balancing day. And with a closer look, you can identify smaller balancing areas within a single day. Trends can occur within bracketing markets, and long-term trends are occasionally interrupted by shorter-term balancing areas. For this reason, we would suggest that day-timeframe traders operating within a bracketing environment perform a running analysis. That way they will always be aware of changing conditions within that bracket.

In Figure 8.9, the letter A identifies multiple examples of excess, which mark the ending of one auction and the beginning of another auction in the opposite direction. Numbers 1 through 4 provide examples of smaller internal balance areas within the larger bracket. Common successful day trades, as we have said, involve fading moves to the balance-area extremes on low volume, and looking for breakouts from the balance ranges on such moves that attract increasing volume.

One of the most interesting trading opportunities occurs when price auctions just beyond a balance area's extreme. Because balance areas are by definition visual, you can expect to find stops just beyond their extremes—stops that are likely to be irresistible to short-term traders. When these stops are taken out and the activity in the direction of the

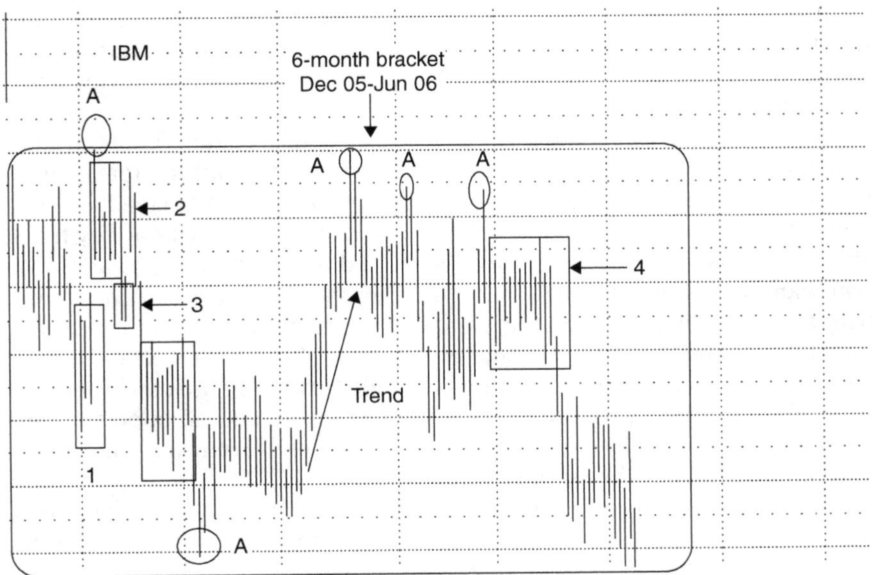

FIGURE 8.9 Six-month bracket occurring in IBM (International Business Machines): December 2005 through June 2006, daily bar chart.

bracket's boundary simply dries up, then you can be relatively sure that the move was caused by day traders pushing price just high enough to take out the stops placed there. This is a good opportunity to fade, as the market will likely reverse and plunge back into the bracket. If, on the other hand, the stops are taken out and the market settles there for a while, the odds are good that a balance-area breakout has occurred, which requires that you place a trade with the breakout. Next in this chapter, we discuss how to monitor such a trade for continuation.

The arrow marked "trend" in Figure 8.9, though within an intermediate-term bracket, should be traded just like any trend: go with it, don't fade it. These intra-bracket trends tend to originate at one extreme of the bracket and once underway often auction all the way to the opposite extreme. It can be difficult to place the correct trade when a trend starts from a bracket-area extreme, because it's likely that you just witnessed several days of the market auctioning, or stair-stepping, in the direction opposite the new trend. But if you have been keeping a written record and have described the bracket correctly, you will realize that such trade location is ideal—the distance to the opposite end of the bracket is much greater than a potential move in the opposite direction, back beyond the bracket extreme, which should trigger an exit. We discuss other exit strategies later in this chapter.

We continually stress the importance of understanding context, and knowing where you are within a bracket is a contextual matter. Unless you have accurately recorded the bracket's description and placed the current price correctly within that context, rapid market activity at key transitional points is likely to appear blurred and indecipherable. That's why you want to continually perform your analysis, comparing volume numbers and assessing the inventory situation of your competitors. In real estate, for example, you hear the mantra "location, location, location." When day- and short-term trading, continually think, "inventory, inventory, inventory." Our position is that markets are not efficient, and all opportunities are not equal, so it follows that just like in blackjack, what has already been played changes the odds of the next hand.

Up to now, we have been reviewing the past from the top down. Let's now focus even more sharply on the previous day as yet another step in preparing for a successful day trade.

YESTERDAY'S TRADE

Every day, we begin by asking ourselves *What was the market attempting to do yesterday, and how successful was that attempt?* The four elements we will initially examine are attempted direction, value-area placement, profile shape, and volume. We will conduct this examination via three examples.

Example 1

Looking at the "discussion day" in Figure 8.10, we see that the previous day was a trend day up, closing on the high. On the day in question, the market opened near the high for the day and attempted to sell off for the first two periods before finding balance almost exactly in the center of the profile—a progression that is much clearer in Figure 8.11, which shows the same profile with each time period noted separately. You will notice that while price was lower for the day, value was clearly higher, as the previous day's value was below the late upward price spike. We continue to stress that value is far more important than price. Price is simply the mechanism the market employs to advertise for opportunities; some opportunities are accepted, while others are rejected.

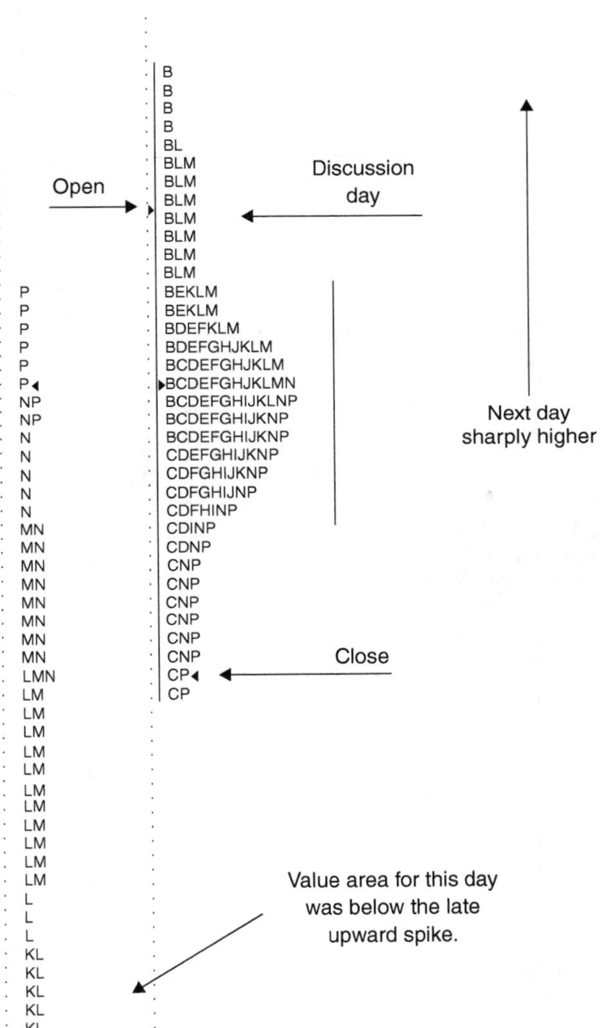

FIGURE 8.10 Example One: S&P 500 daily profile.

The split profile reveals that during the first two periods, B and C, the market auctioned lower without any ability to establish lower value for the day. Price traders could feel that the market was weak to neutral, as price was lower to unchanged for most of the day. Value traders, on the other hand, recognized that *value* was clearly higher. Late in the afternoon, the market attempted to break out of the nine period balance area called out in

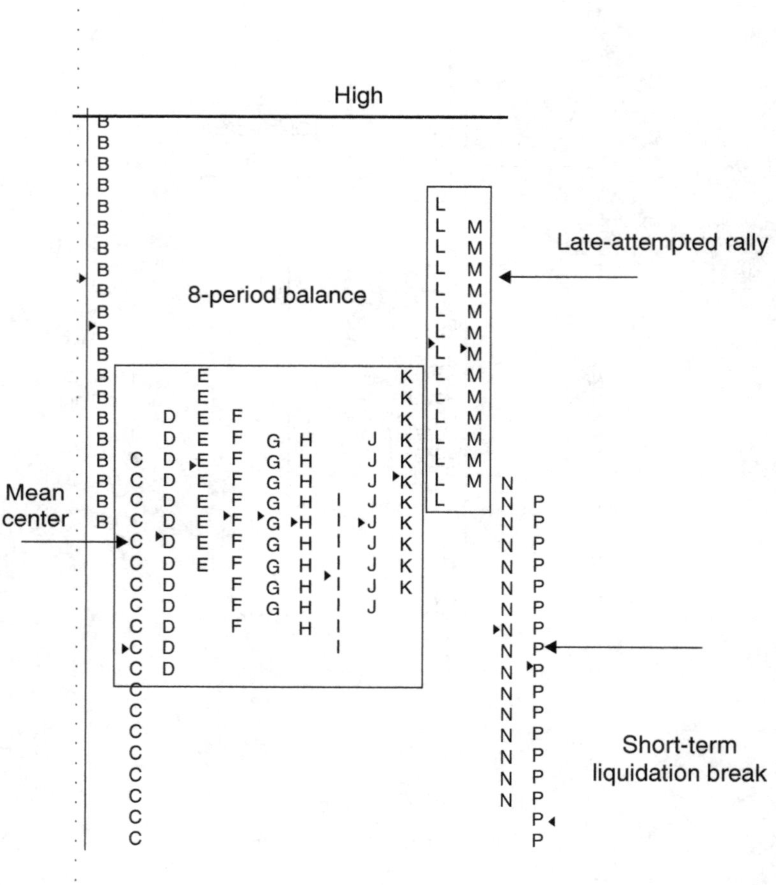

FIGURE 8.11 Example One: S&P 500 split profile.

the square box. Volume was weak during the attempted breakout, and the market was unable to take out the previous day's high—two key indicators that set the stage for a reversion-to-the-mean trade (see mean center in Figure 8.10).

What we are really observing, here, is a short-term liquidation situation, as anyone getting long late in the day was accumulating inventory at prices near the high for the past several days. The lack of upside follow-through, combined with the fact that daytime trading would close in an hour, forced many local and day traders to liquidate. Failure to differentiate between long liquidation of short-term inventory versus new shorts being placed in the market would lead you to starkly divergent views; new shorts would be a clear sign of market weakness, while short-term long liquidation would be just that, and not an overall sign of weakness. Remember: value was clearly higher.

The following day opened sharply higher, setting new short-term highs. Had price traders gotten short near the highs late on this day and held through the close, they would likely have thought, *This feels pretty good—why not take this trade home short and see what happens tomorrow?* A trader that focuses on value would have been in a better position to recognize that the security remained strong, and would probably auction higher on the following day.

Volume was not a consideration in this example, because we only employ overall volume when we can be certain of which direction the market was attempting to auction throughout the day, and the day in Figure 8.11 exhibited no such clarity.

Example 2

The day discussed in Figure 8.12 exhibited the classic b formation as the market traded toward the multiple-day low. We have already discussed the market's tendency to go after stops, and there would almost certainly have been stops just below the price that represented the low for the past several days. If the market was truly weak in the day timeframe, the short-term traders would have been able to push below that price and trigger the stops lurking there. It's important to be able to distinguish between the various timeframes: the day timeframe is not weak enough to push the auction below recent lows, and the next longer timeframe is showing more weakness as price is being accepted, over time, at this lower level. If these lower prices were *too low*, for the day timeframe, you would see single print buying tails at these lows.

This is an extremely complex discussion, and probably one of the most meaningful concepts for a day-timeframe trader to grasp. If you can master what is occurring in Figure 8.12, then you are beginning to develop advanced market knowledge. If you can also execute profitable trades around this knowledge, then you have successfully combined "market" understanding with "self" understanding.

The belly of the b, indicated on the "Initial discussion day" in Figure 8.12, represents the mean for the day, and unless we see price move away from this level on substantial volume, we are likely to see these prices

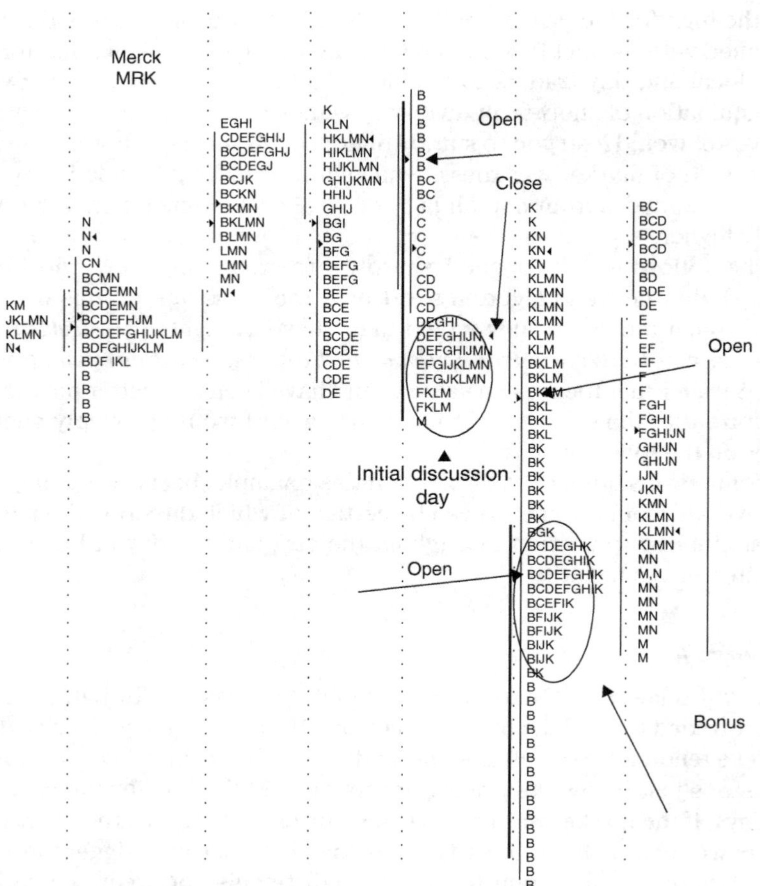

FIGURE 8.12 Example Two: S&P 500 daily profiles.
Source: Copyright © 2006 CQG, Inc. All rights reserved worldwide. www.cqg.com.

revisited. We are always looking for clues today about what is likely to transpire tomorrow, and so I would look for an opportunity to sell above the b or buy below the b on the next trading day with the expectation that this level would be revisited.

On the following day, the market opens slightly lower and auctions beneath the multiple-day low, triggering the stops we suspected were just beneath that level and sending the market down sharply. In the same period, however, the market does indeed work its way back up toward and finally through the fat part of the previous day's b loop.

We have a bonus day in this example, as we can see the mirror image of the b formation—the p formation—as the market rallies from the early morning lows back toward the low of the initial day. For the day following, I would look to sell above or buy below the p, with the expectation that price will revisit price levels in the fat part of the p loop. A good question to ask, at this point, would be, "Why did the market trade sharply above the p late on the bonus day, only to return to this level the following day?" The answer is probably that most of the morning selling was a consequence of the stops we discussed. Once those were "hit" (elected), sending prices lower, momentum sellers piled on, getting short in the hole. In addition, some price-based systems had their selling indicators triggered as prices broke to new recent lows. In the initial period (B), we observed a very long buying tail at the low, which alerted us to the fact that at least the next longer timeframe buyer was accepting the advertised opportunity to buy MRK (Merck) below value. This buying squeezed the shorts, and those who hadn't gotten their day timeframe shorts back as the market approached the close were forced to cover.

We hope you feel the complexity of the short-term market. But at the same time recognize that it is tradable if you can keep an open, flexible mind, and appreciate the importance of developing structure. Market structure varies every day, minute to minute, and the auction process constantly evolves, providing us with an objective, multidimensional glimpse of real time market activity. I view recognizable trading ranges, such as those that manifest during short covering and long liquidation, as structural weaknesses that have to be re-inspected—that's where opportunity lies.

Example 1 was primarily a balancing day that failed to auction successfully out of balance to either side of the mean because each attempt failed to attract sufficient volume to successfully migrate price to new value areas. Remember, either value will be pulled to the new price, or price will return to value.

Example 2 was more complex, as the market attempted a downside breakout from several days of overlapping price and value. That attempt failed, because the early selling was met by aggressive responsive buyers (as evidenced by the long buying tail). These buyers were strong enough to force the morning shorts to cover. What these two days have in common is that short-term traders were best served by fading the exploratory price moves. Both examples offered sufficient clues with which to set early expectations for the following days. Let's now examine a day that suggests continuation.

Example 3

Figure 8.13 is a bar chart of S&P futures, with the final two days highlighted as *Example 3*.

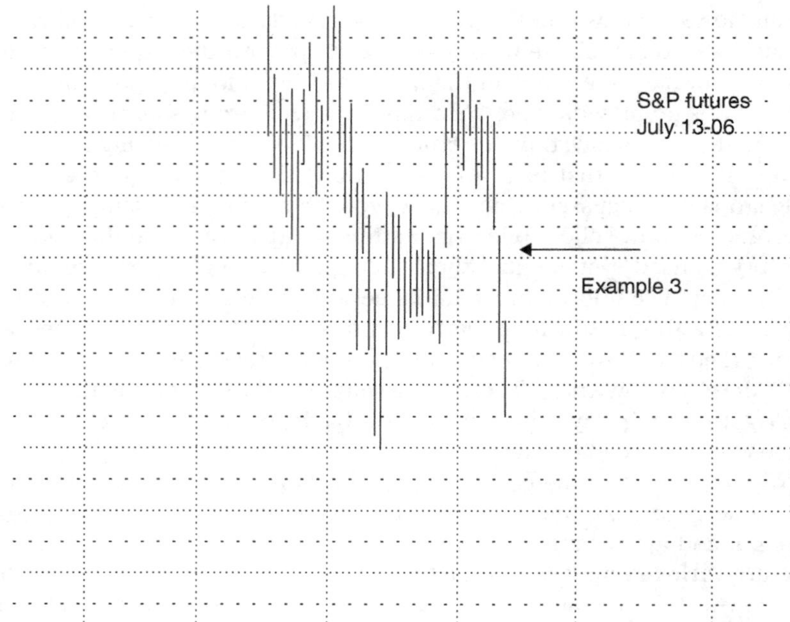

FIGURE 8.13 Example 3: Break in the S&P 500 (focus days), daily bar chart.
Source: Copyright © 2006 CQG, Inc. All rights reserved worldwide. www.cqg.com.

Figure 8.14 displays the profile graphics that correspond to these same two days.

Let's look at the downside breakout in the S&Ps to see what market structure suggested for the following day. The market gapped lower on the opening, which is a sign of crisis or reorganization (Kuhn's "paradigm change"). The day's profile remained elongated, and late in the afternoon prices accelerated to the downside, still seeking enough buyers to enable the market to come into balance. Earlier, we provided an average volume range with 1.6 billion shares on the lower end and 2 billion on the upper end. Volume for this day was 1.8 billion. Now let's put it all together: the gap, elongation, decent volume, and a close near the low suggest downside continuation on the following day. Looking ahead, you can see that the market did, indeed, continue its downward march.

Before actually placing and managing a day trade, make sure you standardize your decision-making process, to some extent; the goal is not to enforce rigid thinking, but to make sure you are looking at the potential trade within its proper context. From experience, I expect any serious trader to design their own checklist, but the following section will give you some guidance on where to start.

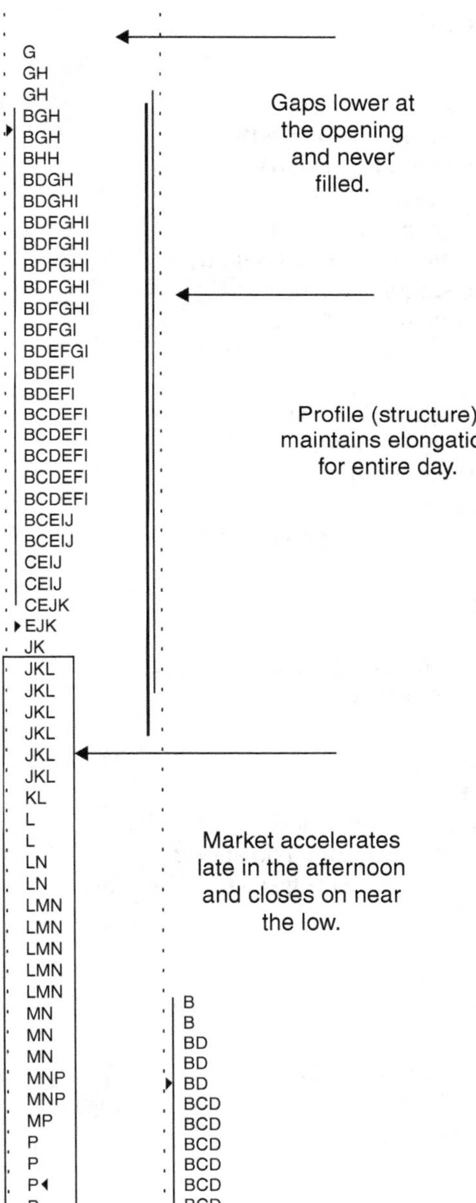

FIGURE 8.14 Example 3: Break in the S&P 500 (focus days), daily profile.
Source: Copyright © 2006 CQG, Inc. All rights reserved worldwide. www.cqg.com.

Trader Checklist

Top Down

- ✔ What is driving the market?
  - ✔ Fundamentals (yes/no)
  - ✔ Economics (yes/no)
  - ✔ Stock specific(yes/no)
- ✔ Market has conviction. (yes/no)
- ✔ Flight to safety? (yes/no)
- ✔ Other contributing factors:
- ✔ What is the market condition?
- ✔ Trending (yes/no)
  - ✔ Early—maturing—late
  - ✔ Inventory too long? Too short?
- ✔ Bracketing? (yes/no)
  - ✔ Lower center—lower
  - ✔ Inventory too long? Too short?

Bottom Up

- ✔ Intermediate term bracket: High: Low:
- ✔ Current price location
  - ✔ Lower
  - ✔ Center:
  - ✔ Upper
  - ✔ Current price location:
  - ✔ Inventory too long? Too short?
- ✔ Short term trading ranges within bracket
  - ✔ High: Low:
  - ✔ High: Low:
  - ✔ High: Low:
  - ✔ Inventory too long? Too short?
  - ✔ Volume on up days:
  - ✔ Volume on down days:
- ✔ Yesterday's trade (describe the following)
  - ✔ Attempted direction:
  - ✔ Value area placement:
  - ✔ Volume analysis:
  - ✔ Shape:
  - ✔ Directional expectations for tomorrow:
  - ✔ Ideal trades you would like to execute based on intermediate term bracket analysis:

✔ Ideal trades you would like to execute based on analysis of yesterday's trade:

Earlier in the book, we defined the two primary functions of the market's two-way auction process: (1) the efficient and fair allocation of bids and offers; and (2) the constant search for information. As part of this ongoing process, the market often explores above the previous day's highs and lows, weekly highs and lows, monthly highs and lows, prior balance areas highs and lows, long-term bracket highs and lows, and so on. The permutations are too numerous to list and change constantly depending on context and timeframe. Therefore, it's important that you develop the expertise that will enable you to identify these reference points, so that when the market gets a response at one of these pivotal levels, you will be prepared to judge its importance. You should begin each day with your own list of reference points—they will be your roadmap to successful trading.

THE MARKET IS OPEN

Once the market opens, the key question is this: *In what direction is the market attempting to auction, and how successful does the auction appear to be?* It can be helpful to personify the concept, and think in terms of how much "confidence" the auction appears to have. Years ago, Peter Steidlmayer classified openings into four categories, which I still believe are valid. We view these four types of openings as initial gauges of early market conviction:

1. Open-Drive
2. Open-Test-Drive
3. Open-Rejection-Reverse
4. Open-Auction

Open-Drive

The strongest and most definitive type of open is the *Open-Drive*, in which the market opens and auctions aggressively in one direction. In *Mind over Markets*, the analogy we used was that of a race horse that explodes out of the gate and never looks back. The Open-Drive results in the lowest odds of opening prices being revisited, which provides you with an early market reference point; if price returns to the opening, you know that something has changed since the early morning, and chances are much higher that the day will end with the market auctioning in the opposite direction. Figure 8.15 illustrates this type of opening.

Before we define the other three types of openings, let's take a moment to review that old familiar concept: *context.* Imagine yourself sitting in a seminar. You're being taught how to profit using market-generated information, and I say, "Now we will define the four types of openings and how to profit from them." This kind of declaration is generally accompanied by a wave of comfort radiating throughout the audience, as each participant readies their pencil and paper to take careful notes on the four different types of openings—notes that will be concrete and easily memorized. (After all, isn't that why you attended the seminar?) While these notes will appear absolute to many, they are merely a starting point.

Ask.com defines cognition with a lot of descriptive words and phrases. Among them are: "a very broad term, which is not easy to describe," and "mechanisms involved in such process in human beings as perception, attention, learning, thought, concept formation, reading, problem solving, and the development of such behavior." True cognitive learning only begins when you realize that you have to transcend the limitations of fixed definitions in order to discover how markets really operate. Each opening has to be placed within a much broader context. On several occasions, we have used the phrase "immersed in the markets." This is just another way of saying that you have to be deeply, personally involved in the markets before you can begin to discover just how much of your creative energy is required before you can begin to travel down the path toward being an expert trader.

Now, back to those "notes."

The Open-Drive is the highest-confidence opening; the first example (Figure 8.15) shows the Open-Drive followed by a sharp downward trend that continued throughout the entire day, gapping lower on the following day. Now let's review the same Open-Drive in different contexts. Figure 8.16 shows the same day illustrated in Figure 8.15, but with more perspective provided; we've added the day prior, which was an inside day (its entire range contained within the range of the previous day). As we have stated, inside days are a form of balance, and when a market comes out of balance it is likely to attract multiple timeframes, which adds to the resulting volatility. In this instance, the market had already turned down (not shown), so the Open-Drive in question was also *with* the current trend.

Figure 8.17 also illustrates an Open-Drive. However, the circumstances are somewhat different. In Figure 8.16, the auction had already turned down and the opening was with the intermediate-term trend; in Figure 8.17, the long-term auction was still up (not shown) and so the Open-Drive occurred *against* the intermediate-term trend, and within the prior day's range, which means that it is still within balance and unlikely to

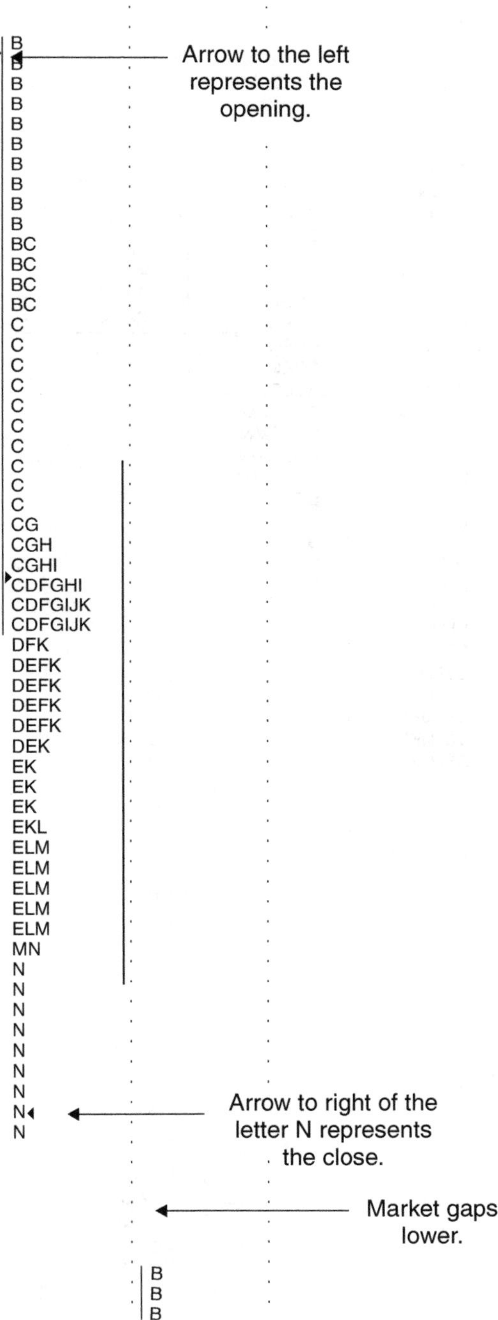

FIGURE 8.15 Open-Drive in the S&P 500, daily profile.
Source: Copyright ©2006 CQG, Inc. All rights reserved worldwide. www.cqg.com.

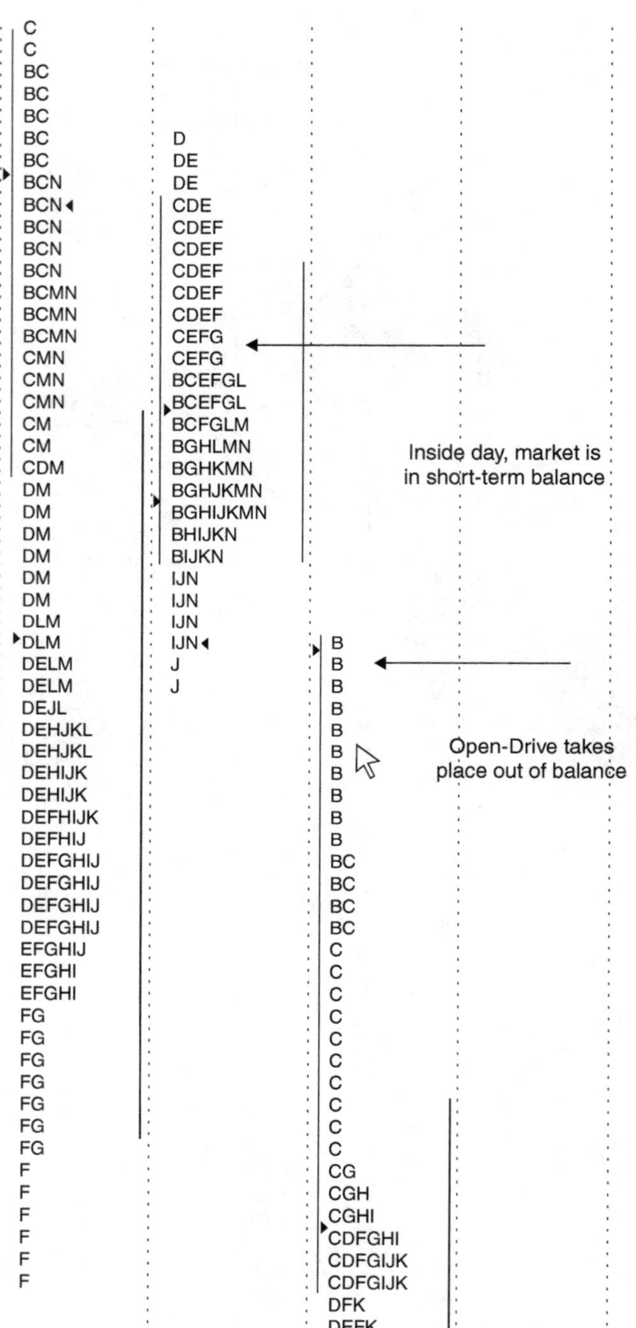

FIGURE 8.16 Open-Drive with the intermediate-trend in the S&P 500, daily profile.

attract as much attention. The context for both examples is quite different, resulting in different expectations going into the following day for each. To reiterate, Figure 8.16 displays an Open-Drive with the trend and out of balance to the downside, and as a result, large downward movement in both price and value occur; the Figure 8.17 Open-Drive is against the major auction and within balance, resulting in only moderate changes in price, with value overlapping to slightly lower.

By definition, an Open-Drive starts out with high confidence, and if that confidence continues throughout the day, you would expect to see the profile elongate, with value being gradually pulled along with price. Remember, price is the fastest moving element, and value develops much more slowly. On the day following an Open-Drive, you would expect to see the market open outside of value in the direction of the Open-Drive, or at least value beginning to build outside of the previous day's value area.

When you start to see developments that contradict the descriptions above, you should quickly realize that the confidence level is declining, and if your day trade is in the same direction as the Open-Drive, your risk is increasing along with the odds of a reversal. If the market continues as expected, on the other hand, then maintain your position and let the market work for you, monitoring activity for signs that the initial optimism inherent in the Open-Drive is beginning to wane, which would suggest that you should exit your trade; your goal should be to become proficient at exiting trades of your own free volition, rather than waiting for stops to take you out. This practice will boost your confidence level (not to mention your bank account).

Open-Test-Drive

An *Open-Test-Drive* is similar to the Open-Drive, except that the market lacks the initial confidence necessary to drive immediately following the opening bell. During this type of opening, the market generally opens and tests beyond a known reference point—such as a previous high or low—to make sure there is no business to be done in that direction. The market then reverses and quickly auctions back through the opening; a failed test in one direction followed by a strong reversal often secures one of the extremes for the day.

In the late 1980s, when I was responsible for an institutional trading desk, it was quite common to receive large institutional orders with instructions to wait 15 minutes before beginning to execute the trade—the institution didn't want to be embarrassed if there was substantial business to be done in the direction opposite their order. For example, if they were selling, they didn't want to sell at $40 per share if the market was going to auction quickly to $42 per share. An Open-Test-Drive is the second most

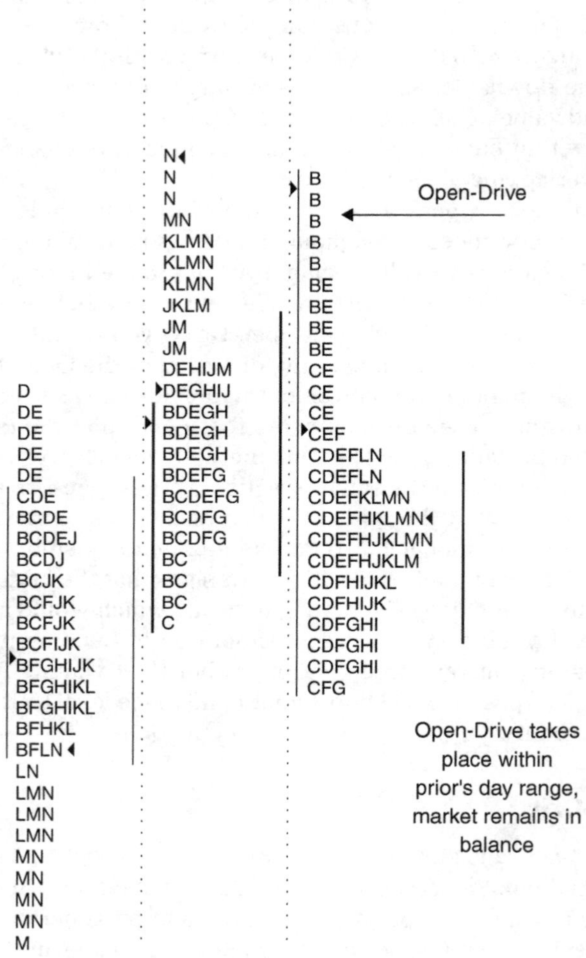

FIGURE 8.17 Open-Drive against the intermediate-term trend in the S&P 500, daily profile.

reliable type of opening. Once the market has tested in the opposite direction and found strong opposite activity, the odds are high that the initial extreme will not be revisited for the remainder of the day.

Figure 8.18 illustrates an Open-Test-Drive. While we didn't show it in the example, the upward test auctioned up to the previous day's high, where sellers quickly stepped in and sold with confidence. The analysis

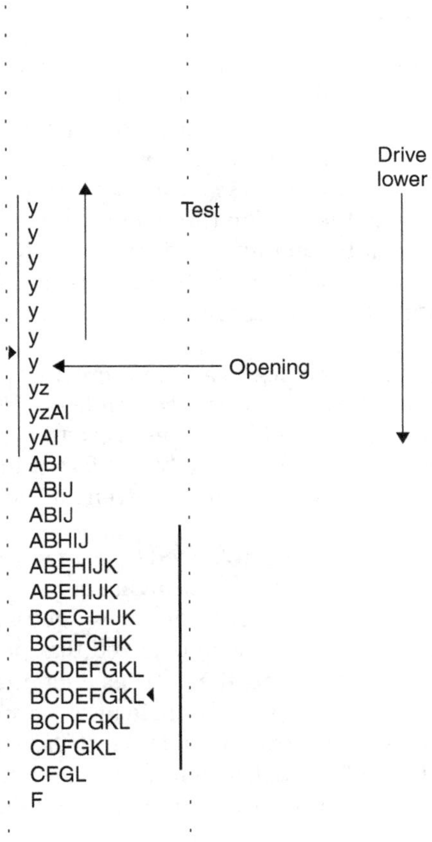

FIGURE 8.18 Open-Test-Drive type of opening, daily profile.

following the "Drive" portion of an Open-Test-Drive is exactly the same as discussed for the Open-Drive: you would expect to see elongation, lower value and price, and so on. Once again, the contradictions—like footnotes to an accounting document—are where the real information is hidden.

Training yourself to constantly think in terms of *market confidence* is a meaningful way to help to decide when to enter and exit trades. For example, while the Open-Test Drive is a high-confidence opening, the confidence is not quite as high as an Open-Drive, which should lead you to adjust your expectations accordingly.

Open-Rejection-Reverse

The *Open-Rejection-Reverse* is characterized by a market that opens, trades in one direction and then meets opposite activity strong enough to reverse the auction and drive it back through the opening range. The thinking process following this kind of open should be along the same lines as what we discussed before: *Ask yourself how much confidence is embodied by the market's early auctions.* The three types of openings we have described thus far differ in the amount of confidence that surrounds them. The weaker the opening, the greater the odds that price auctions back and forth through both the opening range and the early morning highs and lows.

When a market finally decides to auction directionally, we are always trying to determine how long to stay with the trade—a decision that should be based around how much confidence the market is exhibiting in the directional move. The opening type is simply one factor in assessing market confidence. Probably the most used and least reliable confidence indicator is price.

Figure 8.19 shows the opening followed by a downward auction that is rejected, as evidenced by the single print buying tail in y period. The prices that were being offered as the market made a new auction low were quickly accepted by the responsive buyer, who believed that prices were too low and represented a good deal. Had the market auctioned at these lower prices in two consecutive time periods, instead of only one (as shown in the box), the market would have shown a lesser degree of confidence. The fast rejection reveals the fact that buyers had confidence, at least in the early going. The market then reversed and auctioned higher—thus the label "Open-Rejection-Reverse."

The confidence at the lower extreme—because the direction wasn't determined from the opening bell—would be classified as "lower." This simply means that the possibility of the market reversing, later in the day, has to be given serious consideration. Nothing should be viewed in isolation, however, as there are many factors that help us judge the strength of an auction. We've already noted factors such as developing value area placement, volume associated with the auction, and elongated profile structure, which at a glance reveals a higher degree of confidence than a profile that has begun to fatten.

The example in Figure 8.20 demonstrates another sign of auction confidence, which is best explained visually.

Once the rejection occurred in y period, no subsequent half-hour time period trades below the previous period's lowest price. We call this type of activity a *one-way auction*, or an auction that is *one-timeframing*. A costly error traders make is fading a one-timeframing auction. Even if

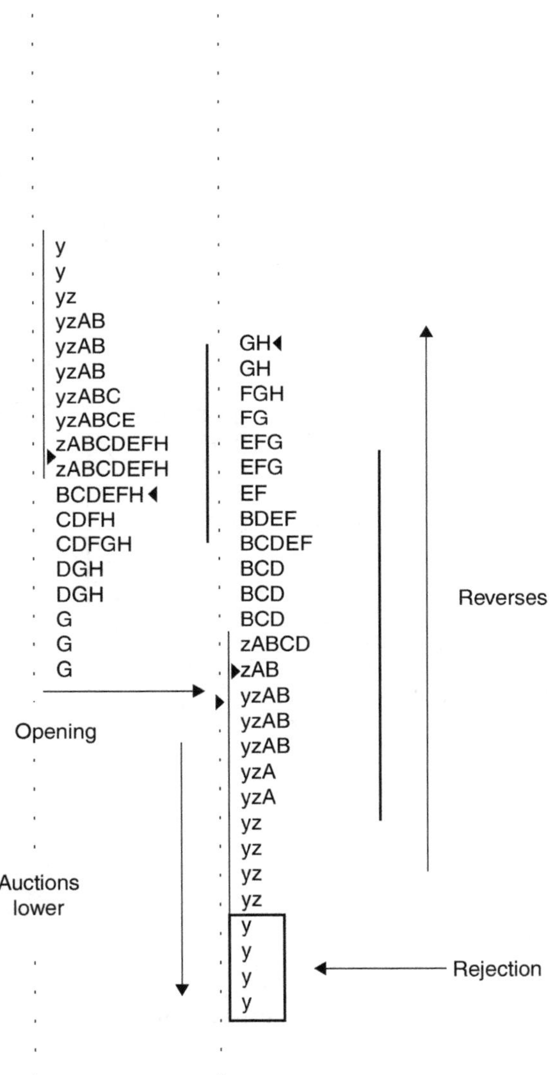

FIGURE 8.19 Open-Rejection-Reverse type of opening, daily profile.

the auction is not supported by volume, or any number of reasons, you are usually better off not stepping in the way of a market that is on the march, though gradually; there will be a better time and price for your trade.

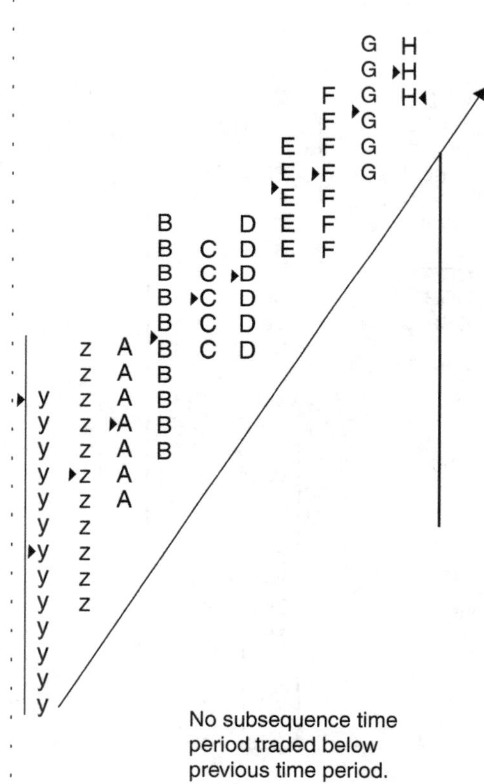
No subsequence time period traded below previous time period.

FIGURE 8.20 One-timeframing auction following an Open-Rejection-Reverse opening, daily split profile.

Open-Auction

Open-Auction activity initially reflects a market with no conviction at all. The market opens and appears to randomly auction above and below the opening range. In reality, the conviction reflected by the Open-Auction largely depends on where the market opens *relative to the previous day.* An Open-Auction that occurs inside the previous day's range, for example, conveys a much different opinion regarding potential day-timeframe development than an Open-Auction that occurs outside that range. In general, if a market opens and auctions within the previous day's value area and range, then a nonconvictional day will usually develop. The same opening occurring *outside* yesterday's range, however, demonstrates a market that is out of balance relative to the previous day, which greatly increases the odds of a dramatic price move in either direction. If the market quickly returns to the previous day's range and reenters the value area, the odds are good that the market will continue on to the opposite extreme of that day's range. Failure to return to yesterday's range increases the odds of a meaningful, directional move in the direction of the out-of-balance opening.

Figure 8.21 demonstrates an Open-Auction, with price trading both above and below the opening for each of the first five periods. When you hear people talk about successful trading requiring patience, that principle is never more applicable in the day timeframe than after an Open-Auction. Whether the market is in or out of balance, there is no reason for a day-timeframe trader to trade during the first five periods of an Open-Auction day. When the market lacks conviction for that long, the odds favor limited range development for the remainder of the day, which translates to limited opportunities. (*Mind over Markets* covers day-time directional development relative to these openings in much greater detail than space allows in this book.)

In sum, the lack of short-term conviction surrounding the opening range suggests that day traders should wait patiently until the market arrives at a directional consensus.

DAY TRADER'S CHECKLIST

As was stated earlier, every experienced trader has his or her own system of checks and balances. The following checklist is designed to get you further down the road to developing your own personal preparation process.

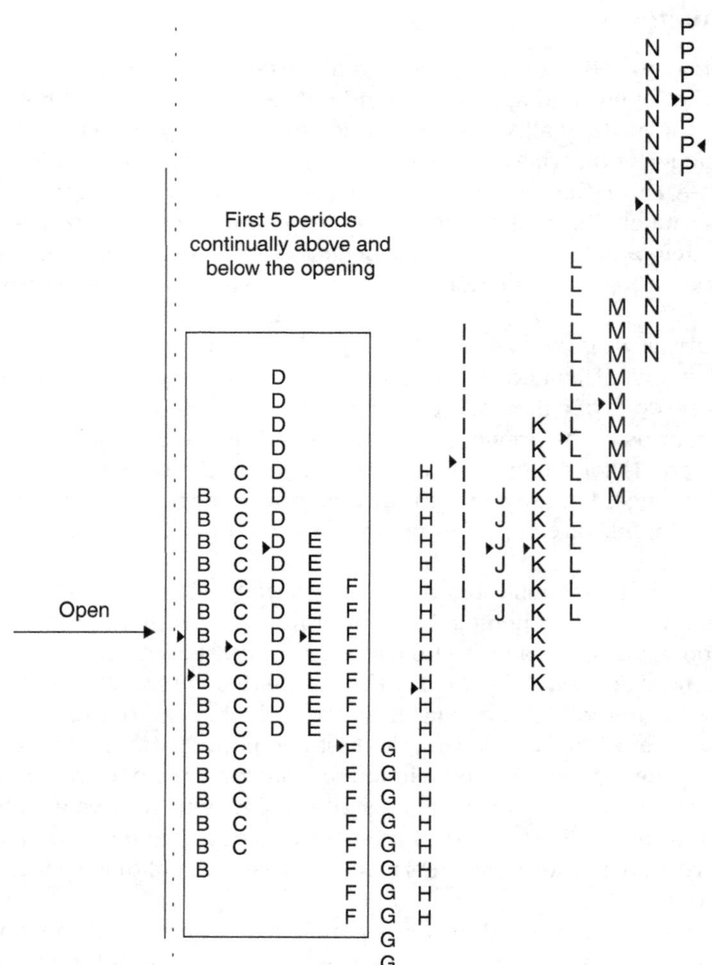

FIGURE 8.21 Open-Auction type of opening.
Source: Copyright © 2006 CQG, Inc. All rights reserved worldwide. www.cqg.com.

- ✔ Review yesterday's profile for clues as to what to expect today. Make a note of possible trades, based on varying developments.
- ✔ Review the overnight markets for any unusual price movement or early indications for the day.
- ✔ Compare the expected opening to the previous day. Is it within or outside the previous day's range? Value area? To the upside or downside?
- ✔ Relative to the expected opening, identify three references points, both above and below the expected opening. These could be the

previous day's high and low, weekly high or low, the top and bottom of the previous day's value area, or the high or low of a recent trading range. (There is no set answer—you should be guided by your past observations of where price slowed or accelerated, as well as past areas of heavy or light volume.)

- ✔ Note what kind of opening is occurring, as well as what you'd want to see in order to quickly judge the resulting directional confidence.
- ✔ Note whether or not there is clear attempted direction, and whether that activity is supported by volume.
- ✔ Does the market appear to be within balance or out of balance?
- ✔ Visualize the remainder of the day. Will it look elongated, squat, fairly normal like a bell-shaped curve, and the like. Note any unusual shapes or patterns that may suggest something unexpected is happening.
- ✔ Estimate how much effort is being expended to move price directionally, and note what that suggests about the inventory conditions of your competitors—too long, too short, above water, below water, etc.
- ✔ If there is a major news announcement scheduled, be aware that there could be unexpected volatility. Let the market provide short-term interpretation of resulting activity by observing developing structure. Unless the day-timeframe structure is extremely strong and unlikely to be reversed by such an announcement, we recommend that day traders be flat in front of significant numbers.

Let's examine three different markets, beginning with the opening bell. This discussion both summarizes and abbreviates this checklist.

Example 1

The first example (see Figure 8.22) enables us to view two high-confidence openings occurring within different contexts—one takes price outside of balance and one results in price maintaining equilibrium. To recap, when price moves outside of balance, the odds are that there will be more volatility and a greater range than when price remains within balance. Here's another way to think about this: The status quo is maintained when the market remains within balance, but the status quo has changed once the market leaves balance, which generally results in additional timeframes joining the fray.

We labeled the different types of openings to facilitate their description. But please remember that the labels are far less important than the amount of *confidence* that is indicated by each opening. Day 1 shows high confidence, selling from the opening bell with price rapidly auctioning below both the value area and the range for the prior day. It doesn't take long for you to visualize lower value for Day 1; you should quickly short this

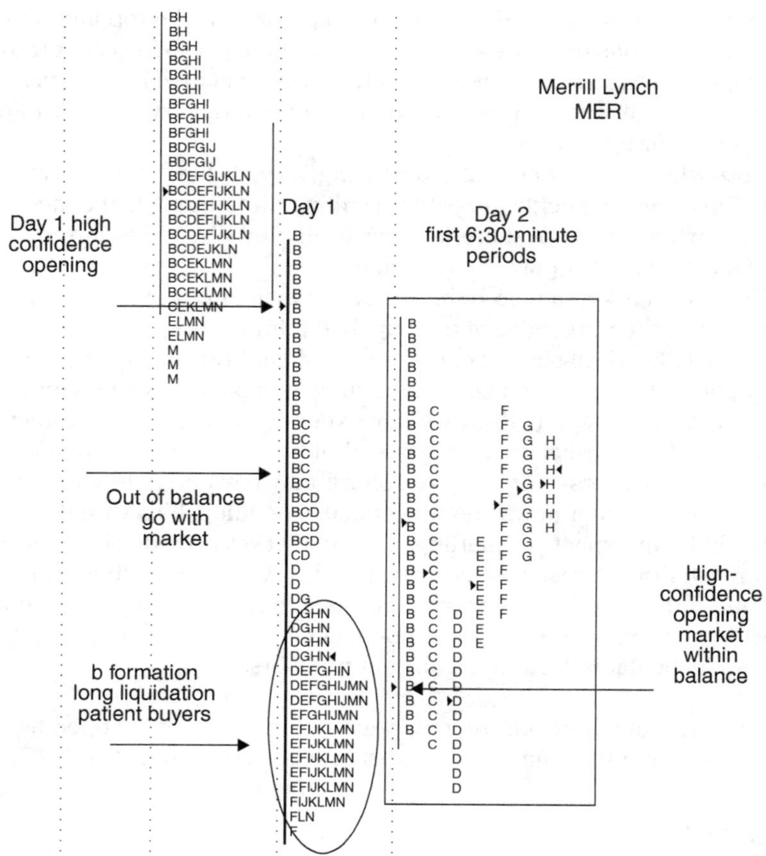

FIGURE 8.22 Example 1: Two high confidence openings occurring in different contexts.
Source: Copyright © 2006 CQG, Inc. All rights reserved worldwide. www.cqg.com.

market—go with the open—once price moves below the previous day's range, with the expectation that value will be pulled down to price. You should also track volume to assure yourself that lower prices are attracting additional activity.

The b pattern begins to form in the fifth time period of Day 1, and continues to develop for the remainder of the day. The expected market structure for a day with early high confidence would be an elongated profile shape; as soon as it becomes clear that the expected is not going to happen, it's time to exit a short position—even if the market continues lower, the odds are building against you. Mechanically, this was a simple day trade, but the emotional ramification of such a trade is far more complex. You had to act quickly, you had to sell something cheaper than you could have sold it for at any time during the prior day, and there was nothing to really measure your risk against. A different mindset would see risk as low due to all the selling that is forcing prices lower. But your mind should have awakened when the market failed to go much lower relative to the fifth time period—*time to cover*. The goal is to exit trades based upon market structure, not based upon price; your observations, not a stop. When a stop is triggered, the market is responsible for the outcome. When you exit a trade on deteriorating structure, then *you* are clearly in charge.

The b pattern that developed on Day 1 tells us that the odds are high that we'll have to trade to the upside at some point tomorrow. The short evidence says that the sellers on this day were not new sellers, but rather short term long stock liquidators. The b patterns provides evidence that the selling was being accumulated by a longer timeframe that expected to take new longs home overnight.

Day 2 also had a high-confidence opening, with the major difference being that price remained within the previous day's value area, which demonstrates a market without much confidence. The strong upward opening that was searching for sellers found those sellers near the opening of Day 1, which was just below the bottom of that day's value area. Our upper references should have been: (1) the previous day's low; (2) the previous day's opening; and (3) the low of the previous day's value area. There was never any price acceptance at any of these reference points—the market did not spend enough time there to reestablish value. Because Day 1 had a wide range, indicating acceptance, and Day 2 fails to auction above Day's 1 high, the expectation would be for a narrow, range-bound day. By periods 6 and 7 (G and H), it appears that this is, in fact, a narrow balancing day with limited opportunities. The key to developing this insight early is to put yourself in the buyers' shoes, examining their mindset.

Figure 8.23 demonstrates Day 2 in its entirety—it remained within the range established by its opening period, which signaled that the odds of any real change were low. You should have quickly visualized that this market was unlikely to do anything meaningful over the rest of this day; there was never any real, new long-term buying, as the combination of short covering and new long-term buying would have caused the profile to elongate.

Example 2

The day that preceded Day 1 in Figure 8.24 exhibits unusual width in the lower portion of the profile (circled area). By now we know that the

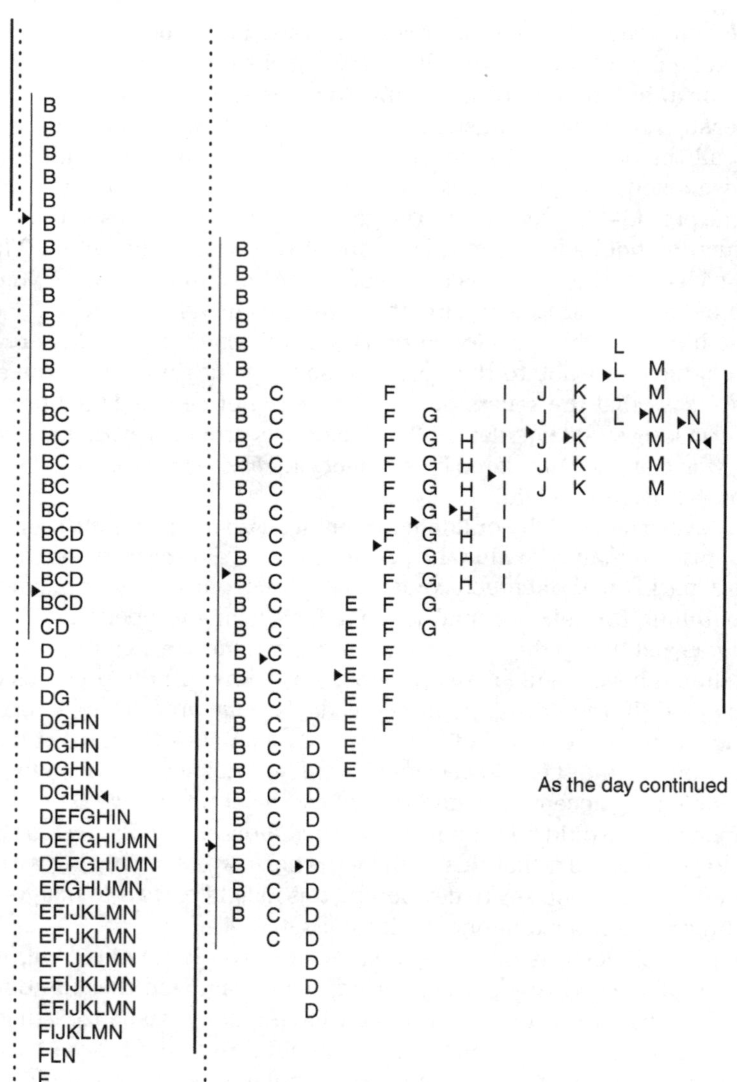

FIGURE 8.23 Example 1: Day 2 daily and split profiles.

odds of revisiting a prominent price level like this are above average—the wider the line of TPOs, the greater the approximate volume. The odds of price returning to such a lever are even greater on days that exhibit

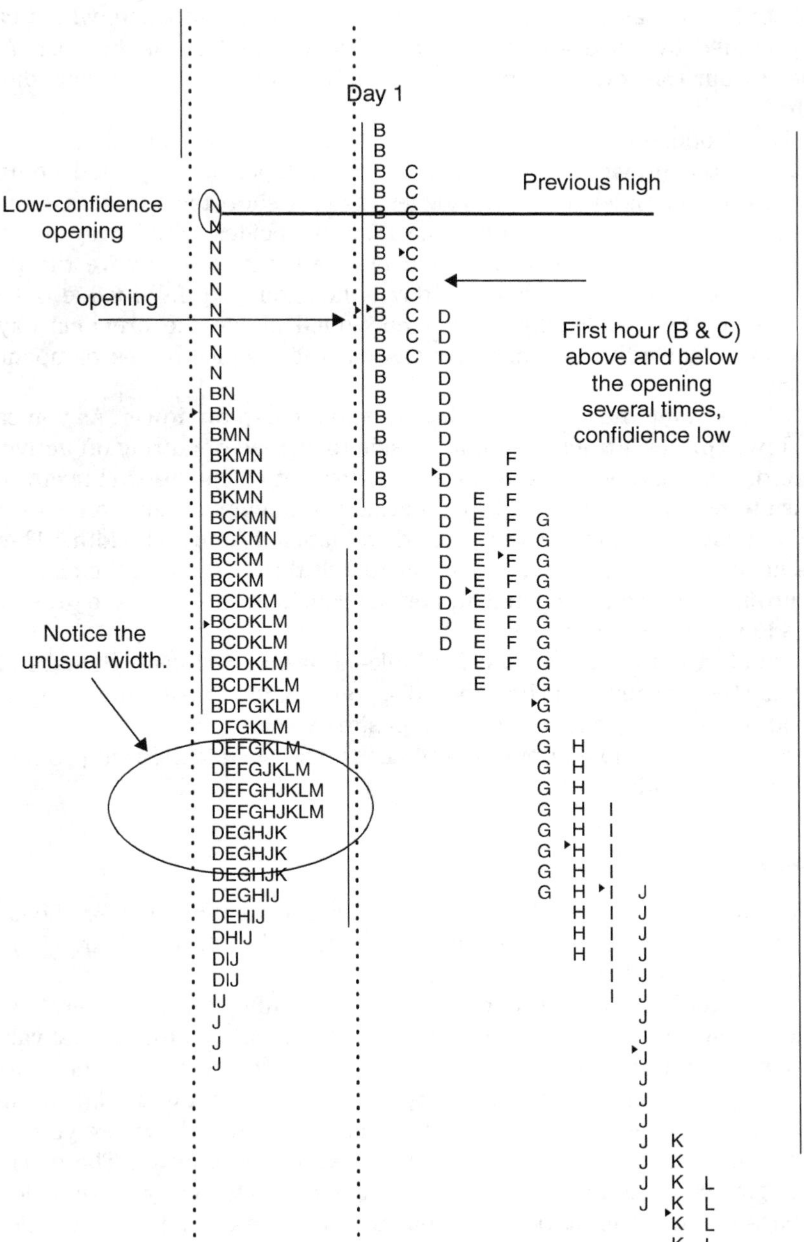

FIGURE 8.24 Example 2: Day with a low confidence opening.

low confidence, as the market is effectively seeking guidance, which can be provided by price levels that have drawn attention in the past. Another of our top reference points for Day 1 would be the previous day's high.

Day 1 opened and traded both above and below the opening, as well as above the previous day's high, in the first period. C period continued this low-confidence action, suggesting that short-term traders should be patient and wait to act until the market decides which way it's going to trade. The failure to find acceptance (over time) above the previous day's high tells us that this day is not going to build value out of balance to the upside; the market auctioned above the previous day's high and discovered that activity was cut off—higher prices dampened activity.

At this point, the market can be expected to explore lower. As you can see, lower prices attracted additional sellers instead of cutting off activity, therefore the market needs to continue lower until it can lure in buyers and return to balance. Notice that in G period the downward auction accelerated quickly, reaching the area circled and labeled "unusual width." There was never any reason for a day trader to exit this trade until the close, as the profile remained elongated and price again accelerated as the previous day's low was taken out.

One last note: once an auction looks above a previous high and fails, or looks below a previous low and fails, you should immediately recognize the possibility of an auction to the opposite extreme.

Figure 8.25 simply allows you to see the finished, collapsed profile of the day we just discussed.

Example 3

We're concluding Chapter 8 with the example shown in Figure 8.26 because it addresses the essence of day trading: *What is the market attempting to do, and what grade does it get for its effort?*

In Example 3, the market opens with low confidence. However, lower price gets accepted in B and C periods, which increases the odds that value will also migrate lower. Periods D and E extend the auction to the downside, giving the impression that this will continue to be a weak day. A rally in G period carries the auction back to the C period high, where you will notice that it also trades back into the previous day's range. The market once again sells off, but doesn't even come close to the early morning low. On days like this the market can appear to be weak, trapping you unless you continually ask yourself, "What is the market getting for its effort?" In this case, while the market has continually sold off, the net effect is very little change, and by the end of the day price actually closes higher.

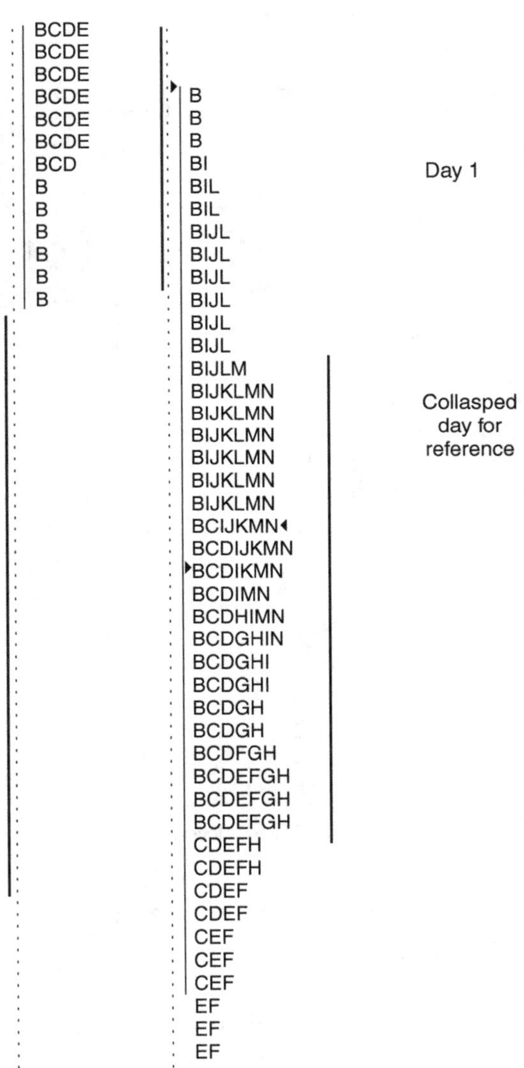

FIGURE 8.25 Example 2: Completed profile for Day 1.
Source: Copyright © 2006 CQG, Inc. All rights reserved worldwide. www.cqg.com.

Confidence was low surrounding the opening, and the constant reentry into the previous day's range—when the market was attempting to auction lower—reveals more proof of low confidence on the downside. You must continually ask yourself: *What is the inventory position of my competitors, and can I anticipate their actions as the day goes on?*

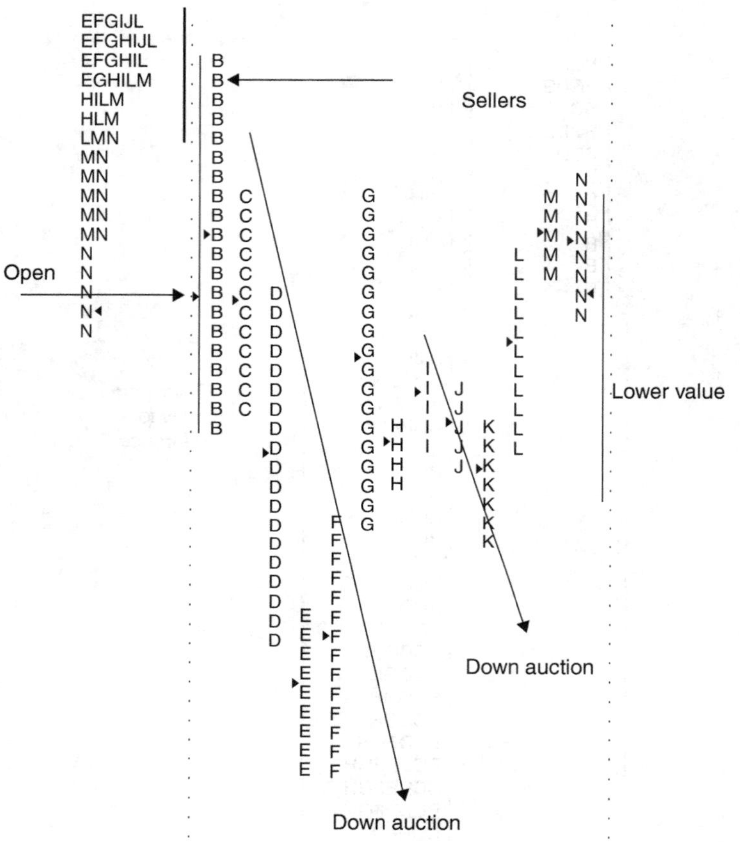

FIGURE 8.26 Example 3: Day with a low confidence opening: Assessing what the market is attempting to do.
Source: Copyright © 2006 CQG, Inc. All rights reserved worldwide. www.cqg.com.

All of the examples just discussed are applicable for round-turn day traders as well as institutional clients who are executing one side of a trade. Remember the question often posed by institutional traders: *I have a large order, should I fill it now or will I have the whole day to work on it?*

PRACTICE, PRACTICE, PRACTICE

We generally think of the type of analysis we've conducted in this chapter as something purely objective and logical. But we are all human and subject to our uniquely shifting emotional currents. Without factoring in emotion, you can't even begin to understand risk—of any kind. As objective as your analysis might be, if you are too emotionally involved, your decision-making abilities will suffer and you may find yourself focusing only on worst-case scenarios. Successful analysis must therefore take into account the way you *process* information, which is part of the larger context in which you trade and invest. The whole-brained trader does not get lost in unrelated particulars or subjective desire, instead continually seeking to understand a sense of the larger whole.

It is important to note here that this holistic insight ultimately has no bearing on how well you *implement* your understanding. You can intuitively grasp the fundamental concepts we're discussing, but you must also spend a substantial amount of time engaged in real work—researching on your own, studying patterns until they come second nature, mastering your emotional involvement in the financial implications of trading—before you can ascend to the ranks of the top performing money traders.

I once read that the best way to learn is to practice something over and over, subtly altering circumstances on each iteration. This is how we gain experience and the flexibility required to make rapid adjustments. The analogy I have used before is that of an experienced surgeon: while the surgeon does considerable prep work—looking at X-rays, reviewing the patient's medical history, etc.—once the incision is made there will always be minute differences to which he or she must adjust on the fly. But because the doctor has experienced untold numbers of similar situations, the slight variations are taken in stride, are accommodated with calm efficiency, and the operation proceeds without mishap.

Top professionals in any field are mentally prepared, they are engaged, and they have the right mental state with which to perform their duties with a clear, open mind—without being overwhelmed by conflicting stimulus or emotion.

CHAPTER 9

Profiting from Market-Generated Information

A common fallacy is the idea that the majority sets the pattern and the trends of social, economic, and religious life. History reveals quite the opposite: the majority copies or imitates the minority and this establishes the long-run developments and socio-economic evolutions.

—Humphrey Neill

Life is endlessly complex and mysterious. It's no wonder people tend to favor clean lines and clear objectives. And as much as we like to think of ourselves as individuals and freethinkers, we all long for easy, straightforward answers. When you consider the demands of modern living—cell phones ringing, bills to pay, relationships to nurture, endless e-mail cascading through the ether—it's no wonder everyone's looking for that magical black box. But, of course, there's no such thing.

One of the core directives of this book is that learning isn't *linear*, and that to successfully trade, you must train your mind to be agile, able to fluidly shift between timeframes and mindsets to accommodate the ever-changing auction. You have to accept the fact that you will never be *certain*, but if you improve your market understanding in conjunction with a better understanding of how you process information and make decisions, you can develop a more intuitive ability to identify those situations when the odds are in your favor (over time, you'll recognize that they occur more often than you might think).

Nietzsche said, "Belief in truth begins with doubting all that has hitherto been believed to be true." This mirrors the Humphrey Neill quote at the beginning of this chapter. If you sense the power and potential in this book, then *welcome to the minority.* It is only the minority—the "innovators" and "early adopters"—that first respond to a change in the dominant paradigm. All this talk of "asymmetric trade location" challenges, by its very nature, the status quo. But think on this: *In trading, as in all things, it is the well-positioned minority that benefits from the actions of the majority.*

TIMEFRAME DIVERSIFICATION

We've come at last to the simple question that lies at the heart of this book: *Why not have a portfolio that is both long and short?* Most would agree that such an approach makes perfect sense. Yet few actually do it. If you've already done your homework on individual securities—and you're any good at it—then you should have come across both long and short opportunities. When you consider the risks inherent in being "all one way" in markets that have repeatedly proved that they can reverse on a dime, *timeframe diversification* is a far more efficient use of your resources because it enables you to employ *all* of your research to develop market ideas—not just the results that indicate possible long positions. The May nonlinear break in stocks that we used for so many of our illustrations was also a marvelous example of the benefits of timeframe diversification. Case in point: On July 14, I received the following e-mail from a friend at State Street Global Advisors in Boston:

> ***From:*** *Brian Shannahan*
> ***Date:*** *July 14, 2006*
> ***To:*** *Jim Dalton*
> ***Subject:*** *since the peak in early May*
> *A thing of beauty. . .<.79> vs <6.22> net 5.44.*
>
> *State Street Global Advisors is one of the top five institutional money managers in the world. They are number one in institutional assets with approximately $1.5 trillion under management. Prior to my retirement from UBS Financial Services, I had asked State Street to develop a long-short portfolio for our clients based upon our specifications—basically 70 percent long and 30 percent short securities—with directions to rebalance to the 70/30 mix any time the shorts reached either 25 percent or 35 percent.*

Brian's e-mail was informing me that, since the May nonlinear break, this portfolio had a return advantage of positive 5.44 percent over its benchmark. This is just one illustration of the power of the concepts that we've discussed in this book.

Timeframe diversification evolves from the recognition that neither individual securities nor individual markets—such as the S&P 500 or 100, Dow, Russell 1000, 2000, or 3000—always move in a single direction. Even if a market is in a long-term trend, there will be meaningful countertrends, which we refer to as *intermediate-term auctions*. These countertrend auctions can easily retrace 5 percent to 10 percent of the trend, and can actually be healthy developments in that they enable markets to come into balance in order to prepare for the next significant leg of the trend. There is also general agreement that not all sectors, industries, or individual securities advance or decline together. In fact, it is more common to see contrary movement or rotations. Because diversification among industries, sectors, and individual securities is widely accepted and encouraged, is it such a reach to accept that portfolios should also be diversified by being short securities or markets that are likely to diverge? The State Street example provided a real-life illustration of this concept: 5.44 percent positive difference for a portfolio of approximately half a billion dollars is real money.

While we believe that investors who rely on fundamental information as the basis for their investment decisions can and do make money over the long run, we don't believe that fundamental information alone can ever guarantee an *absolute* profit or even a relative advantage over competitors. At the time fundamental investors place their trades, they have no way of knowing how much, if any, of that fundamental information has already been incorporated into the price they paid or received. That is the Achilles' heel that is exposed when one relies solely on fundamental information.

Consider that the forces that push a security away from fundamental value tend to be *behavioral* in nature, particularly at the end of extreme moves when the risk of price movement is greatest. The further behavioral forces drive the price of a security, the more interested the fundamentalists get, as they base their decisions (at least in the abstract) on perceived value. When prices have been driven too low, for example, aggressive value buyers appear. Extreme examples would include buyouts, mergers, and spin-offs. In these types of occurrences, timeframe diversification would include lightening up on hedges placed when the security was too high. These hedges might include raising cash, moving into defensive securities, selling options on either indexes or individual portfolio securities, buying index puts on the overall market, industries or sectors, and so on.

The point here is that *just as there is fundamental information, there is also behavioral information.* Fundamentalists forecast, but there is little evidence that suggests there's any merit to their augury. So why not combine the analytical power of fundamental information with a real-time understanding of market activity, employing intermediate timeframe diversification in order to secure a competitive edge?

Fundamental information reflects (or is an estimate of, based on all known contributing factors) the core long-term value of a security. Shorter-term behavioral forces can drive price away from this fundamental value—often times *far* away. The challenge for fundamental investors—and most professional asset managers fall into this camp—is determining whether behavioral or fundamental forces are driving the price of a security, to what extent, and what (if anything) can be done to protect or improve their portfolio profitability. That is precisely where market-generated information and the concepts presented in this book become invaluable.

THE NEW PARADIGM

> *This new paradigm claims that the prices of securities are not always the best estimate of the true underlying value of the firm. It argues that prices can be influenced by speculators and momentum traders, as well as by insiders and institutions that often buy and sell stocks for reasons unrelated to fundamental value, such as for diversification, liquidity and taxes. In other words, prices of securities are subject to temporary shocks that I call "noise" that obscures their true value. These temporary shocks may last for days or for years, and their unpredictability makes it difficult to design a trading strategy that consistently produces superior returns.*
>
> —Jeremy Siegel

When a professor of Wharton Business School is trumpeting the "new paradigm," the world stands waiting for a new theory. Siegel states that it is difficult to build a "strategy" because of the unpredictability inherent in market activity. *Markets in Profile* puts forth just such a strategy, based on a continual reevaluation of the risk of being long or short in any given market.

We have explored two themes: market understanding and self-understanding. We have campaigned for what we believe to be a more consistently reliable, objective source of information—the market itself. Using the market profile conforms to the way our brains receive and process information. We have offered suggestions and sources to help you hone your own process of self-understanding, emphasizing the importance of unlearning old habits in order to clear your mind, so you can assimilate market-generated information in the present tense.

It's a simple thing to say, "Clear your mind." It's quite another to put into practice. Giving up an idea that you have clung to for a long time can be extremely painful, and it is labor intensive to replace it with another—especially one that lacks clear, easily parsed directives. You have to be secure in yourself to let go of the status quo; secure people have confidence that they will assimilate new information and processes and get back on an even keel.

The key to unraveling the flux of market-generated information, as understood from the context of your own evolving emotional and cognitive makeup, is to accept the fact that *all decisions are made under some degree of uncertainty.* That is the fundamental nature of humanity.

Nothing is certain. The agile mind, however, when properly trained and prepared, can discern in the elegant array of evolving market-generated information occasional patterns—like oases of opportunity—that enable the execution of trades that offer greater reward with diminished risk. That beats average any day.

APPENDIX A

Market Update

In Chapter 6, we discussed how markets rarely go from bull to bear or from bear to bull, but rather transition from bull or bear to *bracketing*. Once the bracketing process is complete, markets either return to the previously established trend or begin a new auction in the opposite direction.

In latter chapters, we showed you a market that began to break hard in May 2006 (which was occurring as we were writing that portion of the book). Our explication was bold, as the low hadn't been established and we had only the theories expounded in this book to guide us. Because we were writing about real-time market activity, we promised that we would provide an update on how the market played out when we completed the book. Today is October 23, 2006—two days before we submit the final edits to our publisher. So far, using the December 2006 S&P 500 futures chart (shown in Figure A.1), the market's high in May 2006 was 1353 with a low of 1239 on June 14, and a recovery high of 1380 on October 18. The process may not be complete; however, from the market low the recovery has retraced 100 percent of the break that began in May and has begun to auction higher.

As you may recall, we also stated that the initial break was not unexpected, because the rally to the new highs in May 2006 were made on extremely light volume. Toward the end of the summer once "proof" that the market was weak had arrived, numerous portfolio managers on the talk-show circuit began to turn bearish—well after the lows were established and far too late to provide a competitive advantage.

FIGURE A.1 Continuation of a bracketing market. December 2006 S&P 500 futures.

There is a better way to understand and read markets. Long-term investors and traders armed with market-generated information and the insight provided by the concepts, techniques, and high-probability indicators discussed in this book will be better prepared to act before the herd has turned, positioning themselves favorably in the ever-changing market.

About the Authors

JIM DALTON

After spending several years trading and mentoring traders, Jim was asked to return to UBS Financial Services in 2001 to direct and reorganize its non-proprietary hedge fund research. This opportunity greatly expanded his exposure to many of the world's most successful traders and their strategies. Jim then retired in August 2005 after having held the titles of manager, Hedge Fund Research, and director of research for managed accounts. He currently trades for his own account and is the lead author of *Markets in Profile*. His earlier book, *Mind Over Markets* (by the same authors), was originally published in 1990 and continues to be popular among professional traders, providing a wealth of tactical trading strategies based on the Market Profile. The book was recently translated into Chinese.

Jim has been a member of both the CBOT and CBOE, and he served as executive vice president of the CBOE during its early formative years. Additional experience includes four years active duty in the Marine Corp. and several years with IBM and Merrill Lynch. From his experience, he has learned that "expert opinion" rarely pans out in the active market. He has also observed that superior trading results over the longer term are always the result of a more flexible, adaptive approach to markets. These observations set the stage for Jim's introduction to the Market Profile, a method of arranging data that enables the visualization of evolving market structure.

ROBERT BEVAN DALTON

After a brief stint as assistant editor of a small-town Midwestern newspaper, Rob pursued a hodgepodge of endeavors, from wandering the Middle East to crafting hardwood floors in Tucson and playing at rock star in Greenwich Village. He returned to the written word in the guise of a PR hack for various fashion agencies in Manhattan before fleeing the East Coast for sunny Seattle, where he founded Jie23, a new media design firm. He is now a freelance writer living in the woods on Bainbridge Island with his wife and two young boys. When he's not servicing clients like Microsoft, Vail, Holland America, and British Airways, he crafts the occasional poem and writes for a strange melange of start-ups, creative collaboratives, and arts and environmental nonprofits. Not to mention the occasional book on neuroeconomics.

ERIC JONES

Eric Jones began his career around markets, investing and trading while working as a foreign exchange analyst at a small commodity research and investment management firm founded by his father. It was there that he developed an appreciation for the power of quantitative trading systems. Also while there he met Jim Dalton, who introduced him to the Market Profile, the concept of market-generated information and the tremendously expanded potential of organizing data according to price, time, and volume, instead of just price alone, as was traditionally done.

On and off over the years, Jim and Eric have worked together in various capacities: as partners in a futures market research and trading firm, as investment advisors to clients, as developers of new investment products and platforms, and as leaders of investment research teams. Most recently, Eric was senior vice president, director of product development and investment manager research for UBS Financial Services' Advisory and Consulting Solutions, a unit comprised of managed account, alternative investment and fee-based brokerage products. In this role, Eric was responsible for the strategic development, integration, and market positioning of managed account and alternative investment products and platforms.

In addition to *Mind Over Markets* and *Markets in Profile*, Eric is also coauthor of *Hedging Foreign Exchange, Converting Risk to Profit* (Wiley, 1986).

Index